The Columbia Book of Civil War Poetry

The Columbia Book of

CIVIL WAR POETRY

Richard Marius, *Editor*

Keith Frome, *Associate Editor*

Columbia University Press ❧ New York

Columbia University Press

New York   Chichester, West Sussex

Copyright © 1994 Columbia University Press

All rights reserved

Library of Congress Cataloging-in-Publication Data

The Columbia book of Civil War poetry / Richard Marius, editor ; Keith
W. Frome, associate editor.

    p. cm.

  Includes index.

  ISBN 0-231-10002-7

  1. United States—History—Civil War, 1861-1865—Poetry. 2. War
poetry, American. I. Marius, Richard. II. Frome, Keith W.

PS595.C55C65 1994

811.008'0358—dc20   94-6481

                                    CIP

∞

Casebound editions of Columbia University Press books are printed on permanent and durable acid-free paper.

Printed in the United States of America

c 10 9 8 7 6 5 4 3 2 1

CONTENTS ❧

Introduction   *xiii*

The Horrors of War

SEVERN TEAKLE WALLIS (1816–1894) A Prayer for Peace   3

HENRY WADSWORTH LONGFELLOW (1807–1882) Killed at the Ford   6

HERMAN MELVILLE (1819–1891) Ball's Bluff   8

WALT WHITMAN (1819–1892) Vigil Strange I Kept on the Field One Night   10

    Dirge for Two Veterans   12

    A March in the Ranks Hard-prest, and the Road Unknown   14

    The Wound-Dresser   17

THADDEUS OLIVER (1826–1864) All Quiet along the Potomac Tonight   20

BRET HARTE (1836–1902) A Second Review of the Grand Army   23

STEPHEN VINCENT BENÉT (1898–1943)

    The Congressmen Came Out to See Bull Run   27

ROBERT PENN WARREN (1905–1989) Two Studies in Idealism   32

ELIZABETH BISHOP (1911–1979) From Trollope's Journal   36

JILL BRECKENRIDGE General John Cabell Breckinridge   38

ANDREW HUDGINS (1951–) At Chancellorsville   41

After the Wilderness   43

Around the Campfire   45

Moral Fervor

ELYMAS PAYSON ROGERS (1815–1861)   In 'Fifty Congress Passed a Bill   49

UNKNOWN, *attributed to* CHARLES SPRAGUE HALL *and to*

    THOMAS BRIGHAM BISHOP   John Brown's Body   53

JULIA WARD HOWE (1819–1910)   The Battle Hymn of the Republic   55

GEORGE F. ROOT (1820–1895)   The Battle-Cry of Freedom   57

JAMES RYDER RANDALL (1839–1908)   My Maryland   59

HENRY TIMROD (1829–1867)   Carolina   63

    Charleston   67

WILLIAM CULLEN BRYANT (1794–1878)   The Death of Slavery   71

RALPH WALDO EMERSON (1803–1882)   Boston Hymn   75

    Voluntaries   79

HENRY WADSWORTH LONGFELLOW (1807–1882)   The Building of the Ship   85

JOHN GREENLEAF WHITTIER (1807–1892)   The Furnace Blast   99

    Laus Deo!   103

HENRY CLAY WORK (1832–1884)   Marching through Georgia   106

JAMES MONROE WHITFIELD (1822–1871)   From Year to Year the Contest Grew   109

UNKNOWN, *attributed to* THOMAS *and* ELLEN SNOWDEN *and to*

    DANIEL DECATUR EMMETT (1815–1904)   Dixie   114

EDWARD W. WILLIAMS (1863–1891)   At Harper's Ferry Just before the Attack   116

STEPHEN VINCENT BENÉT (1898–1943)   John Brown's Prayer   120

MURIEL RUKEYSER (1913–1980)   The Soul and Body of John Brown   123

WILLIAM VAUGHN MOODY (1869–1910)

    An Ode in Time of Hesitation   130

UNKNOWN   Enlisted Today   141

HERMAN MELVILLE (1819–1891)   The March into Virginia   144

HENRY WADSWORTH LONGFELLOW (1802–1887)   The Cumberland   147

HERMAN MELVILLE (1819–1891)   A Dirge for McPherson   150

 The Conflict of Convictions   153

 The College Colonel   158

 The House-Top   160

WALT WHITMAN (1819–1892)   As I Lay with My Head in Your Lap Camerado   162

 A Sight in Camp in the Daybreak Gray and Dim   164

 Give Me the Splendid Silent Sun   166

 Beat! Beat! Drums!   168

 Cavalry Crossing a Ford   171

 Bivouac on a Mountain Side   172

 The Artilleryman's Vision   174

 An Army Corps on the March   176

 Come up from the Fields Father   178

UNKNOWN   Hospital Duties   180

THOMAS BUCHANAN READ (1822–1872)   Sheridan's Ride   184

HERMAN MELVILLE (1819–1891)   Sheridan at Cedar Creek   187

JAMES MADISON BELL (1826–1902)   Though Tennyson the Poet King   190

WILL HENRY THOMPSON (1848–1918)   The High Tide at Gettysburg   194

EDGAR LEE MASTERS (1869–1950)   The Battle of Gettysburg   198

PAUL LAURENCE DUNBAR (1872–1906)   The Colored Soldiers   206

 When Dey 'Listed Colored Soldiers   211

ROBERT PENN WARREN (1905–1989)

 A Confederate Veteran Tries to Explain the Event   213

CHARLES OLSON (1910–1970)   Anecdotes of the Late War   217

RANDALL JARRELL (1914–1965) A Description of Some Confederate Soldiers   225

ELEANOR ROSS TAYLOR (1920–) A Few Days in the South in February   227

JOHN UPDIKE (1932–) Richmond   235

SUZANNE RHODENBAUGH (1944–) The Civil War   237

JANE KENYON (1947–) Gettysburg, July 1, 1863   238

ANDREW HUDGINS (1951–) Serenades in Virginia   242

     Burial Detail   246

     A Soldier on the Marsh   250

Pantheon

HERMAN MELVILLE (1819–1891) The Portent   255

FRANCIS TICKNOR (1822–1872) Little Giffen   256

GEORGE MOSES HORTON (1797?–1883?) General Grant—the Hero of the War   258

JAMES RUSSELL LOWELL (1819–1910) Memoriae Positum R. G. Shaw   261

JULIA WARD HOWE (1819–1910) Robert E. Lee   265

FATHER ABRAHAM JOSEPH RYAN (1839–1894) The Sword of Robert Lee   267

W. T. MEREDITH (b. 1839) Farragut, Farragut   269

CONSTANCE FENIMORE WOOLSON (1840–1894) Kentucky Belle   273

KATE BROWNLEE SHERWOOD (1841–1941) Albert Sidney Johnston   279

JOHN REUBEN THOMPSON (1823–1873) Lee to the Rear   283

     Obsequies of Stuart   288

     The Burial of Latané   293

JOHN WILLIAMSON PALMER (1825–1906) Stonewall Jackson's Way   296

BRET HARTE (1836–1902) John Burns of Gettysburg   300

JOHN GREENLEAF WHITTIER (1807–1892) Barbara Frietchie   306

SIDNEY LANIER (1842–1881) The Dying Words of Stonewall Jackson   310

PAUL LAURENCE DUNBAR (1872–1906) Robert Gould Shaw   312

     Frederick Douglass   313

Douglass | 315

ROBERT HAYDEN (1913–) Frederick Douglass | 316

PAUL LAURENCE DUNBAR (1872–1906) The Unsung Heroes | 317

LANGSTON HUGHES (1902–1967) Frederick Douglass: 1817–1895 | 319

PAUL HORGAN (1905–) Tintype of a Private of the Fifteenth Georgia Infantry | 322

DONALD DAVIDSON (1922–) Lee in the Mountains | 323

Lincoln

WILLIAM CULLEN BRYANT (1794–1878) The Death of Abraham Lincoln | 331

HERMAN MELVILLE (1819–1891) The Martyr | 333

WALT WHITMAN (1819–1892) When Lilacs Last in the Dooryard Bloom'd | 335

O Captain! My Captain! | 345

EDWIN MARKHAM (1852–1940) Lincoln, The Man of the People | 348

EDGAR LEE MASTERS (1869–1950) Anne Rutledge | 351

EDWIN ARLINGTON ROBINSON (1869–1935) The Master | 352

VACHEL LINDSAY (1879–1931) Abraham Lincoln Walks at Midnight | 355

JOHN GOULD FLETCHER (1886–1950) Lincoln | 357

CARL SANDBURG (1878–1967) The Long Shadow of Lincoln | 361

LANGSTON HUGHES (1902–1967) Lincoln Monument: Washington | 366

Aftermath

JOHN GREENLEAF WHITTIER (1807–1892) The Battle Autumn of 1862 | 369

JAMES RUSSELL LOWELL (1819–1891)

Ode Recited at the Harvard Commemoration, July 21, 1865 | 372

HERMAN MELVILLE (1819–1891) Malvern Hill | 387

Memorial on the Slain at Chickamauga | 391

WALT WHITMAN (1819–1892) To a Certain Civilian | 392

Spirit Whose Work Is Done   393

JOHN REUBEN THOMPSON (1823–1873) Music in Camp   394

CAROLINE AUGUSTA BALL (b. 1825) The Jacket of Gray   399

BAYARD TAYLOR (1825–1878) Gettysburg Ode   402

FRANCIS MILES FINCH (1827–1907) The Blue and the Gray   411

PATRICK SARSFIELD GILMORE (1829–1892)

    When Johnny Comes Marching Home   414

HENRY TIMROD (1829–1867) Ode ("Sleep sweetly in your humble graves")   417

INNES RANDOLPH (1837–1887) The Rebel   419

KATE PUTNAM OSGOOD (1841–1910) Driving Home the Cows   423

AMBROSE BIERCE (1842–1914?) To E. S. Salomon   426

    The Confederate Flags   430

    The Hesitating Veteran   433

    The Death of Grant   436

    General B. F. Butler   438

MAURICE THOMPSON (1844–1901)

    An Address by an Ex-Confederate Soldier to the Grand Army of the Republic   439

    To the South   443

EDGAR LEE MASTERS (1869–1950) Veterans of the Wars   446

MINNA IRVING (b. 1872) Marching Still   448

ROBERT FROST (1874–1963) The Black Cottage   450

ALLEN TATE (1899–1979) Ode to the Confederate Dead   455

JOHN BERRYMAN (1914–1972) Boston Common   460

DUDLEY RANDALL (1914–) Memorial Wreath   466

ALAN DUGAN (1923–) Fabrication of Ancestors   469

ROBERT LOWELL (1917–1977) For the Union Dead   471

ELEANOR ROSS TAYLOR (1920–) This Year's Drive to Appomattox   476

DEREK WALCOTT (1930–) The Arkansas Testament   478

Stillness

HERMAN MELVILLE (1819–1891)

    An Uninscribed Monument on One of the Battlefields of the Wilderness   495

    Shiloh, a Requiem   497

MARGARET JUNKIN PRESTON (1820–1897) A Grave in Hollywood Cemetery,

    Richmond (J. R. T.)   498

UNKNOWN   Confederate Memorial Day   501

MAURICE THOMPSON (1844–1901) Lincoln's Grave   503

CARL SANDBURG (1878–1967) Cool Tombs   517

EDGAR LEE MASTERS (1869–1950) Gettysburg   518

ROBERT PENN WARREN (1905–1989) History among the Rocks   521

DONALD DAVIDSON (1922–) Sequel of Appomattox   523

JAMES DICKEY (1923–) Hunting Civil War Relics at Nimblewill Creek   525

Acknowledgments   527

Illustrations   *531*

Index of Authors, Titles, and First Lines   *535*

INTRODUCTION ✒

The Civil War was not only the bloodiest conflict in the history of the United States; it was also the most peculiar war we have ever fought—the "anomalous war," historian Charles Royster has called it.[1] Both the horror and the peculiarity are reflected in poetry inspired by the war. In this collection, we have included a cross-section of work, most by poets who lived during the war but much, too, by those who came afterward and found in the conflict inspiration to poetic reflection.

Poetry at the time of the Civil War had an audience modern poets can only envy. Nineteenth-century Americans expected poetry to be served up on every occasion and devoured it when it was set before them. Henry Wadsworth Longfellow's lugubrious "Evangeline" went through six American editions within six months of its publication in the spring of 1847. Translated into German and other European languages, it enjoyed a similarly enthusiastic reception abroad. The poem made Longfellow enough money to grant the poet his heart's desire—to quit teaching at Harvard.[2]

Poetry in the nineteenth century was a public act, appended routinely to political oratory, to celebratory occasions, and to sermons, memorized in schools and recited by children, declaimed by the poets themselves at small gatherings and civic functions. Poetry was expected to be didactic and uplifting, and if it made its audience weep, so much the better. Nineteenth-century readers and auditors loved to wash their cheeks in noble tears.

Whitman, Melville, and a few others from the time produced poems that still have a timeless power to move us. Others are dated by the tastes that created them. Too many nineteenth-century American poets display an unremitting talent for industrious rhymes. The effect is sometimes more amusing than inspiring. But if much poetry generated by our greatest war was less than powerful, the emotions that inspired it were strong and deep—even if they were as perplexing and contradictory as the war itself. The Civil War made us a nation. As historian David Donald once argued in a landmark essay, Abraham Lincoln's Gettysburg Address signaled a transformation. The key word in the address, Donald says, was "nation." Before that time, Lincoln had spoken most frequently of saving the Union. In a public letter to Horace Greeley, the mercurial editor of the New York *Tribune*, Lincoln wrote in August 1862:

> My paramount object in this struggle is to save the Union, and is not either to save or destroy slavery. If I could save the Union without freeing any slave, I would do it, and if I could save it by freeing all the slaves, I would do it, and if I could save it by freeing some and leaving others alone, I would also do that. What I do about slavery and the colored race, I do because I believe it helps to save the Union; and what I forbear, I do because I do not believe it would help to save the Union.[3]

With the opening words of the Gettysburg Address, Lincoln summoned biblical language to declare:

> Four score and seven years ago, our fathers brought forth on this continent a new nation. . . .

The "Union" was a federation of States. A nation is a communion of people united by what Lincoln, in his First Inaugural Address, called the "mystic chords of memory," a powerful sense of common identity however vaguely expressed. The Civil War affirmed once and for all that there was one American people whose fundamental loyalty was to the nation rather than to the states where they happened to reside. By 1861, restless Americans moved readily from one state to another, from east to west, north to south, south to north. But few left the jurisdiction of the national government to find new homes. If they did migrate to Mexico or California or the Oregon Territory before the Civil War or to Hawaii afterward, they quickly pulled their government along after them.

After the war, multitudes moved off the land, away from the rhythms of plowing, planting, and harvest, away from labor measured by sunrise and sunset and governed by weather, to become resident in another world—the town or the city—to lives regulated by the precise and relentless ticking and striking of myriads of clocks and by the factory whistle that signaled the beginning and the end of the working day. They accepted impersonality in daily human relations; with crowds swirling around them, strangers did not nod or speak to each other in the streets. They were governed by men they did not know.

True, most Americans remained rooted to the land. But those who went to the cities wrote the literature—including the poetry. Just as important, urban dwellers bought books and gave writers the paying audience necessary for a literary career. The tastes of urban readers ran to nostalgia for a lost rural Arcadia. Writers obliged them. Longfellow, Whittier, and countless lesser poets sang sweetly of farmland and the cycles of nature—while Americans fled the land in a relentless migration to the excitements and opportunities of city life.

Modern nationalism is an urban phenomenon—a substitute for the localism of farm and village, the identity of the uprooted. Charles Royster has argued that the South never succeeded in developing a national sentiment.[4] How could it have done so without large cities? Urban Americans avidly embraced nationalism's religious trappings—hymns, the flags, bunting, Fourth of July oratory, its mystic feelings of solidarity, and, finally, the imperial crusade. Nationalism lifted them from anonymity and gave them pride and purpose and emotional release and an irresistible sense of belonging to a mighty enterprise.

After the collapse of the Confederacy, the literate population in the defeated South was swept along with the North in this rush of nationalism. Like other Americans, most Southerners remained on the land. Edward L. Ayres has pointed out that only Birmingham among Southern cities possessed an economy built on manufacturing.[5] Yet Southerners were also on the move. Ayres says that from the end of Reconstruction in 1877 to 1900 "the South built railroads faster than the nation as a whole."[6] The railroad brought faster communication with the rest of the country, including easier access to Northern newspapers and magazines, with their fashion plates and news of a wider world. Southerners went north to school and on business, and Northerners moved below the Mason-Dixon Line to invest in what Henry Grady of the Atlanta *Constitution* glowingly portrayed as the "New South."[7] Southern cities clamored for

Northern investment.[8] As they have ever done, Southerners hungered for the respect and admiration of the Northern public. Northern audiences, seeking refuge from the smoke and dirt and clamor and the increasing strangeness of their own cities, greeted Southern writers with adulation and wallowed in Southern nostalgia. Literate Southerners were drawn back into the triumphant nation as though into the vortex of a whirlpool. Poetry, like fiction and journalism, became a unifying force.

It is a cliché of writing conferences that the South is peculiar because it is the only region in the United States that has known defeat. Like most clichés, this one offers a stain of truth in the bottom of the cup. Defeat rankled. Many unreconstructed rebels continued to sing "Dixie" and to deliver the Rebel Yell on command. Some, such as Innes Randolph in this book, wrote occasional poetry expressing unquenched hostility toward the Federal Union. But even Randolph may be putting us on. Given the popularity in the North of such Southern novelists as George Washington Cable and Thomas Nelson Page, we may suspect a profit motive in some effusions for a lost cause.[9] Southerners gone north have always delighted in parading their eccentricities, in part because Northerners expect them and reward Southerners for them.

But the sense of defeat was not as bitter or as enduring as it has often been portrayed. Most leaders of the Confederacy returned quickly to the nation and felt no desire to undo the results of the war. Robert E. Lee swore a loyalty oath to the Federal government within two months after Appomattox, and to Southerners everywhere he counseled submission.[10] His old warhorse James Longstreet became a Republican and resumed his friendship with Ulysses S. Grant. Tennessee's fire-eating governor Isham G. Harris did more than any other man to push his reluctant state into secession in 1861. Harris served on the staffs of several Confederate generals, fled to England for a while after the war—and spent the last twenty years of his life representing Tennessee in the United States Senate. Jefferson Davis never applied for pardon and until his death steadfastly refused the loyalty oath. But he was content to be an icon of the Lost Cause with no thought of lending another armed insurrection his moral authority. In his last speech, delivered when he was almost eighty years old, he told a convention of young Southerners:

> The past is dead; let it bury its dead, its hopes, and its aspirations. Before you lies the future, a future full of golden promise, a future of expanding national glory, before which all the world shall stand amazed. Let me beseech you to lay aside all rancor, all bitter sectional feeling, and to take

your places in the ranks of those who will bring about a consummation devoutly to be wished—a reunited country.[11]

Such healing sentiments were no less strong on the Northern side. In May 1885, Major DeWitt C. Sprague read a long poem to the sixteenth annual reunion of the Union Army of the Potomac. (We have mercifully omitted it from this collection.) Its penultimate verse expresses a common mood in North and South:

Ye gallant men who wore the Southern Gray!
Ye valiant men who wore the loyal Blue
Ye all were to the cause ye fought for True
But ye are all Americans today.[12]

On the Southern side similar sentiments came from Maurice Thompson in his "Address by an Ex-Confederate Soldier to the Grand Army of the Republic" (which we have included).

The reasons for the appropriation of American nationalism by the South are not far to seek. The United States in the decades following the war swept forward into the glittering successes of its gilded age, a period of miraculous economic growth and world influence. Meanwhile Southerners discovered that the end of slavery did not mean the end of white supremacy. With the moral embarrassment of slavery out of the way, Americans, both in the North and South, could happily concur in the conviction that people of color were too inferior to participate in the national life. This dubious principle paved the highway along which Southern whites marched into an enthusiastic nationalism.

The process seems appallingly simple in retrospect. Whatever Southern leaders might have said about states' rights before 1861, the fuel that fired sectional antagonism was slavery. Slavery ignited the moral indignation of the North—amply demonstrated in many of the poems we present here.

In the South, a persistent terror before the lurid fantasy of the freed black man fired orators and writers. More than one of every three human beings in the South was a slave. The ratio terrified those who brooded on it, and many did. Many white Southerners feared that having shaken off their shackles, the freed slaves would rise against their former masters. The occasional slave insurrection was quickly drowned in blood but still created terrifying forebodings among white masters.[13] Like the Native Americans, blacks evoked among whites two extreme images—on the one hand the docile servant of doglike devotion who loved "ole Massa" and all the white folks, and on the other the vicious beast, not fully human, restrained from plunder and rape only by fear of the lash and the noose. The notion of sending freed slaves back to Africa, especially to Liberia, was created by the desire to rid the country of a curse. Its premise was that free blacks and whites in large numbers could never coexist peacefully.

Reconstruction aimed at educating the freed blacks and bringing them into political life as responsible Republicans. It was a doomed effort. In 1877 as the last units of the occupying Federal Army withdrew from the South, unceasing violence and threats of violence had already begun to reduce Southern blacks to a peonage nearly as onerous as slavery itself. Northerners shared the common white Southern opinion that blacks were, as Frederick Law Olmsted declared, "little better than a cunning idiot and a cowed savage."[14] Preoccupied with their own problems—industrialization, the rise of gargantuan corporations, class conflict, and the polyglot flood of immigration from the Old World—Northern whites quickly lost interest in obtaining civil rights for freed black Americans. In 1913 when Woodrow Wilson made racial segregation in the Civil Service the official policy of the Federal government, protests were few and ineffectual.

Southern whites therefore lost far less in defeat and abolition than they had feared beforehand. With white supremacy assured, the old Confederacy could rejoin the North in an exuberant nationalism, sealed finally by the passions released by the Spanish-American War. In 1898 young Southerners and old veterans of the Confederate armies volunteered in droves to fight in the national army that "liberated" Cuba, Puerto Rico, and the Philippines. Confederate General FitzHugh Lee, nephew of Robert E. Lee and veteran of Antietam and Gettysburg, fought as a general in the United States Army in Cuba and when he died in 1905 was buried in his Federal uniform.

Memories of the Civil War drifted into nostalgia. Like a bouquet of slightly fading gardenias on the windowsill, the romantic spirit has lent its over-sweet odor to Southern life and literature without in the least threatening national unity or even having much influence on Southern society. Woodrow Wilson's five-volume *History of the American People*, published in 1905, sold well without arousing much comment about his vitriolic comments on the Thirteenth, the Fourteenth, and especially the Fifteenth amendments to the Constitution. If any single work of nonfiction represents a renewed unity of Northern and Southern white Americans around the assumption of black inferiority, this was it.[15] D. W. Griffith's landmark film

Birth of a Nation, with its exaltation of the Ku Klux Klan, came a decade later and aroused enthusiasm all over the country.

All this makes the Civil War peculiar. After the bloodiest war in Western history to that time, the two sides settled down together in an astonishingly united nation. No smoldering fires beneath the surface ever broke out into anything like the strife and slaughter in Central Europe, renewed now after almost seventy years of apparent unity, following the breakup of the Soviet Union. On the contrary, for North and South the Civil War has become a common stage on which are played out from time to time interpretations of the nation, nearly always in an elegiac spirit of wonder that something so tremendous could pass so utterly away. "I had not thought death had undone so many." Eliot's line might serve as epigraph to our most recent look at the conflict—the captivating television documentary directed by Ken Burns.

The war has been prolific in myths and legends. Royster says, "In the last third of the nineteenth century Southerners found it easy, or at least expedient, to forget a great deal of what they had known about the Confederacy, to reshape its history, and to remember things that had not occurred."[16] Northerners have been equally avid in this enterprise. In 1939 and 1940, "Gone With the Wind" conquered New York, Chicago, and Los Angeles, as well as every city in the South.

The peculiarities of the war and the stages of sentiment about it are reflected in the poetry in this volume. On the Northern side, the conflict quickly became a crusade to save the Union and free the slaves. On the Southern side the North appeared as the heartless aggressor of the Motherland, an aggressor whose ironbound legions had neither decency nor chivalry.

First in early importance as an ideological poem is "John Brown's Body Lies A-Mould'ring in the Grave." It memorializes the half-mad abolitionist whose cockamamie scheme to seize the arsenal at Harper's Ferry, Virginia, and provoke a slave revolt stirred the imagination of both North and South. In October 1859, Brown's ragtag followers failed in their fantastic effort. Most were killed when troops under the command of Colonel Robert E. Lee stormed the building where the conspirators had taken refuge. Vengeance was swift. Brown was tried for treason against the state of Virginia, condemned, and hustled to the gallows. On December 2 he died unrepent, with great dignity, leaving behind a scribbled prophecy: "I, John Brown, am now quite *certain* that the crimes of this *guilty* land will never be purged *away* but by blood."

Most Southern whites saw him as a fanatic representing a Northern desire to loose savage blacks against innocent whites, especially white women. Multitudes of Northerners saw him as saint, a martyr as innocent as Christ himself on the cross. In the late Spring of 1861, Federal troops marched into Washington to defend the city, singing to a thumping rhythm:

John Brown's body lies a-mould'ring in the grave,
John Brown's body lies a-mould'ring in the grave,
John Brown's body lies a-mould'ring in the grave,
   His soul is marching on.
   Glory, glory, hallelujah!
   Glory, glory, hallelujah!
   Glory, glory, hallelujah!
   His soul is marching on!

Here, at the red dawn of the war, almost two years before the Emancipation Proclamation, the song conveyed an unmistakable message: The fight to preserve the Union was indissolubly bound to a crusade to abolish slavery.

Then came Julia Ward Howe, taking the tune to "John Brown's Body" and using her sublime biblical metaphors to create the "Battle Hymn of the Republic," published first in February 1862 in the *Atlantic Monthly*. Howe's most powerful image is inspired by the grim vision of Isaiah 63:1–6. There the avenging angel of God appears in garments stained with blood to tread a sinful people in the winepress of his anger. The "fateful lightning of his terrible swift sword" evokes the vision of the Apocalypse, where Christ appears on Judgment Day with a two-edged sword flashing from his mouth to destroy the wicked. Howe makes slavery a cosmic wickedness, and she flings her images of vengeance and doom at the South with remorseless jubilation. The sublime climax in the last verse likens death in the battle for freedom to the sacrifice of Christ. The "Battle Hymn" announces the apotheosis of a nation purged from the curse of slavery.

Other songs sanctified the Union cause. George F. Root's "Battle-Cry of Freedom" and Henry Clay Work's "Marching through Georgia" are more fervid and less enduring examples of the type. Both are noteworthy for the emphasis they put on the flag of the United States as the emblem of freedom—a significance it has had ever since. [17]

Against the moral claims of the North, the South offered love of the homeland. Since most fighting in the war took place on Southern soil, Southern patriotism was enough to unite Southern whites—even the majority of the population that did not own slaves—against the Yankee flood. This unity was far from complete, and it disintegrated under the pounding of Northern victories after 1863. But it was sufficient to sustain a horrifying war set to music. The irresistible "Dixie," or "Dixie's Land," was perhaps written by a black man gone north. The words are usually taken to have been the creation of Daniel Decatur Emmett (1815–1904), a wandering singer and composer. Only the first verse is well known, and that seems ever to have been so.

It is no irony that the words of "Dixie" are written in Negro dialect. One of the more romantic and perfervid affirmations of Southern whites was that blacks liked being slaves and loved their masters and their plantations—when these same slaves were not being ravaging, insurrectionary beasts, of course. Note, however, that the words are spoken—or sung—by a black person who has left "Dixie's land" and looks back on it with homesick longing. They are emblematic of an American population already in motion before the war began and of the romantic nostalgia that infected the literature of both North and South. For that mood, nothing was really good until it had been truly lost.

Modern wars begin in ideological passions. They are fought in stoic resignation, sorrow, terror, stuporous waiting, frantic instinctive combat, and yearning for peace, any kind of peace. Americans had no experience to prepare them for the carnage of the Civil War. John Keegan has written, "News of a death in battle was a comparatively rare family tragedy at any time before the nineteenth century."[18] Only a handful of pitched battles marked the American Revolution and the War of 1812. The Mexican War was fought far away in an almost mythical land, with few casualties on the American side, and it resulted in quick and overwhelming victory.

Even European countries had no war to compare with this one. Napoleon's Grand Army invaded Russia in 1812 with some 600,000 men, cobbled together from all France's allies. It was the largest army assembled in the western world up to that time. It would have been insufficient for the American Civil War.

How many fought? We are not sure. The Federal army counted enlistments exactly—but some men enlisted several times, renewing their vows, so to speak, when the old enlistment ran out. The total number of enlistments on the Northern side was 2,778,304, of whom 2,489,836 were whites, 178,975 were blacks, and 3,530 were Indians. The navy and marines added another 105,963. The generally accepted estimate is that about two million men altogether served on the Union side. Confederate enlistments are estimated at between 750,000 and 1,227,890.[19] In the Union Army 360,222 men died; the Confederates lost about 258,000.[20] Contagion swept camps on both sides. About sixty percent of the fatalities were the result of disease. The United States lost more American soldiers in the Civil War, says John Keegan, "than the total number killed in the two world wars, Korea, and Vietnam."[21]

At Antietam Creek near Sharpsburg, Maryland, on September 15, 1862, the Army of Northern Virginia under Robert E. Lee suffered some 11,000 casualties; the Union Army lost over 12,000. About 5,000 of these were dead.[22] At Gettyburg, less than a year later, the Confederate losses amounted to nearly 28,000 men killed, wounded, and captured in three days of battle; Federal losses amounted to 23,049.[23]

Men on both sides enlisted with the fervor of knights riding off to chivalric exploits in the manner of the romantic novels of Sir Walter Scott. Mark Twain, not entirely facetiously, blamed the entire war on Scott's influence on the Southern character.[24]

Chivalry meant celebration. Anyone today looking at drawings or paintings of Civil War soldiers must be struck by the variety of the uniforms on both sides. Zouaves from Louisiana and New York went up to kill each other in red fezzes and, sometimes, bright red trousers. Regimental bands with enthusiastic drummers accompanied troops into battle. Both North and South loved parades and had frequent opportunity to enjoy them as the crisis thickened into war. But from the first real battles until the last, the aim of both armies was to kill as many of the enemy as possible by any means available. In this goal, they were extraordinarily successful. As an awareness of the carnage spread on both sides, a certain grim sense of irony ruled spirits tuned to writing poetry.

In mid-July 1861, General Irvin McDowell led the newly formed Union Army out of Washington and into Virginia, accompanied by Congressmen, other gentlemen, and women with picnic baskets. His green troops threw away their rations, including some ammunition, broke ranks to pick berries in the summer heat, and treated the whole affair as a Saturday picnic. Then they collided with a Confederate army waiting for them at a little creek, called locally "Bull Run" and near a rail junction at a hamlet called

Manassas.[25] By the end of that day Union soldiers and civilians alike were fleeing for their lives to the safety of the Potomac and the capital. Casualties amounted to 387 dead Confederates, 481 Union soldiers killed; among the wounded were 1,582 Confederates and 1,124 Federals. Herman Melville, and much later on Stephen Vincent Benét, reflected poetically on this picnic turned into massacre. At the time, Horace Greeley was so horrified that he wrote Lincoln begging him "to make peace with the rebels at once and on their own terms."[26]

Bull Run was a conventional battle even if casualties were enormous compared to previous fights on American soil. It was perhaps the battle of Ball's Bluff in October on the Potomac that demonstrated to the country at large the unchivalric character of this conflict. Federal forces crossed from Maryland into Virginia, landing near a one-hundred-foot-high bank called "Ball's Bluff," and advanced on a Confederate encampment. The Confederates counterattacked and pushed the Federals down the bluff and into the river. Terrified Union soldiers jumped into the water weighed down by their heavy equipment and sank like stones. Those who could swim lunged out into the river while from the heights Confederate riflemen picked them off like gleeful boys shooting frogs in a pond. John Keegan has noted that this was an American illustration of a principle of many battles, where retreating soldiers are likely to be slaughtered by the victors almost as sport.[27] Here was no courtly romance; here was murder. (Among the wounded was young Oliver Wendell Holmes who stopped two bullets with his chest and lived to sit on the Supreme Court of the United States).[28]

The battle forced Herman Melville into reverie. He mused on the contradiction between the parades of "Young soldiers marching lustily / Unto the wars, / With fifes and flags in mottoed pageantry; / While all the porches, walks, and doors / Were rich with ladies cheering royally." These gay gallants died miserably at Ball's Bluff, leaving the poet to lie awake, musing "while in the street / Far footfalls died away till none were left."

Shortly after the battle of Antietam, photographer Matthew Brady opened an exhibit at his gallery in New York City. He displayed some of the photographs of the dead that we include in this book. These mute and contorted corpses offered no image to be palliated by marching bands and pounding drums or by tales of knighthood in flower. Brady's stark work brought home the wisdom that William Tecumseh Sherman was later to express in a pithy sentence: "War is hell."

Families at home received news from battle that sons, husbands, fathers had died. Some of the most affectingly sentimental poetry in this book was inspired by this common experience, new to Americans, Northern and Southern. If the news of the soldier's death was accompanied by some memento, such as a last letter or a lock of hair, the poignancy was all the more powerful. Thaddeus Oliver's "All Quiet along the Potomac Tonight" became one of the most popular poems of the war because it caught the irony of sudden and violent death in the midst of the bucolic American land. Longfellow's "Killed at the Ford," less popular, made much of the same feeling.

The slaughter seems inevitable in retrospect. The efficient technology of war in an industrial age, the psychology of battle, and the primitive state of medicine made for horrendous casualties. Officers and ordinary soldiers expected to expose themselves to enemy fire with a public nonchalance that proved to one another that they were brave. They took chances with fate and often lost. The cannon and rifled musket were deadly at long range against attacking infantry. But the spirit of Civil War tactics might be summed up in one word—"Charge!"

The principle of the charge seemed simple enough. Columns of men rushed forward to attack, expecting to take the bullets of a line of defenders. But if they could run fast and hard without flinching, they could swarm over the defensive line, overwhelm it, break through to the rear, and send the defenders fleeing in panic. Again and again that tactic ruled the day. Again and again it failed—not only at Antietam, Fredericksburg, Gettysburg, and Cold Harbor, but at dozens of lesser battles and skirmishes during the war. The charging force was regularly butchered.

In Robert E. Lee this passion for the offensive had an unblinking champion. Many Civil War historians believe that had the South remained on the defensive from the beginning, the Confederacy might have worn down Northern spirits.[29] But Lee's daring offensive thrusts spent thousands of lives that could not be replaced. Grant could be no less audacious. At Cold Harbor, Virginia, in June 1864, he sent three assaults plunging forward to disaster against Confederate earthworks. Before the attack, Union troops, knowing what lay ahead of them, sewed papers with their names and addresses into their coats so their bodies could be identified after they were dead.[30] The wounded lay between the lines for forty-eight hours before Lee and Grant agreed on a truce to allow them to be picked up. By that time all but two of them had died. Grant wrote in his laconic memoirs, "I have always regretted that the last assault at Cold Harbor was ever made."[31] He seemed to have learned his lesson; at the last of the war, he was content to place Petersburg under a siege that lasted six months and finally wore Lee's army to a remnant.

Medical arts were primitive, antisepsis and infection scarcely understood. Wounds could be cleaned and bound up, and limbs could be cut off; otherwise the body had to heal itself. Walt Whitman, looking for his brother George in Virginia after the battle of Fredericksburg, came on a pile of amputated arms and legs outside a field hospital "cut, bloody, black and blue, swelled, and sickening."[32]

The conditions of battle were miserable. Everyone at Cold Harbor remembered the heat and the dust. Dr. John Gardner Perry, a surgeon there with the Army of the Potomac, wrote to his wife, "The heat is intolerable, and the roads are covered with dust six or eight inches deep, which every gust of wind sweeps up, covering everything with a dirty, white coating."[33] A few days later Dr. Perry wrote again: "I am up to my neck in work. It is slaughter, slaughter, slaughter. . . . Horses and mules die by the hundreds from continued hard labor and scant feed. The roads are strewn with them, and the decay of these, with that of human bodies in the trenches, causes malaria of the worst kind."[34]

Poetry was expected to be read by women, and the details of the carnage did not often get into verse. But a bleak mood in the face of such bloodiness could not be held at bay. Whitman seemed to express better than any other poet this growing horror of the mutilation and death in the war. His "Dirge for Two Veterans" commemorates the deaths of a father and son—reminiscent of Shakespeare's *Henry VI* where the feeble old king sees sons and fathers killing each other in a land torn asunder by civil war. Whitman did not identify the side for which the father and son of his poem died. The horrors of war were impartial. His graphic autobiographical poem "The Wound-Dresser" came out of his observations in the military hospitals in and near Washington. Says Whitman's best biographer, Justin Kaplan, "By the end of the war Whitman figured he had made over six hundred hospital visits and tours, often lasting for several days and nights, and in some degree had ministered to nearly a hundred thousand of the sick and wounded of both sides."[35]

In the face of this horror, one senses in the nation a certain wavering, a hesitation before ultimate things. What did it all mean? What was the final vindication for such sacrifice? Where was God in this war? Few poets acquainted with the fighting tried to answer such questions, and their religious sentiments are distinctly ambiguous.

God appears now and then as he does in the prose of Abraham Lincoln, especially in Lincoln's Second Inaugural Address—God the Almighty, inscrutable force ruling the cosmos and directing events but whose designs are hidden in impenetrable darkness. Or else God is, as for James Russell Lowell in

"Ode Recited at the Harvard Commemoration," a synonym for truth and all the best in the human spirit, a God available in our sense of beauty and the sublime. But Lowell's God is not a person, not the living God of the Bible and Christian sermonizing. Stripped of Lowell's manufactured fervor, his God might as well be the "invisible hand" of Adam Smith, so beloved by nineteenth-century liberal economists, a progressive and rational deity regulating the marketplace of human values to final good regardless of catastrophe to this or that individual along the way. Lowell even throws in a note of social Darwinism. The war has proved the nobility of American manhood—"a new imperial race."

As we have already seen, God is more grim and terrible in "The Battle Hymn of the Republic." In Whittier's "Laus Deo!" he is the predestinating God of the New England Puritans who finally vindicates the righteous. But the personal, living God whose eye is on the sparrow and who lifts up the fallen and heals the afflicted is scarcely evident in this poetry. The war was too much for him.

Among the educated in both Europe and America the skeptical tide of the nineteenth century was running at the full before the war began. Darwin's *Origin of Species* appeared in 1859, but religious skepticism did not wait for Darwin to become widespread. Tennyson's "In Memoriam," with its line "Nature red in tooth and claw," is a literary antecedent to the "survival of the fittest"—Herbert Spencer's term to describe Darwinism. Victor Hugo in France and Henry Wadsworth Longfellow in America were alike in shunning confessional religion in favor of lofty and vague sentiments. Outright expressions of atheism or agnosticism were rare in the United States but not unknown. Americans generally believed that an irreligious person could not be morally good. Or it may have been that they feared to renounce the God in whom they did not truly believe—a not uncommon human experience. Years after the war, Oliver Wendell Holmes wrote to Harold Laski, "I thought I was original in saying that I didn't believe in Hell but was afraid of it until I saw it quoted in a newspaper from Madam de Staël."[36]

A few were outspoken agnostics. The orator Robert Green Ingersoll (1833–1899), a veteran of the Union Army, scandalized the orthodox and scotched his political career with his witty attacks on Christianity and the Bible. Given the public temper, discretion for most religious doubters seemed the better part of valor. William Cullen Bryant published "Thanatopsis" in 1817, expressing a stoic view of death unconditioned by the consolation of orthodox religion. But he did so without overt attacks on traditional Christian doctrines or sensibilities, and the last verse of his beloved poem "To a Waterfowl" expressed a faith in divine providence.

In relative silence, therefore, a subterranean unbelief flowed in the American consciousness and was probably more substantial than many scholars have supposed. As anyone visiting a large nineteenth-century cemetery (especially in New England) can attest, religious inscriptions on tombstones became more and more rare. Those that did appear express laconic and vague sentiments capable of ambiguous interpretation.

Now and then soldiers were swept by religious enthusiasms as they are in any war. The Rev. R. E. McBride, a fighting veteran of the Union Army, recalled long afterward a revival "of extraordinary interest" during the winter lull of 1864–1865. The soldiers had no minister. "No! They themselves were ministers of God, anointed from on high for this work." McBride spoke glowingly of a "remarkable" conversion "during a meeting of peculiar power." The convert "fell in battle, March 31st, and died in the arms of his comrades, who were trying to carry him back when our line was broken and routed."[37] McBride, having become a minister after the war, does not tell us whether this example encouraged the others. Stonewall Jackson was notorious for his mumbled ritual prayers that prefaced almost every act and for his ceaseless and unsuccessful struggle to make his troops keep the Sabbath.[38] He believed that Southern victory was ordained by God and that if it were not, the fault lay with the sinfulness of the Southern people. Yet Royster estimates that only one third of Jackson's troops were church members, and, he says, "Revivals in the Confederate army did not touch the great majority of men."[39]

Much more typical, it seems, was the experience of Walt Whitman. Justin Kaplan mentions Whitman's disgust at the "Delegates of the Christian Commission" who visited military hospitals "distributing an appalling total of thirty-nine million pages of pious tracts and lecturing the legless on the evils of dancing." Whitman wrote, "You ought to see the way the men as they lie helpless in bed turn away their faces from the sight of these Agents, Chaplains, &c. (*hirelings* as Elias Hicks would call them—they seem to me always a set of foxes & wolves)."[40] A nurse wrote her husband, "There comes that odious Walt Whitman to talk evil and unbelief to my boys. . . . I think I would rather see the Evil One himself."[41]

For those who fought in it and lived to reflect on it, the horrors of massacre in combat seemed far beyond the thin power of any theology to knit together into some coherent framework of ultimate meaning. The war was too big to be a sign of something else—of divine providence or any other religious value; it was its own eternity. Wrote Whitman in "As I Lay with My Head in Your Lap Camerado":

And the threat of what is call'd hell is little or nothing to me

And the lure of what is call'd heaven is little or nothing to me;

Dear camerado! I confess I have urged you onward with me, and still urge you, without the least idea

    what is our destination,

Or whether we shall be victorious, or utterly quell'd and defeated.

Soldiers could not discern in the fighting the hand of God. Edgar Lee Masters, born after the war was over, looked back at "The Battle of Gettysburg" and said it was all staged by "the treacherous Tyche," the Greek goddess of chance, her image a rudder with which she guides the affairs of humankind for her own bleak purposes. In 1918 Oliver Wendell Holmes wrote to his friend Laski and demonstrated an attitude toward the divine akin to Whitman's:

I can't help an occasional semi-shudder as I remember that millions of intelligent men think that I am barred from the face of God unless I change. But how can one pretend to believe what seems to him childish and devoid alike of historical and rational foundations. . . . I am glad to remember that when I was dying after Ball's Bluff I remembered my father's saying that death-bed repentances generally meant only that the man was scared and reflected that if I wanted to I couldn't [repent] because I still thought the same. The last is the point, for I see no virtue in being brave against the universe—against the source of the power that enables you to raise your defiant fist.[42]

Perhaps Herman Melville's "The Conflict of Convictions" expresses a common religious mood among people educated well enough to write literate poetry. Here faith and doubt strive against each other.

But He who rules is old—is old;

Ah! faith is warm, but heaven with age is cold.

    (Ho ho, ho ho,

    The cloistered doubt

Of olden times
Is blurted out!)

The conclusion is ambiguous, an allusion to the appearance of God to Job to respond to the sufferer's plea for understanding:

Yea and nay—
Each hath his say,
But God He keeps the middle way.
None was by
When He spread the sky;
Wisdom is vain, and prophesy.[43]

Perhaps Whittier's "Battle Autumn of 1862" is as good an epitome as any to the religious doubts raised by random destruction. Here God is frankly Nature; after all the death and "bitter grief," she will bring "flower and leaf" to mock "the war-field's crimson stain." But whatever soaring hopes might be placed in Nature's capacity to redeem herself, death remains final in these poems. We find in them only shadowy expectations of eternal life or else no expectations at all. This attitude may account for the excessive sentimentality of some of them. It is as though the authors tried to stave off oblivion by multiplying adjectives, by trying to pump up emotion so that it might in itself be a kind of immortality. But sentimentality fails because it is the fervent declaration of beliefs that one does not and cannot hold in the face of events.

The vanity of such efforts was the inspiration of both Allen Tate and Robert Lowell long afterward in their meditations on the Confederate and Union dead respectively. Tate was a romantic about the Confederacy, the Lost Cause, the chivalric ideal that might have been. He thought that the nobility of this great vision was forgotten by a hurrying, industrial nation. His "Ode to the Confederate Dead" meditates on ephemeral memory and creeping oblivion. It glows with a sad wonder that the patiently accumulating years should make of such hot and gallant chivalry only a quiet, autumnal graveyard swirling with falling leaves. It is not merely a requiem for the Confederate dead but for a nation no longer interested in its own past.

In much the same mood, Tate's younger friend Robert Lowell wrote "For the Union Dead." Lowell fixes his attention on the Augustus Saint-Gaudens monument to Robert Gould Shaw and the 54th Massachusetts Infantry on the Boston Common opposite the Massachusetts State House on Beacon Street. Here is a slender Colonel Shaw on horseback, riding stiff and brave with his black regiment, soon to be cut to pieces by Confederate fire at Fort Wagner in South Carolina. Lowell's images are not of a quiet military graveyard settling into oblivion, but of the whirl and buzz of a modern city streaming by the Shaw Memorial, indifferent to its meaning and to the cause of justice for which these men, black and white, died.

Yet despite its horror, for its survivors the war was the most intense experience of their lives. Nothing afterward was the same. Some discovered, long before Wallace Stevens put the thought into words, that death was the mother of beauty. The senses were heightened with the desperate knowledge that time and death were speeding, that a vigorous young man astride his horse in the sun might be a mutilated corpse in an hour, in weeks an anonymous skeleton in an unmarked grave. Men learned that they were capable of bravery they could not have imagined before the war. Afterward they recalled their own deeds with amazement, although in a trance of mysterious recognition they remembered strangers on a stage doing incredible things. And momentary fragments of lost days glittered in their memories.

Whitman expressed these feelings most boldly and most eloquently, catching poetic snapshots of action—"Cavalry Crossing a Ford," "Bivouac on a Mountain Side," "An Army Corps on the March," "The Artilleryman's Vision." He thrilled to the war almost in spite of himself, and at the end, in his "Spirit Whose Work Is Done," he regretted the departure of its stupendous fervor.

Those who lived through the perils were forever changed and removed from the civilians who stayed at home. "To a Certain Civilian" Whitman wrote, "And go lull yourself with what you can understand, and with piano-tunes, / For I lull nobody, and you will never understand me." War provided a terrible wisdom that those who had not experienced it could never have. Says Daniel Aaron: "The 'civilian'— untested, insulated from the quintessential experience of violence and death—inhabited a different country and spoke in a different tongue. He was likely to be a 'patriot,' an idealist, an amateur; he believed in God and Providence, hated the enemy, and had not an inkling of the soldier's austere trade."[44]

As we have already noted, the common experience of battle brought veterans of both sides closer to each other than to the civilians in their own camps. Veterans streamed to reunions and created a fellowship of Blue and Gray that helped to seal the bonds of nationhood. In 1913, on the fiftieth anniversary of the battle of Gettysburg, 54,000 old soldiers from both sides gathered to remember together those distant hot and bloody days.[45] Twenty-five years later 1800 of them returned to hear Franklin Roosevelt speak of an old war at home while a new and more terrible conflict was brewing abroad.[46] By then the Civil War had become our national epic, our Troy, and our Agincourt, and the generals and common soldiers who fought in it had been lifted to a pantheon of myth.

Lincoln was the first to be the subject of apotheosis because he died at the hand of an assassin only two days after the telegraph brought news to Washington of Lee's surrender. Lincoln was martyr to the great cause. He inspired the best poetry of this type because Whitman was there to write it—although even Whitman wrote too much of it. But in some respects the poetry that gushed out to honor Lincoln was typical of verse in praise of famous and obscure heroes. Lincoln had been as reviled as any President in our history, not only in the South but also in the North. Yet the poetry about him cleansed away all criticism and elevated him to an alabaster sainthood. The same was true of poetry in honor of Stonewall Jackson, Robert E. Lee, Albert Sidney Johnston, Philip Sheridan, David G. Farragut, Ulysses S. Grant, and less notable men and women. The postwar poetry in this collection has little to say about profiteers, deserters, doubters, spies, bawds, cowards, and other such riffraff who plagued both sides throughout the great conflict. As the poets looked back on it, the war was a temple of demi-gods; it purified and burnished with glory everyone it touched.

Like Lincoln the Railsplitter, these are democratic heroes with the common touch. They are humble and selfless, akin to Everyman, a mirror of us all, but when duty calls, something glorious takes hold of them and lifts them to sublime accomplishment.

Seldom mentioned by white poets are the black soldiers who fought for the Union and the black slaves for whom the war was waged. Had it not been for the white Colonel Robert Gould Shaw of the 54th Massachusetts Infantry, mention of them would have been even more rare. Bret Harte's ghostly "Second Review of the Grand Army" presents the dead from the war marching at midnight through Washington. Among them

Came the dusky martyrs of Pillow's fight,

With limbs enfranchised and bearing bright;

I thought—perhaps 'twas the pale moonlight—

   They looked as white as their brothers!

Paul Laurence Dunbar (1872–1906), a black poet, whose short life came after the war, looked back on the pride of "The Colored Soldiers" fighting for their own liberty. But Dunbar lived in the days of Jim Crow, and his tone was forlorn. He addresses the image of Robert Gould Shaw, but in despair "Since thou and those who with thee died for right / Have died, the Present teaches, but in vain!"

Attitudes towards Shaw differ. He died heroically at the head of the 54th Massachusetts Infantry, the first regiment enlisted in the Union Army, and the Saint-Gaudens Memorial inspired several of the poems in this collection, including, as we have seen, Robert Lowell's "For the Union Dead." But James Russell Lowell's vapid "Memoriae Positum R. G. Shaw" offers not a hint that Shaw's men were black or that they did any fighting. Shaw is a paladin, the eternal golden youth. Lowell's attitude was shared by the makers of the monument. Only Shaw's name was inscribed on it when it was unveiled in May 1897. The names of the black troops of the 54th were not added until after World War II, long after all of them were dead. Robert Lowell, Langston Hughes, and John Berryman, meditating on the monument, include the black soldiers in their poetic reflections about Shaw. But theirs is a twentieth-century consciousness.

Bruce Catton called the final volume in his major history of the Civil War *A Stillness at Appomattox*. It is a striking title, evoking a mood found in many of our poets. The Civil War was without doubt the noisiest war in all history to that time. John Keegan notes that "at Agincourt noise would have been chiefly human and animal and would have overlaid the clatter of weapon-strokes." But, he says, "The noise of Waterloo assaulted the whole being."[47] That was 1815. Accounts of the Civil War—including much poetry—are filled with efforts to describe the various sounds of exploding shells, whirring bullets, roaring cannon, and yelling and screaming men, all in clouds of thick and rolling smoke. Confederate General E. Porter Alexander described the artillery and rifle fire at Gettysburg when Pickett's infantry charged on the third day. "The grand roar of nearly the whole artillery of both armies burst in on the silence, almost as suddenly as the full notes of an organ would fill a church. . . . The enemy's position seemed to have broken out with guns everywhere, and from Round Top to Cemetery Hill was blazing like a volcano."[48]

In all major battles, orders had to be written out because they could not be heard. No one either in poetry or in prose captured battle better than Whitman in "The Artilleryman's Vision," which actually celebrates the noise of conflict.

Then the war ended, and silence came again. The fields of Gettysburg went back to wheat and to monuments. At Shiloh Church and at Antietam and on the heights of Fredericksburg the placid routines of an ordinary life returned, and it was as if the furious chaos of war had never been. In orderly cemeteries the bones of dead soldiers leached into the soil, and moss crept over the stones. To this day the little stream called Bull Run still runs sluggishly across the fields where two great battles were fought, and the pond at Shiloh, where men of both sides drank during the battle, is clear of blood and reflects the sky amid silent trees. The Emmitsburg Road is paved now, and cars swish along it in and out of Gettysburg. Its line is unchanged from the torrid afternoon when Pickett's men swept across it with a continuous yell against a tumult of cannonfire and musketry—and shortly came back again, bleeding and beaten and uncaring at that moment for the glory to come when their effort would be remembered. Monuments stand everywhere on hundreds of fields—carved soldiers, gallant and mute forever in marble and granite, their stone images a doomed effort to recall furious days of blazing sound and fury, now passed away into silence. It is one of the ironies of American life that among the most peaceful places in the United States are the battlefields of our fiercest war.

William A. Frassanito has spent most of his life studying Civil War photography. His intriguing book *Grant and Lee: The Virginia Campaigns 1864–1865*[49] features many photographs taken during the war, matched with photographs he has taken of those same sites in recent times. It is uncanny to see houses, churches, fields, insignificant outbuildings, streets, and the configurations of the land itself, recognizable and ordinary today, and yet the scenes of tremendous events in the fading past. We see a great tree at Fredericksburg shading wounded Union soldiers and a medical man, and in an adjoining photograph we see that same tree standing today, alive on the same grassy mound, solitary and huge where children have played, unconscious of the drama of life and death enacted here.[50]

From the end of the war, this strangeness of ordinary places has haunted Americans, including their poets, when they have tried to recapture the conflict in their imaginations. We include at the end of this anthology a section we call "Stillness." It perhaps encompasses as much as any word can the uncanny and the sublime feelings that come to us when we visit these places of roaring tumult and shouting, fear and death, and find there serenity, meditation, and sadness at the erosions of time. It was our strangest war, and the wonder of it endures and draws generation after generation of us to itself. R. M.

Endnotes

1. Charles Royster, *The Destructive War* (New York: Alfred A. Knopf, 1991), pp. 144–92.

2. Richard Marius, "Non-Authorial Revisions in the Page-proofs for Evangeline," in *The Marks in the Fields: Essays on the Uses of Manuscripts*, ed. by Rodney G. Dennis (Cambridge, Mass.: The Houghton Library, 1992), pp. 77–85.

3. Quoted in Shelby Foote, *The Civil War: A Narrative—Fort Sumter to Perryville* (New York: Random House, 1958), p.706.

4. Royster, *Destructive War*, pp. 172–77.

5. Edward L. Ayres, *The Promise of the New South: Life after Reconstruction* (New York: Oxford University Press, 1992), p. 56.

6. Ibid., p. 9.

7. Ibid., p. 21. Ayres says that in a speech in 1886 to the New England Society of New York, "Grady serenely exaggerated the changes that had come to the South in the preceding few years in politics, in race relations, in industrial and agricultural growth."

8. Royster, *Destructive War*, p. 168. Royster says that six years after it was burned and pillaged by Sherman's army in February 1865, Columbia, South Carolina, published a 65-page booklet portraying the town as ideal for Northern investment and declaring, "The nationality or nativity of no man is questioned."

9. Ayres, *Promise of the New South*, pp. 30–33.

10. Shelby Foote, *The Civil War: A Narrative—Red River to Appomattox* (New York: Random House, 1974), pp. 1048–49.

11. Ibid., p. 1058.

12. Major DeWitt C. Sprague, "Poem," in *The Society of the Army of the Potomac: Report of the Sixteenth Annual Reunion, May 6 & 7, 1885* (New York: MacGowan and Shipper Printers, 1885), p. 22.

13. Daniel Aaron, *The Unwritten War* (Madison: University of Wisconsin Press, 1987), p. 255. Aaron comments on Mary Chesnut's attitude towards slaves and her "fears that the slaves were simply biding their time."

14. Ibid., p. 333.

15. For Woodrow Wilson's attitudes on race, see Richard Marius, "Many an Extravagant Prank and Mummery: Wilson, Race, and the Brahmin Historians," *Soundings* (Winter 1993): 439–65.

16. Royster, *Destructive War,* p. 172.

17. Ibid., pp. 148–49. Royster discusses Edward Everett Hale's short story "The Man without a Country," published in 1863, which makes much of the sacred symbol of the flag of the United States in the war.

18. John Keegan, *A History of Warfare* (New York: Alfred A. Knopf, 1993), p. 360.

19. *The Civil War: Master Index* (Alexandria, Virginia: Time-Life Books, 1987), p. 136.

20. Richard W. Murphy, *The Nation Reunited: War's Aftermath* (Alexandria, Virginia: Time-Life Books, 1987), p. 25.

21. John Keegan, *History of Warfare,* p. 356.

22. Foote, *Civil War: A Narrative—Fort Sumter to Perryville,* p. 702.

23. Champ Clark, *Gettysburg* (Alexandria, Virginia: Time-Life Books, 1985), pp. 145, 150.

24. Jonathan Raban, Introduction to *Life on the Mississippi,* by Mark Twain (New York: Vintage Books and the Library of America, 1991), pp. 284–85.

25. Foote, *Civil War: A Narrative—Fort Sumter to Perryville,* pp. 73–74.

26. Quoted in Foote, *The Civil War: A Narrative—Fort Sumter to Perryville,* p. 85.

27. John Keegan, *The Face of Battle* (Harmondsworth: Penguin Books, 1984), pp. 152–53, 314.

28. Ronald H. Bailey, *Forward to Richmond: McClellan's Peninsular Campaign* (Alexandria, Virginia: Time-Life Books, 1983), pp. 38–53.

29. Alan T. Nolan, *Lee Considered: General Robert E. Lee and Civil War History* (Chapel Hill: University of North Carolina Press, 1991), pp. 68–106.

30. Foote, *Civil War: A Narrative—Red River to Appomattox,* p. 290.

31. Ulysses S. Grant, *Memoirs and Selected Letters* (New York: The Library of America), p. 588.

32. Quoted in Justin Kaplan, *Walt Whitman: A Life* (New York: Simon and Schuster, 1980), p. 268.

33. *Letters from a Surgeon of the Civil War,* comp. by Martha Derby Perry (Boston: Little, Brown and Company, 1906), p. 189.

34. Ibid., p. 207.

35. Kaplan, *Walt Whitman,* p. 277.

36. *Holmes-Laski Letters: The Correspondence of Mr. Justice Holmes and Harold J. Laski, 1916–1935,* ed. by Mark DeWolfe Howe, with a foreword by Felix Frankfurter (Cambridge: Harvard University Press, 1953), p.153.

37. R. E. McBride, *In the Ranks: Wilderness to Appomattox Court-House* (Cincinnati: Walden & Stowe, 1881), pp. 159–60.

38. Royster, *Destructive War,* pp. 52–53.

39. Ibid., pp. 268–69.

40. Kaplan, *Walt Whitman*, p. 280.

41. Ibid., p. 276.

42. *Holmes-Laski Letters*, p. 154.

43. Compare Job 38:4–7: Where wast thou when I laid the foundations of the earth? declare, if thou hast understanding. Who hath laid the measures thereof, if thou knowest? or who hath stretched the line upon it? Whereupon are the foundations therefore fastened? or who laid the corner stone thereof; when the morning stars sang together, and all the sons of God shouted for joy?

44. Aaron, *Unwritten War*, p. 188.

45. Jack McLaughlin, *Gettysburg: The Long Encampment* (New York: Appleton-Century, 1963), p. 211.

46. Ibid., p. 223.

47. Keegan, *Face of Battle*, p. 141.

48. *Battles and Leaders of the Civil War*, ed. by Ned Bradford (New York: Fairfax Press, 1979), p. 395.

49. William A. Frassanito, *Grant and Lee: The Virginia Campaigns, 1864–1865* (New York: Charles Scribner's Sons, 1983).

50. Ibid., p. 75.

The Columbia Book of Civil War Poetry

Horrors of War ❧

SEVERN TEACKLE WALLIS (1816–1894) 🍂

A Prayer for Peace

Peace! Peace! God of our fathers grant us Peace!
Unto our cry of anguish and despair
Give ear and pity! From the lonely homes,
Where widowed beggary and orphaned woe
Fill their poor urns with tears; from trampled plains,
Where the bright harvest Thou hast sent us rots—
The blood of them who should have garnered it
Calling to Thee—from fields of carnage, where
The foul-beaked vultures, sated, flap their wings
O'er crowded corpses, that but yesterday
Bore hearts of brother, beating high with love
And common hopes and pride, all blasted now—
Father of Mercies! not alone from these
Our prayer and wail are lifted. Not alone
Upon the battle's seared and desolate track!
Nor with the sword and flame, is it, O God,
That thou hast smitten us. Around our hearths,
And in the crowded streets and busy marts,
Where echo whispers not the far-off strife

That slays our loved ones; in the solemn halls
Of safe and quiet counsel—nay, beneath
The temple roofs that we have reared to Thee,
And 'mid their rising incense—God of Peace!

The curse of war is on us. Greed and hate
Hungering for gold and blood; Ambition, bred
Of passionate vanity and sordid lusts,
Mad with the base desire of tyrannous sway
Over men's souls and thoughts, have set their price
On human hecatombs, and sell and buy
Their sons and brothers for the shambles. Priests,
With white, anointed, supplicating hands,
From Sabbath unto Sabbath clasped to Thee,
Burn in their tingling pulses, to fling down
Thy censers and Thy cross, to clutch the throats
Of kinsmen, by whose cradles they were born,
Or grasp the hand of Herod, and go forth
Till Rachel hath no children left to slay.
The very name of Jesus, writ upon
Thy shrines beneath the spotless, outstretched wings
Of Thine Almighty Dove, is wrapt and hid
With bloody battle-flags, and from the spires
That rise above them angry banners flout
The skies to which they point, amid the clang
Of rolling war-songs tuned to mock Thy praise.

All things once prized and honored are forgot;
The freedom that we worshipped next to Thee;
The manhood that was freedom's spear and shield;
The proud, true heart; the brave, outspoken word,

Which might be stifled, but could never wear
The guise, whate'er the profit, of a lie;
All these are gone, and in their stead have come
The vices of the miser and the slave—
Scorning no shame that bringeth gold or power,
Knowing no love, or faith, or reverence,
Or sympathy, or tie, or aim, or hope,
Save as begun in self, and ending there.
With vipers like to these, oh! blessed God!
Scourge us no longer! Send us down, once more,
Some shining seraph in Thy glory clad,
To wake the midnight of our sorrowing
With tidings of good-will and peace to men;
And if that star, that through the darkness led
Earth's wisdom the guide, not our folly now,
Oh, be the lightning Thine Evangelist,
With all its fiery, forked tongues, to speak
The unanswerable message of Thy will.

Peace! Peace! God of our fathers, grant us peace!
Peace to our hearts, and at Thine altars; peace
On the red waters and their blighted shores;
Peace for the 'leaguered cities, and the hosts
That watch and bleed around them and within,
Peace for the homeless and the fatherless;
Peace for the captive on his weary way,
And the mad crowds who jeer his helplessness;
For them that suffer, them that do the wrong
Sinning and sinned against. O God! for all;
For a distracted, torn, and bleeding land—
Speed the glad tidings! Give us, give us Peace!

HENRY WADSWORTH LONGFELLOW (1807–1882) 🌿

Killed at the Ford

A dirge for a bright young soldier killed at random, probably by a sharpshooter—the antithesis of the death prized in chivalric legends where brave men fought face to face. Longfellow was probably the most famous and most beloved poet in America, one of the few Northern poets much appreciated in the South despite his consistent antislavery sentiments.

He is dead, the beautiful youth,
The heart of honor, the tongue of truth,
He, the life and light of us all,
Whose voice was blithe as a bugle-call,
Whom all eyes followed with one consent,
The cheer of whose laugh, and whose pleasant word,
Hushed all murmurs of discontent.

Only last night, as we rode along,
Down the dark of the mountain gap,
To visit the picket-guard at the ford,
Little dreaming of any mishap,
He was humming the words of some old song:
"Two red roses he had on his cap
And another he bore at the point of his sword."

Sudden and swift a whistling ball
Came out of a wood, and the voice was still;
Something I heard in the darkness fall,

And for a moment my blood grew chill;
I spake in a whisper, as he who speaks
In a room where some one is lying dead;
But he made no answer to what I said.

We lifted him up to his saddle again,
And through the mire and the mist and the rain
Carried him back to the silent camp,
And laid him as if asleep on his bed;
And I saw by the light of the surgeon's lamp
Two white roses upon his cheeks,
And one, just over his heart, blood red!

And I saw in a vision how far and fleet
That fatal bullet went speeding forth,
Till it reached a town in the distant North,
Till it reached a house in a sunny street,
Till it reached a heart that ceased to beat
Without a murmur, without a cry;
And a bell was tolled in that far-off town,
For one who had passed from cross to crown,
And the neighbors wondered that she should die.

HERMAN MELVILLE (1819–1891)

Ball's Bluff

A Reverie
(October 1861)

*For the battle of Ball's Bluff, see
the Introduction. Melville had
published* Moby Dick *in 1851,
but he found few readers, and by
the time the Civil War came, he
thought himself a failure. He
published his Civil War poetry in
1866 in a volume he called* Battle
Pieces and Aspects of the War.

One noonday, at my window in the town,
   I saw a sight—saddest that eyes can see—
   Young soldiers marching lustily
      Unto the wars,
With fifes, and flags in mottoed pageantry;
    While all the porches, walks, and doors
   Were rich with ladies cheering royally.

They moved like Juny morning on the wave,
   Their hearts were fresh as clover in its prime
   (It was the breezy summer time),
      Life throbbed so strong,
How should they dream that Death in rosy clime
    Would come to thin their shining throng?
Youth feels immortal, like the gods sublime.

Weeks passed; and at my window, leaving bed,
   By night I mused, of easeful sleep bereft,
   On those brave boys (Ah War! thy theft);

Some marching feet
Found pause at last by cliffs Potomac cleft;
Wakeful I mused, while in the street
Far footfalls died away till none were left.

WALT WHITMAN (1819–1892) ❧

Vigil Strange I Kept on the Field One Night

Whitman published Leaves of
Grass in 1855, breaking away
from the conventions of rhyme and
meter that stultified so much
nineteenth-century poetry in
America. In December 1862 he
traveled down into Virginia to visit
his brother George who had
suffered a minor wound at
Fredericksburg. This visit exposed
him to the carnage of war, and
afterward when he took up
residence in Washington, he visited
military hospitals and comforted the
wounded of both sides. This poem
in which a father keeps watch over
the corpse of his son reflects the
fairly common occurrence of
fathers and sons going into battle
together. Robert E. Lee's son,
W. H. F. "Rooney" Lee, fought
as a cavalryman in the Army of
Northern Virginia.

Vigil strange I kept on the field one night;

When you my son and my comrade dropt at my side that day,

One look I but gave which your dear eyes return'd with a look I shall never forget,

One touch of your hand to mine O boy, reach'd up as you lay on the ground,

Then onward I sped in the battle, the even-contested battle,

Till late in the night reliev'd to the place at last again I made my way,

Found you in death so cold dear comrade, found your body son of responding kisses, (never
    again on earth responding,)

Bared your face in the starlight, curious the scene, cool blew the moderate night-wind,

Long there and then in vigil I stood, dimly around me the battlefield spreading,

Vigil wondrous and vigil sweet there in the fragrant silent night,

But not a tear fell, not even a long-drawn sigh, long, long I gazed,

Then on the earth partially reclining sat by your side leaning my chin in my hands,

Passing sweet hours, immortal and mystic hours with you dearest comrade—not a tear, not a word,

Vigil of silence, love and death, vigil for you my son and my soldier,

As onward silently stars aloft, eastward new ones upward stole,

Vigil final for you brave boy, (I could not save you, swift was your death,

I faithfully loved you and cared for you living, I think we shall surely meet again,)

Till at latest lingering of the night, indeed just as the dawn appear'd,

My comrade I wrapt in his blanket, envelop'd well his form,

Folded the blanket well, tucking it carefully over head and carefully under feet,

And there and then and bathed by the rising sun, my son in his grave, in his rude-dug grave I deposited,

Ending my vigil strange with that, vigil of night and battle-field dim,

Vigil for boy of responding kisses, (never again on earth responding,)

Vigil for comrade swiftly slain, vigil I never forget, how as day brighten'd,

I rose from the chill ground and folded my soldier well in his blanket,

And buried him where he fell.

WALT WHITMAN (1819–1892) 🪶

Dirge for Two Veterans

The last sunbeam
Lightly falls from the finish'd Sabbath,
On the pavement here, and there beyond it is looking,
    Down a new-made double grave.

Lo, the moon ascending,
Up from the east the silvery round moon,
Beautiful over the house-tops, ghastly, phantom moon,
    Immense and silent moon.

I see a sad procession,
And I hear the sound of coming full-key'd bugles,
All the channels of the city streets they're flooding,
    As with voices and with tears.

I hear the great drums pounding,
And the small drums steady whirring,
And every blow of the great convulsive drums,
    Strikes me through and through.

For the son is brought with the father,
(In the foremost ranks of the fierce assault they fell,
Two veterans son and father dropt together,
   And the double grave awaits them.)

Now nearer blow the bugles,
And the drums strike more convulsive,
And the daylight o'er the pavement quite has faded,
   And the strong dead-march enwraps me.

In the eastern sky up-buoying,
The sorrowful vast phantom moves illumin'd,
('Tis some mother's large transparent face,
   In heaven brighter growing.)

O strong dead-march, you please me!
O moon immense with your silvery face, you soothe me!
O my soldiers twain! O my veterans passing to burial!
   What I have I also give you.

The moon gives you light,
And the bugles and the drums give you music,
And my heart, O my soldiers, my veterans,
   My heart gives you love.

WALT WHITMAN (1819–1892)

A March in the Ranks Hard-prest and the Road Unknown

A vivid and detailed account of a makeshift hospital after battle. The blood and gore of the wounded are in vivid contrast to the church where they lie. In the Civil War, abdominal wounds were almost always fatal because surgeons had no way of dealing with their complications.

A march in the ranks hard-prest, and the road unknown,

A route through a heavy wood with muffled steps in the darkness,

Our army foil'd with loss severe, and the sullen remnant retreating,

Till after midnight glimmer upon us the lights of a dim-lighted building,

We come to an open space in the woods, and halt by the dim-lighted building,

'Tis a large old church at the crossing roads, now an impromptu hospital,

Entering but for a minute I see a sight beyond all the pictures and poems ever made,

Shadows of deepest, deepest black, just lit by moving candles and lamps,

And by one great pitchy torch stationary with wild red flame and clouds of smoke,

By these, crowds, groups of forms vaguely I see on the floor, some in the pews laid down,

At my feet more distinctly a solider, a mere lad, in danger of bleeding to death, (he is shot in
    the abdomen,)

I stanch the blood temporarily, (the youngster's face is white as a lily,)

Then before I depart I sweep my eyes o'er the scene fain to absorb it all,

Faces, varieties, postures beyond description, most in obscurity, some of them dead,

Surgeons operating, attendants holding lights, the smell of ether, the odor of blood,

The crowd, O the crowd of the bloody forms, the yard outside also fill'd,

Some on the bare ground, some on planks or stretchers, some in the death-spasm sweating,

An occasional scream or cry, the doctor's shouted orders or calls,

The glisten of the little steel instruments catching the glint of the torches,
These I resume as I chant, I see again the forms, I smell the odor,
Then hear outside the orders given, *Fall in, my men, fall in;*
But first I bend to the dying lad, his eyes open, a half-smile gives he me,
Then the eyes close, calmly close, and I speed forth to the darkness,
Resuming, marching, ever in darkness marching, on in the ranks,
The unknown road still marching.

Interior view of a military hospital (probably Carver Hospital, near Washington, D.C.)

A detailed account of wounds,
an account much at odds with the
romance of chivalry with which
young men rushed off to war.
The line "Come sweet death! be
persuaded O beautiful death!"
reflects the common nineteenth-
century sentimental theme that
death is beautiful, but it is here
placed in a context beyond
sentimentality.

WALT WHITMAN (1819–1892)

The Wound-Dresser

I An old man bending I come among new faces,
Years looking backward resuming in answer to children,
Come tell us old man, as from young men and maidens that love me,
(Arous'd and angry, I'd thought to beat the alarum, and urge relentless war,
But soon my fingers fail'd me, my face dropp'd and I resign'd myself,
To sit by the wounded and soothe them, or silently watch the dead;)
Years hence of these scenes, of these furious passions, these chances,
Of unsurpass'd heroes, (was one side so brave? the other was equally brave;)
Now be witness again, paint the mightiest armies of earth,
Of those armies so rapid so wondrous what saw you to tell us?
What stays with you latest and deepest? of curious panics,
Of hard-fought engagements or sieges tremendous what deepest remains?

II O maidens and young men I love and that love me,
What you ask of my days those the strangest and sudden your talking recalls,
Soldier alert I arrive after a long march cover'd with sweat and dust,
In the nick of time I come, plunge in the fight, loudly shout in the rush of successful charge,
Enter the captur'd works—yet lo, like a swift-running river they fade,

Pass and are gone they fade—I dwell not on soldiers' perils or soldiers' joys,
(Both I remember well—many the hardships, few the joys, yet I was content.)

But in silence, in dreams' projections,
While the world of gain and appearance and mirth goes on,
So soon what is over forgotten, and waves wash the imprints off the sand,
With hinged knees returning I enter the doors, (while for you up there,
Whoever you are, follow without noise and be of strong heart.)

Bearing the bandages, water and sponge,
Straight and swift to my wounded I go,
Where they lie on the ground after the battle brought in,
Where their priceless blood reddens the grass the ground,
Or to the rows of the hospital tent, or under the roof'd hospital,
To the long rows of cots up and down each side I return,
To each and all one after another I draw near, not one do I miss,
An attendant follows holding a tray, he carries a refuse pail,
Soon to be fill'd with clotted rags and blood, emptied, and fill'd again.

I onward go, I stop,
With hinged knees and steady hand to dress wounds,
I am firm with each, the pangs are sharp yet unavoidable,
One turns to me his appealing eyes—poor boy! I never knew you,
Yet I think I could not refuse this moment to die for you, if that would save you.

III   On, on I go, (open doors of time! open hospital doors!)
The crush'd head I dress, (poor crazed hand tear not the bandage away,)
The neck of the cavalry-man with the bullet through and through I examine,
Hard the breathing rattles, quite glazed already the eye, yet life struggles hard,
(Come sweet death! be persuaded O beautiful death!
In mercy come quickly.)

From the stump of the arm, the amputated hand,
I undo the clotted lint, remove the slough, wash off the matter and blood,
Back on his pillow the soldier bends with curv'd neck and side-falling head,
His eyes are closed, his face is pale, he dares not look on the bloody stump,
And has not yet look'd on it.

I dress a wound in the side, deep, deep,
But a day or two more, for see the frame all wasted and sinking,
And the yellow-blue countenance see.

I dress the perforated shoulder, the foot with the bullet-wound,
Cleanse the one with a gnawing and putrid gangrene, so sickening, so offensive,
While the attendant stands behind aside me holding the tray and pail.

I am faithful, I do not give out,
The fractur'd thigh, the knee, the wound in the abdomen,
These and more I dress with impassive hand, (yet deep in my breast a fire, a burning flame.)

IV Thus in silence in dreams' projections,
Returning, resuming, I thread my way through the hospitals,
The hurt and wounded I pacify with soothing hand,
I sit by the restless all the dark night, some are so young,
Some suffer so much, I recall the experience sweet and sad,
(Many a soldier's loving arms about this neck have cross'd and rested,
Many a soldier's kiss dwells on these bearded lips.)

THADDEUS OLIVER (1826–1864) ❧

All Quiet along the Potomac Tonight

"All quiet along the Potomac to-night!"
    Except here and there a stray picket
Is shot, as he walks on his beat, to and fro,
    By a rifleman hid in the thicket.

'Tis nothing! a private or two now and then
    Will not count in the news of a battle;
Not an officer lost! only one of the men
    Moaning out, all alone, the death-rattle.

All quiet along the Potomac to-night!
    Where soldiers lie peacefully dreaming;
And their tents in the rays of the clear autumn moon,
    And the light of their camp-fires are gleaming.

A tremulous sigh, as a gentle night-wind
    Through the forest leaves slowly is creeping;
While the stars up above, with their glittering eyes,
    Keep guard o'er the army while sleeping.

There's only the sound of the lone sentry's tread,
    As he tramps from the rock to the fountain,
And he thinks of the two on the low trundle bed,
    Far away, in the cot on the mountain.

His musket falls slack, his face, dark and grim,
    Grows gentle with memories tender,
As he mutters a prayer for the children asleep,
    And their mother—"may heaven defend her!"

The moon seems to shine forth as brightly as then—
    That night, when the love, yet unspoken,
Leaped up to his lips, and when low-murmured vows
    Were pledged to be ever unbroken.

Then drawing his sleeve roughly over his eyes,
    He dashes off tears that are welling;
And gathers his gun closer up to his breast,
    As if to keep down the heart's swelling.

He passes the fountain, the blasted pine-tree,
    And his footstep is lagging and weary;
Yet onward he goes, through the broad belt of light,
    Towards the shades of the forest so dreary.

Hark! was it the night wind that rustled the leaves?
    Was it moonlight so wondrously flashing?
It looked like a rifle: "Ha! Mary, good-bye!"
    And his life-blood is ebbing and splashing.

"All quiet along the Potomac to-night!"
    No sound save the rush of the river;
While soft falls the dew on the face of the dead,
    And the picket's off duty forever!

Harte spent the war in California, far from combat. As he suggests in the first line, his knowledge of the war came chiefly from what he read about it. The "Grand Review" of the Army of the Potomac, the Army of Georgia, and the Army of Tennessee featured a parade of about 150,000 soldiers marching down Pennsylvania Avenue from The Capitol through thousands of cheering spectators at the end of the war. So many troops were involved that the parade required two days — May 23 and 24, 1865. The memory of the dead and wounded was preserved by banners of black crepe and by the ambulance wagons that followed each brigade.

BRET HARTE (1836–1902)

A Second Review of the Grand Army
(May 24, 1865)

I read last night of the Grand Review
   In Washington's chiefest avenue, —
Two hundred thousand men in blue,
   I think they said was the number, —
Till I seemed to hear their trampling feet,
The bugle blast and the drum's quick beat,
The clatter of hoofs in the stony street,
The cheers of people who came to greet,
And the thousand details that to repeat
   Would only my verse encumber, —
Till I fell in a revery, sad and sweet,
   And then to a fitful slumber.

When, lo! in a vision I seemed to stand
In the lonely Capitol. On each hand
Far stretched the portico, dim and grand
Its columns ranged, like a martial band
Of sheeted spectres, whom some command
   Had called to a last reviewing.

Grand Review, Washington, D.C.

And the streets of the city were white and bare;
No footfall echoed across the square;
But out of the misty midnight air
I heard in the distance a trumpet blare,
And the wandering night-winds seemed to bear
    The sound of a far tattooing.

Then I held my breath with fear and dread;
For into the square, with a brazen tread,
There rode a figure whose stately head
    O'erlooked the review that morning,
That never bowed from its firm-set seat
When the living column passed its feet,
Yet now rode steadily up the street
    To the phantom bugle's warning:

Till it reached the Capitol square, and wheeled,
And there in the moonlight stood revealed
A well-known form that in State and field
    Had led our patriot sires:
Whose face was turned to the sleeping camp,
Afar through the river's fog and damp,
That showed no flicker, nor waning lamp,
    Nor wasted bivouac fires.

And I saw a phantom army come,
With never a sound of fife or drum,
But keeping time to a throbbing hum
    Of wailing and lamentation:
The martyred heroes of Malvern Hill,
Of Gettysburg and Chancellorsville,

The men whose wasted figures fill
    The patriot graves of the nation.

And there came the nameless dead, — the men
Who perished in fever-swamp and fen,
The slowly-starved of the prison-pen;
    And, marching beside the others,
Came the dusky martyrs of Pillow's fight,
With limbs enfranchised and bearing bright:
I thought — perhaps 'twas the pale moonlight —
    They looked as white as their brothers!

And so all night marched the Nation's dead,
With never a banner above them spread,
Nor a badge, nor a motto brandished;
No mark — save the bare uncovered head
    Of the silent bronze Reviewer;
With never an arch save the vaulted sky;
With never a flower save those that lie
On the distant graves — for love could buy
    No gift that was purer or truer.

So all night long swept the strange array;
So all night long, till the morning gray,
I watch'd for one who had passed away,
    With a reverent awe and wonder, —
Till a blue cap waved in the lengthening line,
And I knew that one who was kin of mine
Had come; and I spake — and lo! that sign
    Awakened me from my slumber.

STEPHEN VINCENT BENÉT (1898–1943) ❦

The Congressmen Came Out to See Bull Run

From: *John Brown's Body*

The congressmen came out to see Bull Run,
The congressmen who like free shows and spectacles.
They brought their wives and carriages along,
They brought their speeches and their picnic-lunch,
Their black constituent-hats and their devotion:
Some even brought a little whiskey, too.
(A little whiskey is a comforting thing
For congressmen in the sun, in the heat of the sun.)
The bearded congressmen with orator's mouths,
The fine, clean-shaved, Websterian congressmen,
Come out to see the gladiator's show
Like Iliad gods, wrapped in the sacred cloud
Of Florida-water, wisdom and bay-rum,
Of free cigars, democracy and votes,
That lends such portliness to congressmen.
(The gates fly wide, the bronze troop marches out
Into the stripped and deadly circus-ring,
"*Ave, Caesar!*" the cry goes up, and shakes

B-5148

Battlefield of Bull Run

The purple awning over Caesar's seat.)
"*Ave, Caesar! Ave*, O congressmen,
We who are about to die.
Salute you, congressmen!"
Eleven States,
New York, Rhode Island, Maine,
Connecticut, Michigan and the gathered West,
Salute you, congressmen!
The red-fezzed Fire-Zouaves, flamingo-bright,
Salute you, congressmen!
The raw boys still in their civilian clothes,
Salute you, congressmen!
The second Wisconsin in its homespun grey,
Salutes you, congressmen!
The Garibaldi Guards in cocksfeather hats,
Salute you, congressmen!
The Second Ohio with their Bedouin-caps,
Salutes you, congressmen!
Sherman's brigade, grey-headed Heintzelman,
Ricketts' and Griffin's doomed and valiant guns,
The tough, hard-bitten regulars of Sykes
Who covered the retreat with the Marines,
Burnside and Porter, Willcox and McDowell,
All the vast, unprepared, militia-mass
Of boys in red and yellow Zouave pants,
Who carried peach-preserves inside their kits
And dreamt of being generals overnight;
The straggling companies where every man
Was a sovereign and a voter—the slack regiments
Where every company marched a different step;
The clumsy and unwieldy-new brigades

Not yet distempered into battle-worms;
The whole, huge, innocent army, ready to fight
But only half-taught in the tricks of fighting,
Ready to die like picture-postcard boys
While fighting still had banners and a sword
And just as ready to run in blind mob-panic,
Salutes you with a vast and thunderous cry,
Ave, Caesar, ave, O congressmen,
Ave, O Iliad gods who forced the fight!
You bring your carriages and your picnic-lunch
To cheer us in our need.

                   You come with speeches,
Your togas smell of heroism and bay-rum.
You are the people and the voice of the people
And, when the fight is done, your carriages
Will bear you safely, through the streaming rout
Of broken troops, throwing their guns away.
You come to see the gladiator's show,
But from a high place, as befits the wise:
You will not see the long windrows of men
Strewn like dead pears before the Henry House
Or the stone-wall of Jackson breathe its parched
Devouring breath upon the failing charge,
Ave, Caesar, ave, O congressmen,
Cigar-smoke wraps you in a godlike cloud,
And if you are not to depart from us
As easily and divinely as you came,
It hardly matters.

                 Fighting Joe Hooker once
Said with that tart, unbridled tongue of his
That made so many needless enemies,

"Who ever saw a dead cavalryman?"

         The phrase

Stings with a needle sharpness, just or not,

But even he was never heard to say,

"Who ever saw a dead congressman?"

And yet, he was a man with a sharp tongue.

ROBERT PENN WARREN (1905–1989) 🪶

Two Studies in Idealism: Short Survey
of American and Human History

(For Allan Nevins)

Warren was a Kentuckian,
educated at Vanderbilt, Yale, and
Oxford, and early a member of the
literary group called the Fugitives,
after a journal called The Futigive
that they published for a time at
Vanderbilt. He was more
ambivalent toward the Southern
rural heritage than such fellow
Fugitives as Allen Tate, Donald
Davidson, and Andrew Lytle.
Two soldiers think they kill for
different reasons and in different
spirits. But both of them kill—and
are killed.

I   Bear Track Plantation: Shortly after Shiloh

Two things a man's built for, killing and you-know-what.
As for you-know-what, I reckon I taken my share,
Bed-ease or bush-whack, but killing—hell, three's all I got,
And he promised me ten, Jeff Davis, the bastard. 'Taint fair.

It ain't fair, a man rides and knows he won't live forever,
And a man needs something to take with him when he dies.
Ain't much worth taking, but what happens under the cover
Or at the steel-point—yeah, that look in their eyes.

That same look, it comes in their eyes when you give 'em the business.
It's something a man can hang on to, come black-frost or sun.
Come hell or high water, it's something to save from the mess,
No matter whatever else you never got done.

For a second it seems like a man can know what he lives for,
When those eyelids go waggle, or maybe the eyes pop wide,

And that look comes there. Yeah, Christ, then you know who you are—
And will maybe remember that much even after you've died.

But now I lie worrying what look my own eyes got
When that Blue-Belly caught me off balance. Did my look mean then
That I'd honed for something not killing or you-know-what?
Hell, no. I'd lie easy if Jeff had just give me that ten.

II   Harvard '61: Battle Fatigue

I didn't mind dying—it wasn't that at all.
It behooves a man to prove manhood by dying for Right.
If you die for Right that fact is your dearest requital,
But you find it disturbing when others die who simply haven't the right.

Why should they die with that obscene insouciance?
They seem to insult the principle of your own death.
Touch pitch, be defiled: it was hard to keep proper distance
From such unprincipled wastrels of blood and profligates of breath.

I tried to slay without rancor, and often succeeded.
I tried to keep the heart pure, though my hand took stain.
But they made it so hard for me, the way they proceeded
To parody with their own dying that Death which only Right should
    sustain.

Time passed. It got worse. It seemed like a plot against me.
I said they had made their own evil bed and lay on it,
But they grinned in the dark—they grinned—and I yet see
That last one. At woods-edge we held, and over the stubble they came
    with bayonet.

Jefferson Davis, President of the Confederate States

He uttered his yell, he was there!—teeth yellow, some missing.
Why, he's old as my father, I thought, finger frozen on trigger.
I saw the ambeer on his whiskers, heard the old breath hissing.
The puncture came small on his chest. 'Twas nothing. The stain then got
    bigger.

And he said: "Why, son, you done done it—I figgered I'd skeered ye."
Said: "Son, you look puke-pale. Buck up! If it hadn't been you,
Some other young squirt would a-done it." I stood, and weirdly
The tumult of battle went soundless, like gesture in dream. And I was
    dead, too.

Dead, and had died for the Right, as I had a right to,
And glad to be dead, and hold my residence
Beyond life's awful illogic, and the world's stew,
Where people who haven't the right just die, with ghastly impertinence.

ELIZABETH BISHOP (1911–1979) 🦅

Bishop wrote about historical themes. The English author Anthony Trollope visited the United States several times and was in this country at the outbreak of the Civil War.

From Trollope's Journal

(Winter, 1861)

As far as statues go, so far there's not
much choice: they're either Washingtons
or Indians, a whitewashed, stubby lot,
His country's Father or His foster sons.
The White House in a sad, unhealthy spot
just higher than Potomac's swampy brim,
—they say the present President has got
ague or fever in each backwoods limb.
On Sunday afternoon I wandered,—rather,
I floundered,—out alone. The air was raw
and dark; the marsh half-ice, half-mud. This weather
is normal now: a frost, and then a thaw,
and then a frost. A hunting man, I found
the Pennsylvania Avenue heavy ground . . .
There all around me in the ugly mud,
—hoof-pocked, uncultivated,—herds of cattle,
numberless, wond'ring steers and oxen, stood:
beef for the Army, after the next battle.
Their legs were caked the color of dried blood;

their horns were wreathed with fog. Poor, starving, dumb
or lowing creatures, never to chew the cud
or fill their maws again! Th'effluvium
made that damned anthrax on my forehead throb.
I called a surgeon in, a young man, but,
with a sore throat himself, he did his job.
We talked about the War, and as he cut
away, he croaked out, "Sir, I do declare
everyone's sick! The soldiers poison the air."

JILL BRECKENRIDGE

General John Cabell Breckinridge

My Recurring Dream: December 2, 1862
From: Civil Blood

*Breckenridge is a modern poet,
and she wrote this poem in 1986.
John Cabell Breckinridge was a
Kentuckian, Vice President of the
United States under President
James Buchanan and Lincoln's
Democratic opponent in the
Presidential election of 1860.
Although he thought that the states
had the right to secede, he was not
sure that secession was wise when
it came. He served as a general in
the Confederate Army and in
December 1862 was serving in the
command of General Braxton
Bragg in Tennessee, south of
Nashville. The significance of the
date December 2 is difficult to
assess, since no major action
occurred on that day. On
December 3, a Confederate force
attacked a Union wagon convoy
foraging for food near Nashville.*

Every night I dream we're fighting, armies raised
high to celestial fields flooded with lunar light.
Up in the sky, everything moves faster in the mercury
of air. The armies step across clouds, brisker than
before, heaviness gone from their feet. Then the
firing begins; one shot, and the white sky crumbles.
A cough, a sigh float across the field. The drummer
boy is fiercely drumming as a big man carries him
across the stream. Bayonets sparkle like winter stars.
The armies advance, blue and gray, December wind punishing
every inch of skin. No blood stains red this nightly war,
fought in black and white. A harvest moon shines on the
jumble of mangled forms. Stands of grass bend and dry
before they burn. A soldier has found his left foot
hiding inside his boot; one gropes for his head, but it
has rolled away. Another limps, using his gun as a crutch.
When fire starts up in the field, the wounded call for help.
Now they're begging. Shells pop like fireworks to punctuate
their screams. I carry wounded men from the field, stumble

Confederate General John C. Breckinridge, of Kentucky

and fall, flames raging closer. Face stinging from the heat,
I smell my mustache burning, run, flames surrounding me,
wake thrashing, wet with perspiration. Rising alone, I
build up the fire, heat some water for coffee to rinse
the taste of gunpowder and smoke from my mouth.

Hudgins assumes the persona
of Sidney Lanier, poet and
Confederate soldier, who became
a poet and lecturer on English
literature at Johns Hopkins
University in Baltimore. As this
poem says, Confederate soldiers
often stripped clothing off dead
Union soldiers on the field of
battle. The Confederates, lacking
clothing factories, suffered terribly
from the lack of shoes and clothing
throughout the war. At
Chancellorsville, Virginia, on the
first four days of May 1863, Lee's
outnumbered Army of Northern
Virginia inflicted a humiliating
defeat on the Army of the
Potomac under the command of
General Joseph Hooker.

ANDREW HUDGINS (1951–)

At Chancellorsville
The Battle of the Wilderness

He was an Indiana corporal
shot in the thigh when their line broke
in animal disarray. He'd crawled
into the shade and bled to death.
My uniform was shabby with
continuous wear, worn down to threads
by the inside friction of my flesh on cloth.
The armpit seams were rotted through
and almost half the buttons had dropped off.
My brother said I should remove
the Yank's clean shirt: "From now on, Sid,
he'll have no use for it." Imagining
the slack flesh shifting underneath
my hands, the other-person stink
of that man's shirt, so newly his,
I cursed Clifford from his eyeballs to
his feet. I'd never talked that way before
and didn't know I could. When we returned,
someone had beat me to the shirt.

So I had compromised my soul
for nothing I would want to use—
some knowledge I could do without.
Clifford, thank God, just laughed. It was good
stout wool, unmarked by blood.
By autumn, we wore so much blue
we could have passed for New York infantry.

The poem suggests the irrationality
that war brings on those who fight
it. The date places this incident in
the battle of Chancellorsville,
although mention of the
"Wilderness" suggests the fighting
between Grant and Lee a year later
in the Wilderness Campaign.

ANDREW HUDGINS (1951–) ✌

After the Wilderness
(May 3, 1863)

When Clifford wasn't back to camp by nine,
I went to look among the fields of dead
before we lost him to a common grave.
But I kept tripping over living men
and had to stop and carry them to help
or carry them until they died,
which happened more than once upon my back.
And I got angry with those men because
they kept me from my search and I was out
still stumbling through the churned-up earth at dawn,
stopping to stare into each corpse's face,
and all the while I was writing in my head
the letter I would have to send our father,
saying Clifford was lost and I had lost him.

I found him bent above a dying squirrel
while trying to revive the little thing.
A battlefield is full of trash like that—
dead birds and squirrels, bits of uniform.

Its belly racked for air. It couldn't live.
Cliff knew it couldn't live without a jaw.
When in relief I called his name, he stared,
jumped back, and hissed at me like a startled cat.
I edged up slowly, murmuring "Clifford, Cliff,"
as you might talk to calm a skittery mare,
and then I helped him kill and bury all
the wounded squirrels he'd gathered from the field.
It seemed a game we might have played as boys.
We didn't bury them all at once, with lime,
the way they do on burial detail,
but scooped a dozen, tiny, separate graves.
When we were done he fell across the graves
and sobbed as though they'd been his unborn sons.
His chest was large—it covered most of them.
I wiped his tears and stroked his matted hair,
and as I hugged him to my chest I saw
he'd wet his pants. We called it Yankee tea.

*Another poem on the random
nature of death in war, ending with
the comment, "From this, I didn't
learn a thing," testifying to the
meaninglessness of the conflict for
the individual soldier. To speak of
"in-coming shells" is anachronistic
language, reminding us of the
Vietnam war when the phrase was
common and reminding us, too, of
the meaninglessness of that war to
many who opposed its carnage.*

ANDREW HUDGINS (1951–) 🖋

Around the Campfire

Around the campfire we sang hymns.
When asked I'd play my flute, and lay
a melody between night's
incessant cannonfire that boomed
irregularly, but with the depth
of kettle drums. Occasionally,
in lulls, we'd hear a fading snatch
of Yankee song sucked to us in
the backwash of their cannonballs.
These are, oddly enough, fond memories.

One night, a Texas boy sat down
and strummed a homemade banjo,
He'd bought it for a canteen full
of corn. He followed me around
and pestered me to teach him notes.
He loved that ragged box but, Lord,
he couldn't play it worth a damn.
Nobody could. I tried to tell him so.

"Hell, I know, Sid," he said. "If I
were any good, it would worry me
too much. This way I can just blame
the instrument."

And this, too, is
a fond instructive memory.

Boom BOOM. "Listen to that," he said.
Then silence once again as Yanks
swabbed out the cannonbarrel and rammed
another charge into the gun. They paused
a minute in their work. *Boom BOOM.*
Our cannon fired in answer to
in-coming shells. "Don't they," he asked
"sound like a giant limping through
the woods in search of us?" I laughed.
It was a peaceful night and we
were working on some liquid corn.
Boom BOOM. I filled my cup again
and said, "He's after us all right."
He laughed. *Boom BOOM.* I sloshed more in
his cup. A shell exploded to our right.
A piece of shrapnel nicked my ear,
and when the smoke had cleared, I saw
him sitting, looking for his cup
and for the hand he'd held it in.

From this, I didn't learn a thing.

Moral Fervor ❧

The Fugitive Slave Law was part
of the Compromise of 1850. It
allowed slave owners to pursue
runaway slaves to any part of the
United States and to bring them
back to slavery in the South. The
word "Confederacy" here means
not the Confederate States, which
had not seceded when the poem
was written, but the Union of
states supposedly preserved by the
Fugitive Slave Law.

ELYMAS PAYSON ROGERS (1815–1861) 🖎

In 'Fifty Congress Passed a Bill
From: "A Poem on the Fugitive Slave Law"

In 'fifty, Congress passed a Bill,
Which proved a crude and bitter pill
At least in many a northern mouth,
Though sweet as honey at the South.
It was the object of this Act
(By priests and politicians backed)
That masters might with ease retake
The wretched slaves who chanced to break
Away from servitude thenceforth,
And sought a refuge at the North.

It was the purpose of this Act
To make the Northern States, in fact,
The brutal master's hunting grounds,
To be explored by human hounds
Who would, for shining gold, again
Bind on the bleeding captive's chain.
This Bill most clearly was designed
To prejudice the public mind

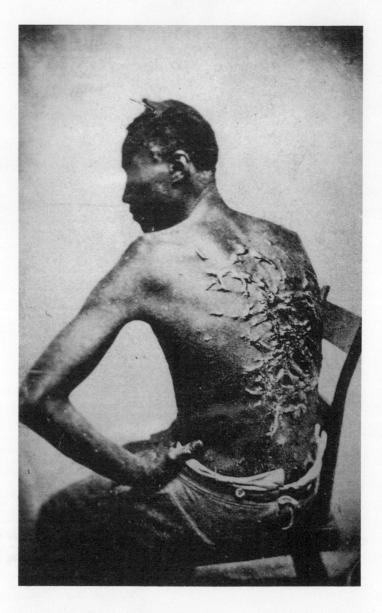

"Overseer Artayou Carrier whipped me. I was two months in bed sore from the whipping. My master came after I was whipped; he discharged the overseer."

The very words of poor Peter as he sat for his picture, April 2, 1863

In favor of the master's claim,
Howe'er circuitous or lame.

From officers of baser sort,
The Bill sought sanction and support:
And lawyers bought of no repute
And bribed the dough-faced judge to boot,
It gave encouragement to knaves,
It mocked the suff'rings of the slaves
By giving, if the slave went free,
The judge five dollars as his fee.
But if the judge bound on his chains,
He won ten dollars for his pains.

Go to yon Capitol and look
On this free nation's statute book,
And there you'll find the monstrous Bill
Upon the nation's records still.
And dough-faced politicians now
Their rev'rence for the Act avow,
And hundreds impudently say
That all should peacefully obey
The Act, and yield to its demands,
And give back to the master's hands
The poor, dejected, bleeding slave,
This great Confederacy to save.
We scarce can quench our indignation,
Aroused by such an intimation,
For government should man befit,
And not man sacrifice to it.
And if the Union long has stood

Cemented with the bondsman's blood;
If human hearts and human bone
Are truly its chief corner stone;
If State from State would soon divide
If not with negro sinews tied;
Then let th' accursed Union go,
And let her drift, or, sink below,
Or, let her quick in sunder break
And so become a shattered wreck.

And is that vile requirement just
Which tramples manhood in the dust?
Shall we arrest escaping slaves
At every beck of Southern knaves?
Shall Northern freemen heed a few
Of that untoward apostate crew,
And, let them hunt upon their soil
And drag to unrequited toil
A man, however rude or raw,
Because of that nefarious law
Which causes liberty to bleed,
And gravely sanctions such a deed?

Only the words to the first verse seem generally agreed upon. The other verses are as varied as folk tradition can make them. But whatever the variations, the song intends to link the war to freeing the slaves. The song, sung in four/four time, is the ideal cadence for a parade march. The left foot would come down on the first syllable of each line and the right foot at the end of each line would signal a pause and a breath to begin the next line. As a marching song it was never supplanted, not even by Julia Ward Howe's "Battle Hymn of the Republic." Sherman's men marching out of Atlanta sang "John Brown's Body."

Attributed to CHARLES SPRAGUE HALL *and to*
THOMAS BRIGHAM BISHOP ✒

John Brown's Body

John Brown's body lies a-mould'ring in the grave,
John Brown's body lies a-mould'ring in the grave,
John Brown's body lies a-mould'ring in the grave,
His soul goes marching on!

Chorus:
Glory, glory! Hallelujah!
Glory, glory! Hallelujah!
Glory, glory! Hallelujah!
His soul is marching on!

He captured Harper's Ferry with his nineteen men so true,
And he frightened old Virginia till she trembled through and through.
They hung him for a traitor, themselves the traitor crew,
But his soul is marching on!

John Brown died that the slave might be free,
John Brown died that the slave might be free,

John Brown died that the slave might be free,
   And his soul is marching on!

The stars of Heaven are looking kindly down,
The stars of Heaven are looking kindly down,
The stars of Heaven are looking kindly down,
   On the grave of old John Brown.

Now has come the glorious jubilee,
Now has come the glorious jubilee,
Now has come the glorious jubilee,
   When all mankind are free.

Howe was an ardent abolitionist and feminist. She and her husband, Samuel G. Howe, edited the Boston Commonwealth, *dedicated to freeing the slaves. Her poem/song is discussed in the Introduction. The war is seen as a Providential Day of Judgment and the introduction of the Day of Jubilee, the Millennium when the nation will live by God's will.*

JULIA WARD HOWE (1819–1910) ✍

The Battle Hymn of the Republic

Mine eyes have seen the glory of the coming of the Lord;
He is trampling out the vintage where the grapes of wrath are stored;
He hath loosed the fateful lightning of His terrible swift sword;
    His truth is marching on.

    Glory! Glory! Hallelujah!
    Glory! Glory! Hallelujah!
    Glory! Glory! Hallelujah!
    His truth is marching on.

I have seen Him in the watch fires of a hundred circling camps
They have builded Him an altar in the evening dews and damps;
I can read His righteous sentence by the dim and flaring lamps;
    His day is marching on.

    Glory! Glory! Hallelujah!
    Glory! Glory! Hallelujah!
    Glory! Glory! Hallelujah!
    His day is marching on.

He has sounded forth the trumpet that shall never call retreat;
He is sifting out the hearts of men before His judgment seat;
Oh, be swift, my soul, to answer Him; be jubilant, my feet;
 Our God is marching on.

 Glory! Glory! Hallelujah!
 Glory! Glory! Hallelujah!
 Glory! Glory! Hallelujah!
 Our God is marching on.

In the beauty of the lilies Christ was born across the sea,
With a glory in His bosom that transfigures you and me;
As He died to make men holy, let us die to make men free;
 While God is marching on.

 Glory! Glory! Hallelujah!
 Glory! Glory! Hallelujah!
 Glory! Glory! Hallelujah!
 While God is marching on.

Root was probably the most popular song writer on the Northern side during the Civil War. His themes tended to be lugubrious. In addition to this poem he wrote "Tramp, Tramp, Tramp, the Boys Are Marching," supposedly in the voice of Union prisoners of war in the atrocious Southern prison camps, awaiting liberation by their victorious comrades. He also wrote "Just before the Battle, Mother," interesting because it is another song in the democratic hero tradition spawned by the Civil War.

GEORGE FREDERICK ROOT (1820–1895) ❧

The Battle-Cry of Freedom

Yes, we'll rally round the flag, boys, we'll rally once again,
   Shouting the battle cry of Freedom;
We will rally from the hillside, we'll gather from the plain,
   Shouting the battle cry of Freedom.

  Refrain:
     The Union forever, Hurrah! boys, Hurrah!
     Down with the traitor, up with the stars;
     While we rally round the flag, boys, rally once again,
     Shouting the battle cry of Freedom.

We are springing to the call of our brothers gone before,
   Shouting the battle cry of Freedom;
And we'll fill the vacant ranks with a million free men more,
   Shouting the battle cry of Freedom.

We will welcome to our numbers the loyal, true, and brave,
    Shouting the battle cry of Freedom;
And although they may be poor, not a man shall be a slave,
    Shouting the battle cry of Freedom.

So we're springing to the call from the East and from the West,
    Shouting the battle cry of Freedom;
And we'll prove a loyal crew for the land we love the best,
    Shouting the battle cry of Freedom.

On April 19, 1861, the 6th
Massachusetts Infantry on its way
to Washington was attacked by a
mob in Baltimore. The troops, in
self-defense, fired on the crowd,
killing a number of civilians.
Randall composed this wretched
poem to commemorate the event
and in hopes of coaxing Maryland
into insurrection, a move that
would have made Washington
untenable. Maryland remained in
the Union, but Randall's poem
became its state song—surely
because it had no competition.

JAMES RYDER RANDALL (1839–1908) ✍

My Maryland

The despot's heel is on thy shore,
    Maryland!
His torch is at thy temple door,
    Maryland!
Avenge the patriotic gore
That flecked the streets of Baltimore,
And be the battle-queen of yore,
    Maryland! my Maryland!

Hark to an exiled son's appeal,
    Maryland!
My Mother State, to thee I kneel,
    Maryland!
For life and death, for woe and weal,
Thy peerless chivalry reveal,
And gird thy beauteous limbs with steel,
    Maryland! my Maryland!

Thou wilt not cower in the dust,
    Maryland!
Thy beaming sword shall never rust,
    Maryland!
Remember Carroll's sacred trust,
Remember Howard's warlike thrust,
And all thy slumberers with the just,
    Maryland! my Maryland!

Come! 'tis the red dawn of the day,
    Maryland!
Come with thy panoplied array,
    Maryland!
With Ringgold's spirit of the fray,
With Watson's blood at Monterey,
With fearless Lowe and dashing May,
    Maryland! my Maryland!

Come! for thy shield is bright and strong,
    Maryland!
Come! for thy dalliance does thee wrong,
    Maryland!
Come to thine own heroic throng
Stalking with Liberty along,
And chant thy dauntless slogan-song,
    Maryland! my Maryland!

Dear mother! burst the tyrant's chain,
    Maryland!
Virginia should not call in vain,
    Maryland!

She meets her sisters on the plain—
"*Sic Semper*," 'tis the proud refrain
That baffles minions back amain,
    Maryland!
Arise in majesty again,
    Maryland! my Maryland!

I see the blush upon thy cheek,
    Maryland!
For thou wast ever bravely meek,
    Maryland!
But lo! there surges forth a shriek,
From hill to hill, from creek to creek,
Potomac calls to Chesapeake,
    Maryland! my Maryland!

Thou wilt not yield the Vandal toll,
    Maryland!
Thou wilt not crook to his control,
    Maryland!
Better the fire upon thee roll,
Better the shot, the blade, the bowl,
Than crucifixion of the soul,
    Maryland! my Maryland!

I hear the distant thunder-hum,
    Maryland!
The old Line's bugle, fife and drum,
    Maryland!
She is not dead, nor deaf, nor dumb;
Huzza! she spurns the Northern scum!

She breathes! She burns! She'll come!
  She'll come!
    Maryland, my Maryland!

HENRY TIMROD (1829–1867)

Carolina

I The despot treads thy sacred sands,
 Thy pines give shelter to his bands
 Thy sons stand by with idle hands
   Carolina!
 He breathes at ease thy airs of balm,
 He scorns the lances of thy palm;
 Oh! who shall break thy craven calm,
   Carolina!
 Thy ancient fame is growing dim,
 A spot is on thy garment's rim;
 Give to the winds thy battle hymn,
   Carolina!

II Call thy children of the hill,
 Wake swamp and river, coast and rill,
 Rouse all thy strength and all thy skill,
   Carolina!
 Cite wealth and science, trade and art,
 Touch with thy fire the cautious mart,

And pour thee through the people's heart,
    Carolina!
Till even the coward spurns his fears,
And all thy fields and fens and meres
Shall bristle like thy palm with spears,
    Carolina!

III   Hold up the glories of thy dead;
Say how thy elder children bled,
And point to Eutaw's battle bed,
    Carolina!
Tell how the patriot's soul was tried,
And what his dauntless breast defied;
How Rutledge ruled and Laurens died,
    Carolina!
Cry! till thy summons, heard at last,
Shall fall like Marion's bugle-blast
Re-echoed from the haunted Past,
    Carolina!

IV   I hear a murmur as of waves
That grope their way through sunless caves,
Like bodies struggling in their graves,
    Carolina!
And now it deepens; slow and grand
It swells, as rolling to the land,
An ocean broke upon the strand,
    Carolina!
Shout! let it reach the startled Huns!

And roar with all thy festal guns!
It is the answer of thy sons,
  Carolina!

V They will not wait to hear thee call;
From Sachem's Head to Sumter's wall
Resounds the voice of hut and hall,
  Carolina!
No! thou hast not a stain, they say,
Or none save what the battle-day
Shall wash in seas of blood away,
  Carolina!
Thy skirts indeed the foe may part,
Thy robe be pierced with sword and dart,
They shall not touch thy noble heart,
  Carolina!

VI Ere thou shalt own the tyrant's thrall
Ten times ten thousand men must fall;
Thy corpse may hearken to his call,
  Carolina!
When, by thy bier, in mournful throngs
The women chant thy mortal wrongs,
'Twill be their own funereal songs,
  Carolina!
From thy dead breast by ruffians trod
No helpless child shall look to God;
All shall be safe beneath thy sod,
  Carolina!

VII   Girt with such wills to do and bear,
      Assured in right, and mailed in prayer.
      Thou wilt not bow thee to despair,
              Carolina!
      Throw thy bold banner to the breeze!
      Front with thy ranks the threatening seas
      Like thine own proud armorial trees,
              Carolina!
      Fling down thine gauntlet to the Huns,
      And roar the challenge from thy guns;
      Then leave the future to thy sons,
              Carolina!

In this poem Timrod provides a
view of Charleston poised to fire on
Fort Sumter in the bright spring of
1861. In this tranquil moment the
city awaits the judgment of fate.

HENRY TIMROD (1829–1867) ❧

Charleston

Calm as that second summer which precedes
    The first fall of the snow,
In the broad sunlight of heroic deeds,
    The city bides the foe.

As yet, behind their ramparts, stern and proud,
    Her bolted thunders sleep, —
Dark Sumter, like a battlemented cloud,
    Looms o'er the solemn deep.

No Calpe frowns from lofty cliff or scaur
    To guard the holy strand;
But Moultrie holds in leash her dogs of war
    Above the level sand.

And down the dunes a thousand guns lie couched,
    Unseen, beside the flood, —
Like tigers in some Orient jungle crouched
    That wait and watch for blood.

Ruins of Charleston, South Carolina, 1865

Meanwhile, through streets still echoing with trade,
    Walk grave and thoughtful men,
Whose hands may one day wield the patriot's blade
    As lightly as the pen.

And maidens, with such eyes as would grow dim
    Over a bleeding hound,
Seem each one to have caught the strength of him
    Whose sword she sadly bound.

Thus girt without and garrisoned at home,
    Day patient following day,
Old Charleston looks from roof and spire and dome,
    Across her tranquil bay.

Ships, through a hundred foes, from Saxon lands
    And spicy Indian ports,
Bring Saxon steel and iron to her hands,
    And Summer to her courts.

But still, along yon dim Atlantic line,
    The only hostile smoke
Creeps like a harmless mist above the brine,
    From some frail, floating oak.

Shall the Spring dawn, and she, still clad in smiles,
    And with an unscathed brow,
Rest in the strong arms of her palm-crowned isles,
    As fair and free as now?

We know not; in the temple of the Fates
    God has inscribed her doom;
And, all untroubled in her faith, she waits
    The triumph or the tomb.

WILLIAM CULLEN BRYANT (1794–1878) 🖋

The Death of Slavery

O thou great Wrong, that, through the slow-paced years,
 Didst hold thy millions fettered, and didst wield
 The scourge that drove the laborer to the field,
And turn a stony gaze on human tears,
   Thy cruel reign is o'er;
   Thy bondmen crouch no more
In terror at the menace of thine eye;
 For He who marks the bounds of guilty power,
Long-suffering, hath heard the captive's cry,
 And touched his shackles at the appointed hour,
And lo! they fall, and he whose limbs they galled
Stands in his native manhood, disenthralled.

A shout of joy from the redeemed is sent;
 Ten thousand hamlets swell the hymn of thanks;
 Our rivers roll exulting, and their banks
Send up hosannas to the firmament!
   Fields where the bondman's toil
   No more shall trench the soil,

Seem now to bask in a serener day;
    The meadow-birds sing sweeter, and the airs
Of heaven with more caressing softness play,
    Welcoming man to liberty like theirs.
A glory clothes the land from sea to sea,
For the great land and all its coasts are free.

Within that land wert thou enthroned of late,
    And they by whom the nation's laws were made,
    And they who filled its judgment-seats obeyed
Thy mandate, rigid as the will of Fate.
            Fierce men at thy right hand,
            With gesture of command,
Gave forth the word that none might dare gainsay;
    And grave and reverend ones, who loved thee not,
Shrank from thy presence, and in blank dismay
    Choked down, unuttered, the rebellious thought;
While meaner cowards, mingling with thy train,
Proved, from the book of God, thy right to reign.

Great as thou wert, and feared from shore to shore,
    The wrath of Heaven o'ertook thee in thy pride;
    Thou sitt'st a ghastly shadow; by thy side
Thy once strong arms hang nerveless evermore.
            And they who quailed but now
            Before thy lowering brow,
Devote thy memory to scorn and shame,
    And scoff at the pale, powerless thing thou art.
And they who ruled in thine imperial name,
    Subdued, and standing sullenly apart,

Scowl at the hands that overthrew thy reign,
And shattered at a blow the prisoner's chain.

Well was thy doom deserved; thou didst not spare
   Life's tenderest ties, but cruelly didst part
   Husband and wife, and from the mother's heart
Didst wrest her children, deaf to shriek and prayer;
         Thy inner lair became
         The haunt of guilty shame;
Thy lash dropped blood; the murderer, at thy side,
   Showed his red hands, nor feared the vengeance due.
Thou didst sow earth with crimes, and, far and wide,
   A harvest of uncounted miseries grew,
Until the measure of thy sins at last
Was full, and then the avenging bolt was cast!

Go now, accursed of God, and take thy place
   With hateful memories of the elder time,
   With many a wasting plague, and nameless crime,
And bloody war that thinned the human race;
         With the Black Death, whose way
         Through wailing cities lay,
Worship of Moloch, tyrannies that built
   The Pyramids, and cruel creeds that taught
To avenge a fancied guilt by deeper guilt—
   Death at the stake to those that held them not.
Lo! the foul phantoms, silent in the gloom
Of the flown ages, part to yield thee room.

I see the better years that hasten by
   Carry thee back into that shadowy past,

Where, in the dusty spaces, void and vast,
The graves of those whom thou hast murdered lie.
The slave-pen, through whose door
Thy victims pass no more,
Is there, and there shall the grim block remain
At which the slave was sold; while at thy feet
Scourges and engines of restraint and pain
Moulder and rust by thine eternal seat.
There, mid the symbols that proclaim thy crimes,
Dwell thou, a warning to the coming times.

RALPH WALDO EMERSON (1803–1882)

Boston Hymn
(Read in Music Hall, January 1, 1863)

The word of the Lord by night
To the watching Pilgrims came,
As they sat by the seaside,
And filled their hearts with flame.

God said, I am tired of kings,
I suffer them no more;
Up to my ear the morning brings
The outrage of the poor.

Think ye I made this ball
A field of havoc and war,
Where tyrants great and tyrants small
Might harry the weak and poor?

My angel, — his name is Freedom, —
Choose him to be your king;
She shall cut pathways east and west,
And fend you with his wing.

Lo! I uncover the land
Which I hid of old time in the West,
As the sculptor uncovers the statue
When he has wrought his best;

I show Columbia, of the rocks
Which dip their foot in the seas
And soar to the airborne flocks
Of clouds and the boreal fleece.

I will divide my goods;
Call in the wretch and slave:
None shall rule but the humble.
And none but toil shall have.

I will have never a noble,
No lineage counted great;
Fishers and choppers and ploughmen
Shall constitute a state.

Go, cut down trees in the forest
And trim the straightest boughs;
Cut down the trees in the forest
And build me a wooden house.

Call the people together,
The young men and the sires,
The digger in the harvest field,
Hireling, and him that hires;

And here in a pine statehouse
They shall choose men to rule
In every needful faculty,
In church and state and school.

Lo, now! if these poor men
Can govern the land and sea
And make just laws below the sun,
As planets faithful be.

And ye shall succor men;
'Tis nobleness to serve;
Help them who cannot help again:
Beware from right to swerve.

I break your bonds and masterships,
And I unchain the slave:
Free be his heart and hand henceforth
As wind and wandering wave.

I cause from every creature
His proper good to flow:
As much as he is and doeth,
So much he shall bestow.

But, laying hands on another
To coin his labor and sweat,
He goes in pawn to his victim
For eternal years in debt.

Today unbind the captive
So only are ye unbound;
Lift up a people from the dust,
Trump of their rescue, sound!

Pay ransom to the owner,
And fill the bag to the brim.
Who is the owner? The slave is owner,
And ever was. Pay him.

Oh North! give him beauty for rags,
And honor, O South! for his shame;
Nevada! coin thy golden crags
With Freedom's image and name.

Up! And the dusky race
That sat in darkness long—
Be swift their feet as antelopes,
And as behemoth strong.

Come, East and West and North,
By races, as snowflakes,
And carry my purpose forth,
Which neither halts nor shakes.

My will fulfilled shall be,
For, in daylight or in dark,
My thunderbolt has eyes to see
His way home to the mark.

"Voluntaries" recounts the efforts made by the North to placate the slave-holders and to preserve the Union. Printed in the Atlantic Monthly of October 1863, several months after the Emancipation Proclamation, it is also a call to arms to the young men needed to fill the ranks of the Union Army. The poem may have been intended to support Lincoln's fresh call for troops and the Conscription Act of May 1863.

RALPH WALDO EMERSON (1803–1882)

Voluntaries

I   Low and mournful be the strain,
Haughty thought be far from me;
Tones of penitence and pain,
Moanings of the tropic sea;
Low and tender in the cell
Where a captive sits in chains,
Crooning ditties treasured well
From his Afric's torrid plains.
Sole estate his sire bequeathed, —
Hapless sire to hapless son, —
Was the wailing song he breathed,
And his chain when life was done.

What his fault, or what his crime?
Or what ill planet crossed his prime?
Heart too soft and will too weak
To front the fate that crouches near, —
Dove beneath the vulture's beak, —
Will song dissuade the thirsty spear?

Harriet Beecher Stowe

Dragged from his mother's arms and breast,
Displaced, disfurnished here,
His wistful toil to do his best
Chilled by a ribald jeer.
Great men in the Senate sate,
Sage and hero, side by side,
Building for their sons the State,
Which they shall rule with pride.
They forbore to break the chain
Which bound the dusky tribe,
Checked by the owners' fierce disdain,
Lured by "Union" as the bribe.
Destiny sat by, and said,
"Pang for pang your seed shall pay,
Hide in false peace your coward head,
I bring round the harvest day."

II   Freedom all winged expands,
Nor perches in a narrow place;
Her broad van seeks unplanted lands;
She loves a poor and virtuous race.
Clinging to a colder zone
Whose dark sky sheds the snowflake down,
The snowflake is her banner's star,
Her stripes the boreal streamers are.
Long she loved the Northman well;
Now the iron age is done,
She will not refuse to dwell
With the offspring of the Sun;
Foundling of the desert far,
Where palms plume, siroccos blaze,

He roves unhurt the burning ways
In climates of the summer star.
He has avenues to God
Hid from men of Northern brain,
Far beholding, without cloud,
What these with slowest steps attain.
If once the generous chief arrive
To lead him willing to be led,
For freedom he will strike and strive,
And drain his heart till he be dead.

III   In an age of fops and toys,
Wanting wisdom, void of right,
Who shall nerve heroic boys
To hazard all in Freedom's fight, —
Break sharply off their jolly games,
Forsake their comrades gay
And quit proud homes and youthful dames
For famine, toil and fray?
Yet on the nimble air benign
Speed nimbler messages,
That waft the breath of grace divine
To hearts in sloth and ease.
So nigh is grandeur to our dust,
So near is God to man,
When Duty whispers low, *Thou must,*
The youth replies, *I can.*

IV   O, well for the fortunate soul
Which Music's wings infold,

Stealing away the memory
Of sorrows new and old!
Yet happier he whose inward sight,
Stayed on his subtile thought,
Shuts his sense on toys of time,
To vacant bosoms brought.
But best befriended of the God
He who, in evil times,
Warned by an inward voice,
Heeds not the darkness and the dread,
Biding by his rule and choice,
Feeling only the fiery thread
Leading over heroic ground,
Walled with mortal terror round,
To the aim which him allures,
And the sweet heaven his deed secures.
Peril around, all else appalling,
Cannon in front and leaden rain
Him duty through the clarion calling
To the van called not in vain.

　　Stainless soldier on the walls,
Knowing this,—and knows no more,—
Whoever fights, whoever falls,
Justice conquers evermore,
Justice after as before,—
And he who battles on her side,
God, though he were ten times slain,
Crowns him victor glorified,
Victor over death and pain.

V   Blooms the laurel which belongs
      To the valiant chief who fights;
      I see the wreath, I hear the songs
      Lauding the Eternal Rights,
      Victors over daily wrongs:
      Awful victors, they misguide
      Whom they will destroy,
      And their coming triumph hide
      In our downfall, or our joy:
      They reach no term, they never sleep,
      In equal strength through space abide;
      Though, feigning dwarfs, they crouch and creep,
      The strong they slay, the swift outstride:
      Fate's grass grows rank in valley clods,
      And rankly on the castled steep, —
      Speak it firmly, these are gods,
      All are ghosts beside.

HENRY WADSWORTH LONGFELLOW (1807–1882) ❧

The Building of the Ship

"Build me straight, O worthy Master!
  Stanch and strong, a goodly vessel,
That shall laugh at all disaster,
  And with wave and whirlwind wrestle!"

The merchant's word
Delighted the Master heard;
For his heart was in his work, and the heart
Giveth grace unto every Art.

A quiet smile played round his lips,
As the eddies and dimples of the tide
Play round the bows of ships,
That steadily at anchor ride.
And with a voice that was full of glee,
He answered, "Erelong we will launch
A vessel as goodly, and strong, and stanch,
As ever weathered a wintry sea!"
And first with nicest skill and art,

Perfect and finished in every part,
A little model the Master wrought,
Which should be to the larger plan
What the child is to the man,
Its counterpart in miniature;
That with a hand more swift and sure
The greater labor might be brought
To answer to his inward thought.
And as he labored, his mind ran o'er
The various ships that were built of yore,
And above them all, and strangest of all
Towered the *Great Harry*, crank and tall,
Whose picture was hanging on the wall,
With bows and stern raised high in air,
And balconies hanging here and there,
And signal lanterns and flags afloat,
And eight round towers, like those that frown
From some old castle, looking down
Upon the drawbridge and the moat.
And he said with a smile, "Our ship, I wis,
Shall be of another form than this!"

It was of another form, indeed;
Built for freight, and yet for speed,
A beautiful and gallant craft;
Broad in the beam, that the stress of the blast,
Pressing down upon sail and mast,
Might not the sharp bows overwhelm;
Broad in the beam, but sloping aft
With graceful curve and slow degrees,
That she might be docile to the helm,

And that the currents of parted seas,
Closing behind, with mighty force,
Might aid and not impede her course.

In the ship-yard stood the master,
    With the model of the vessel,
That should laugh at all disaster,
    And with wave and whirlwind wrestle!

Covering many a rood of ground,
Lay the timber piled around;
Timber of chestnut, and elm, and oak,
And scattered here and there, with these,
The knarred and crooked cedar knees;
Brought from regions far away,
From Pascagoula's sunny bay,
And the banks of the roaring Roanoke!
Ah! what a wondrous thing it is
To note how many wheels of toil
One thought, one word, can set in motion!
There's not a ship that sails the ocean,
But every climate, every soil,
Must bring its tribute, great or small,
And help to build the wooden wall!

The sun was rising o'er the sea,
And long the level shadows lay,
As if they, too, the beams would be
Of some great, airy argosy,
Framed and launched in a single day.
That silent architect, the sun,

Had hewn and laid them every one,
Ere the work of man was yet begun.
Beside the master, when he spoke,
A youth, against an anchor leaning,
Listened, to catch his slightest meaning.
Only the long waves, as they broke
In ripples on the pebbly beach,
Interrupted the old man's speech.

Beautiful they were, in sooth,
The old man and the fiery youth!
The old man, in whose busy brain
Many a ship that sailed the main
Was modelled o'er and o'er again; —
The fiery youth, who was to be
The heir of his dexterity,
The heir of his house, and his daughter's hand,
When he had built and launched from land
What the elder head had planned.

"Thus," said he, "will we build this ship!
Lay square the blocks upon the slip,
And follow well this plan of mine.
Choose the timbers with greatest care;
Of all that is unsound beware;
For only what is sound and strong
To this vessel shall belong.
Cedar of Maine and Georgia pine
Here together shall combine.
A goodly frame, and a goodly fame,
And the *Union* be her name!

For the day that gives her to the sea
Shall give my daughter unto thee!"

The Master's word
Enraptured the young man heard;
And as he turned his face aside,
With a look of joy and a thrill of pride,
Standing before
Her father's door,
He saw the form of his promised bride.
The sun shone on her golden hair,
And her cheek was glowing fresh and fair,
With the breath of morn and the soft sea air.
Like a beauteous barge was she,
Still at rest on the sandy beach,
Just beyond the billow's reach;
But he
Was the restless, seething, stormy sea!

Ah, how skilful grows the hand
That obeyeth Love's command!
It is the heart, and not the brain,
That to the highest doth attain,
And he who followeth Love's behest
Far excelleth all the rest!

Thus with the rising of the sun
Was the noble task begun,
And soon throughout the ship-yard's bounds
Were heard the intermingled sounds
Of axes and of mallets, plied
With vigorous arms on every side;

Plied so deftly and so well,
That, ere the shadows of evening fell,
The keel of oak for a noble ship,
Scarfed and bolted, straight and strong,
Was lying ready, and stretched along
The blocks, well placed upon the slip.
Happy, thrice happy, every one
Who sees his labor well begun.
And not perplexed and multiplied,
By idly waiting for time and tide!

And when the hot, long day was o'er,
The young man at the master's door
Sat with the maiden, calm and still.
And within the porch, a little more
Removed beyond the evening chill,
The father sat, and told them tales
Of wrecks in the great September gales,
Of pirates coasting the Spanish Main,
And ships that never came back again,
The chance and change of a sailor's life,
Want and plenty, rest and strife,
His roving fancy, like the wind,
That nothing can stay and nothing can bind,
And the magic charm of foreign lands,
With shadows of palms, and shining sands,
Where the tumbling surf,
O'er the coral reefs of Madagascar,
Washes the feet of the swarthy Lascar,
As he lies alone and asleep on the turf.
And the trembling maiden held her breath

At the tales of that awful, pitiless sea,
With all its terror and mystery,
The dim, dark sea, so like unto death,
That divides and yet unites mankind!
And whenever the old man paused, a gleam
From the bowl of his pipe would awhile illume
The silent group in the twilight gloom,
And thoughtful faces, as in a dream;
And for a moment one might mark
What had been hidden by the dark,
That the head of the maiden lay at rest,
Tenderly, on the young man's breast!

Day by day the vessel grew,
With timbers fastened strong and true,
Stemson and keelson and sternson-knee,
Till, framed with perfect symmetry,
A skeleton ship rose up to view!
And around the bows and along the side
The heavy hammers and mallets plied,
Till after many a week, at length,
Wonderful for form and strength,
Sublime in its enormous bulk,
Loomed aloft the shadowy hulk!
And around it columns of smoke, upwreathing,
Rose from the boiling, bubbling, seething
Caldron, that glowed,
And overflowed
With the black tar, heated for the sheathing.
And amid the clamors
Of clattering hammers,

He who listened heard now and then
The song of the master and his men: —

"Build me straight, O worthy Master,
    Stanch and strong, a goodly vessel,
That shall laugh at all disaster,
    And with wave and whirlwind wrestle!"

With oaken brace and copper band,
Lay the rudder on the sand,
That, like a thought, should have control
Over the movement of the whole;
And near it the anchor, whose giant hand
Would reach down and grapple with the land,
And immovable and fast
Hold the great ship against the bellowing blast.
And at the bows an image stood,
By a cunning artist carved in wood,
With robes of white, that far behind
Seemed to be fluttering in the wind.
It was not shaped in a classic mould,
Nor like a Nymph or Goddess of old,
Or Naiad rising from the water,
But modelled from the master's daughter!
On many a dreary and misty night,
'T will be seen by the rays of the signal light,
Speeding along through the rain and the dark,
Like a ghost in its snow-white sark,
The pilot of some phantom bark,
Guiding the vessel, in its flight,
By a path none other knows aright!

Behold, at last,
Each tall and tapering mast
Is swung into its place;
Shrouds and stays
Holding it firm and fast!

Long ago,
In the deer-haunted forests of Maine,
When upon mountain and plain
Lay the snow,
They fell,—those lordly pines!
Those grand, majestic pines!
'Mid shouts and cheers
The jaded steers,
Panting beneath the goad,
Dragged down the weary, winding road
Those captive kings so straight and tall,
To be shorn of their streaming hair,
And, naked and bare,
To feel the stress and the strain
Of the wind and the reeling main,
Whose roar
Would remind them forevermore
Of their native forests they should not see again.

And everywhere
The slender, graceful spars
Poise aloft in the air,
And at the mast-head,
White, blue, and red,
A flag unrolls the stripes and stars.

Ah! when the wanderer, lonely, friendless,
In foreign harbors shall behold
That flag unrolled,
'T will be as a friendly hand
Stretched out from his native land,
Filling his heart with memories sweet and endless!

All is finished! and at length
Has come the bridal day
Of beauty and of strength.
To-day the vessel shall be launched!
With fleecy clouds the sky is blanched,
And o'er the bay,
Slowly, in all his splendors dight,
The great sun rises to behold the sight.
The ocean old,
Centuries old,
Strong as youth, and as uncontrolled,
Paces restless to and fro,
Up and down the sands of gold.
His beating heart is not at rest;
And far and wide,
With ceaseless flow,
His beard of snow
Heaves with the heaving of this breast.
He waits impatient for his bride.
There she stands,
With her foot upon the sands,
Decked with flags and streamers gay,
In honor of her marriage day,
Her snow-white signals fluttering, blending,

Round her like a veil descending,
Ready to be
The bride of the gray old sea.

On the deck another bride
Is standing by her lover's side.
Shadows from the flags and shrouds,
Like the shadows cast by clouds,
Broken by many a sunny fleck,
Fall around them on the deck.

The prayer is said,
The service read,
The joyous bridegroom bows his head;
And in tears the good old Master
Shakes the brown hand of his son,
Kisses his daughter's glowing cheek
In silence, for he cannot speak,
And ever faster
Down his own the tears begin to run.
The worthy pastor—
The shepherd of that wandering flock,
That has the ocean for its wold,
That has the vessel for its fold,
Leaping ever from rock to rock—
Spake, with accents mild and clear,
Words of warning, words of cheer,
But tedious to the bridegroom's ear.
He knew the chart
Of the sailor's heart,
All its pleasures and its griefs,

All its shallows and rocky reefs,
All those secret currents, that flow
With such resistless undertow,
And lift and drift, with terrible force,
The will from its moorings and its course.
Therefore he spake, and thus said he:—
"Like unto ships far off at sea,
Outward or homeward bound, are we.
Before, behind, and all around,
Floats and swings the horizon's bound,
Seems at its distant rim to rise
And climb the crystal wall of the skies,
And then again to turn and sink,
As if we could slide from its outer brink.
Ah! it is not the sea,
It is not the sea that sinks and shelves,
But ourselves
That rock and rise
With endless and uneasy motion,
Now touching the very skies,
Now sinking into the depths of ocean.
Ah! if our souls but poise and swing
Like the compass in its brazen ring,
Ever level and ever true
To the toil and the task we have to do,
We shall sail securely, and safely reach
The Fortunate Isles, on whose shining beach
The sights we see, and the sounds we hear,
Will be those of joy and not of fear!"

Then the Master,

With a gesture of command,
Waved his hand;
And at the word,
Loud and sudden there was heard,
All around them and below,
The sound of hammers, blow on blow,
Knocking away the shores and spurs.
And see! she stirs!
She starts,—she moves,—she seems to feel
The thrill of life along her keel,
And, spurning with her foot the ground,
With one exulting, joyous bound,
She leaps into the ocean's arms!

And lo! from the assembled crowd
There rose a shout, prolonged and loud,
That to the ocean seemed to say,
"Take her, O bridegroom, old and gray,
Take her to thy protecting arms,
With all her youth and all her charms!"

How beautiful she is! How fair
She lies within those arms, that press
Her form with many a soft caress
Of tenderness and watchful care!
Sail forth into the sea, O ship!
Through wind and wave, right onward steer!
The moistened eye, the trembling lip,
Are not the signs of doubt or fear.

Sail forth into the sea of life,
O gentle, loving, trusting wife,

And safe from all adversity
Upon the bosom of that sea
Thy comings and thy goings be!
For gentleness and love and trust
Prevail o'er angry wave and gust;
And in the wreck of noble lives
Something immortal still survives!

Thou, too, sail on, O Ship of State!
Sail on, O *Union*, strong and great!
Humanity with all its fears,
With all the hopes of future years,
Is hanging breathless on thy fate!
We know what Master laid thy keel,
What Workmen wrought thy ribs of steel,
Who made each mast, and sail, and rope,
What anvils rang, what hammers beat,
In what a forge and what a heat
Were shaped the anchors of thy hope!
Fear not each sudden sound and shock,
'T is of the wave and not the rock;
'T is but the flapping of the sail,
And not a rent made by the gale!
In spite of rock and tempest's roar,
In spite of false lights on the shore,
Sail on, nor fear to breast the sea!
Our hearts, our hopes, are all with thee,
Our hearts, our hopes, our prayers, our tears,
Our faith triumphant o'er our fears,
Are all with thee,—are all with thee!

Whittier wrote voluminously for the abolitionist cause, urged on by his good friend William Lloyd Garrison, publisher of the Liberator, *which printed many of Whittier's poems. He was a democratic poet, writing fervently of rural life and good rural people, and he was much loved by his Northern audience. The poem was intended to be sung to the tune of Luther's great hymn, "A Mighty Fortress Is Our God."*

JOHN GREENLEAF WHITTIER (1807–1892) ❦

The Furnace Blast

We wait beneath the furnace-blast
   The pangs of transformation;
Not painlessly doth God recast
   And mould anew the nation.
      Hot burns the fire
      Where wrongs expire;
      Nor spares the hand
      That from the land
   Uproots the ancient evil.

The hand-breadth cloud the sages feared
   Its bloody rain is dropping;
The poison plant the fathers spared
   All else is overtopping.
      East, West, South, North,
      It curses the earth;
      All justice dies,
      And fraud and lies
   Live only in its shadow.

What gives the wheat-field blades of steel?
    What points the rebel cannon?
What sets the roaring rabble's heel
    On the old star-spangled pennon?
        What breaks the oath
        Of the men o' the South?
        What whets the knife
        For the Union's life? —
    Hark to the answer: Slavery!

Then waste no blows on lesser foes
    In strife unworthy freemen.
God lifts to-day the veil, and shows
    The features of the demon!
        O North and South,
        Its victims both,
        Can ye not cry,
        "Let slavery die!"
    And union find in freedom?

What though the cast-out spirit tear
    The nation in his going?
We who have shared the guilt must share
    The pang of his o'erthrowing!
        Whate'er the loss,
        Whate'er the cross,
        Shall they complain
        Of present pain
    Who trust in God's hereafter?

For who that leans on His right arm
 Was ever yet forsaken?
What righteous cause can suffer harm
 If He its part has taken?
  Though wild and loud,
  And dark the cloud,
  Behind its folds
  His hand upholds
 The calm sky of to-morrow!

Above the maddening cry for blood,
 Above the wild war-drumming,
Let Freedom's voice be heard, with good
 The evil overcoming.
  Give prayer and purse
  To stay the Curse
  Whose wrong we share,
  Whose shame we bear,
 Whose end shall gladden Heaven!

In vain the bells of war shall ring
 Of triumphs and revenges,
While still is spared the evil thing
 That severs and estranges.
  But blest the ear
  That yet shall hear
  The jubilant bell
  That rings the knell
 Of Slavery forever!

Then let the selfish lip be dumb,
    And hushed the breath of sighing;
Before the joy of peace must come
    The pains of purifying.
        God give us grace
        Each in his place
        To bear his lot,
        And, murmuring not,
    Endure and wait and labor!

*This is a post-war poem,
Whittier's song of triumph at the
ratification of the Thirteenth
Amendment that freed the slaves.
It contains many references to
triumphant Old Testament songs
about God's victories over the
wicked. Yet he speaks of them as
"ancient myth and song and tale."*

JOHN GREENLEAF WHITTIER (1807–1892)

Laus Deo!

*"On hearing the bells ring on the passage of the constitutional
amendment abolishing slavery."*
J. G. WHITTIER

It is done!
　Clang of bell and roar of gun
Send the tidings up and down.
　How the belfries rock and reel!
　How the great guns, peal on peal,
Fling the joy from town to town!

　Ring, O bells!
　Every stroke exulting tells
Of the burial hour of crime.
　Loud and long, that all may hear,
　Ring for every listening ear
Of Eternity and Time!

　Let us kneel:
　God's own voice is in that peal,
And this spot is holy ground.
　Lord, forgive us! What are we,
　That our eyes this glory see,

That our ears have heard the sound!

For the Lord
On the whirlwind is abroad;
In the earthquake He has spoken:
He has smitten with His thunder
The iron walls asunder,
And the gates of brass are broken!

Loud and long
Lift the old exulting song;
Sing with Miriam by the sea,
He has cast the mighty down;
Horse and rider sink and drown;
"He hath triumphed gloriously!"

Did we dare,
In our agony of prayer,
Ask for more than He has done?
When was ever His right hand
Over any time or land
Stretched as now beneath the sun?

How they pale,
Ancient myth and song and tale,
In this wonder of our days,
When the cruel rod of war
Blossoms white with righteous law,
And the wrath of man is praise!

Blotted out!
All within and all about
Shall a fresher life begin;
Freer breathe the universe
As it rolls its heavy curse
On the dead and buried sin!

It is done!
In the circuit of the sun
Shall the sound thereof go forth.
It shall bid the sad rejoice,
It shall give the dumb a voice,
It shall belt with joy the earth!

Ring and swing,
Bells of joy! On morning's wing
Send the song of praise abroad!
With a sound of broken chains
Tell the nations that He reigns,
Who alone is Lord and God!

HENRY CLAY WORK (1832–1884)

Marching through Georgia

Like Root, Work was a popular songwriter during the Civil War. His sentimental tastes appealed to the time. Another of his creations was "Grandfather's Clock." He was a fervent abolitionist. He wrote "Marching through Georgia" to commemorate Sherman's famous march from Atlanta to the sea in November and December 1864. He romanticized the event considerably.

Bring the good old bugle, boys, we'll sing another song,
Sing it with a spirit that will start the world along,
Sing it as we used to sing it, fifty thousand strong,
 While we were marching through Georgia.

 Chorus:
  Hurrah! hurrah! we bring the jubilee!
  Hurrah! hurrah! the flag that makes you free!
  So we sang the chorus from Atlanta to the sea,
  While we were marching through Georgia.

How the darkies shouted when they heard the joyful sound;
How the turkeys gobbled which our commissary found;
How the sweet potatoes even started from the ground,
 While we were marching through Georgia.

Yes, and there were Union men who wept with joyful tears,
When they saw the honoured flag they had not seen for years;
Hardly could they be restrained from breaking forth in cheers,
 While we were marching through Georgia.

Union General William Tecumseh Sherman

"Sherman's dashing Yankee boys will never reach the coast,"
So the saucy rebels said, and 'twas a handsome boast;
Had they not forgot, alas, to reckon with the host,
    While we were marching through Georgia.

So we made a thoroughfare for Freedom and her train.
Sixty miles in latitude, three hundred to the main;
Treason fled before us, for resistance was in vain,
    While we were marching through Georgia.

JAMES MONROE WHITFIELD (1822–1871) ❧

From Year to Year the Contest Grew

From: "A Poem Written for the Celebration of the Fourth Anniversary of President Lincoln's Emancipation Proclamation"

From year to year the contest grew,
    Till slavery, glorying in her strength,
Again war's bloody falchion drew,
    And sluggish freedom, roused at length,
Waked from her stupor, seized the shield,
And called her followers to the field.
And at that call they thronging came,
With arms of strength, and hearts on flame;
Answering the nation's call to arms,
The northern hive poured forth its swarms;
The lumbermen of Maine threw down
    The axe, and seized the bayonet;
The Bay State's sons from every town,
    Left loom and anvil, forge and net;
The Granite State sent forth its sons,
    With hearts as steadfast as her rocks;
The stern Vermonters took their guns,
    And left to others' care their flocks;

Slave pen of Price, Birch & Co., Alexandria, Virginia

Rhode Island and Connecticut
    Helped to fill up New England's roll,
And showed the pilgrim spirit yet
    Could animate the Yankee soul.
The Empire State sent forth a host,
    Such as might seal an empire's fate;
Even New Jersey held her post,
    And proved herself a Union State.
The Key-Stone of the Union arch
    Sent forth an army true and tried;
Ohio joined the Union march,
    And added to the Nation's side
    A force three hundred thousand strong,
    While Michigan took up the song;
    Wisconsin also, like the lakes,
    When the autumnal gale awakes,
    And rolls its surges on the shore,
    Poured forth its sons to battle's roar.
    The gallant State of Illinois
    Sent forth in swarms its warlike boys.
    On Indiana's teeming plain,
    Thick as the sheaves of ripened grain,
    Were soldiers hurrying to the wars
    To battle for the Stripes and Stars.
From Iowa fresh numbers came,
    While Minnesota joined the tide,
And Kansas helped to spread the flame,
    And carry o'er the border side
    The torch the ruffians once applied
    When fiercely, but in vain, they tried
    The people of their rights to spoil,

And fasten slavery on her soil.
From East unto remotest West,
    From every portion of the North,
The true, the bravest, and the best,
    Forsook their homes and sallied forth;
    And men from every foreign land
    Were also reckoned in that band.
    The Scandinavians swelled the train,
    The brave Norwegian, Swede, and Dane,
    And struck as though Thor rained his blows
    Upon the heads of haughty foes;
    Or Odin's self had sought the field
    To make all opposition yield.
Italia's sons, who once had cried
    Loud for united Italy,
And struck by Garibaldi's side
    For union and equality—
    Obtained another chance to fight
    For nationality and right.
The Germans came, a sturdy throng,
    And to the bleeding country brought
Friends of the right, foes of the wrong,
    Heroes in action as in thought,
Sigel, and Schurz, and many others,
    Whose names shall live among the brave,
Till all men are acknowledged brothers,
    Without a master or a slave.
Ireland's sons, as usual, came
    To battle strife with shouts of joy,
With Meagher and Corcoran won such fame
    As well might rival Fontenoy.

Briton and Frank, for centuries foes,
Forgot their struggles, veiled their scars,
To deal on slavery's head their blows,
Fighting beneath the Stripes and Stars.

Attributed to THOMAS *and* ELLEN SNOWDEN *and to*
DANIEL DECATUR EMMETT (1815–1904) 🖎

Dixie

*Attributed to Thomas and Ellen
Snowden, the words by Daniel
Decatur Emmett. The Snowdens
were black musicians and singers
and Dan Emmett (1815–1904)
was a singer and composer. He
also wrote the popular "Old Dan
Tucker." "Dixie" is discussed in
the Introduction. It was one of
Abraham Lincoln's favorite tunes.*

I wish I was in de land ob cotton,
Old times dar am not forgotten,
Look away! Look away! Look away! Dixie Land.
In Dixie Land whar I was born in
Early on one frosty mornin',
Look away! Look away! Look away! Dixie Land.

Chorus:
Den I wish I was in Dixie, Hooray! Hooray!
In Dixie Land I'll take my stand,
To lib and die in Dixie!
Away, away, away down South in Dixie!
Away, away, away down South in Dixie!

Old Missus marry Will de Weaber,
Willium was a gay deceaber,
Look away! Look away! Look away! Dixie Land.
But when he put his arm around 'er,

He smiled as fierce as a forty-pounder,
Look away! Look away! Look away! Dixie Land.

His face was sharp as a butcher's cleaber,
But dat did not seem to greab 'er,
Look away! Look away! Look away! Dixie Land.
Old Missus acted the foolish part,
And died for a man dat broke her heart,
Look away! Look away! Look away! Dixie Land.

Now here's a health to the next old Missus,
And all de gals dat want to kiss us,
Look away! Look away! Look away! Dixie Land.
But if you want to drive 'way sorrow,
Come and hear dis song tomorrow,
Look away! Look away! Look away! Dixie Land.

Dar's buckwheat cakes an' Ingen batter
Makes you fat or a little fatter,
Look away! Look away! Look away! Dixie Land.
Den hoe it down an' scratch your grabble,
To Dixie's land I'm bound to trabble,
Look away! Look away! Look away! Dixie Land.

EDWARD W. WILLIAMS (1863–1891) 🪶

At Harper's Ferry Just before the Attack

This post-war doggerel illustrates the growing sainthood of John Brown and his men in the eyes of those who saw slavery as the most important moral issue of the war. At the time this poem was written in the 1880s, Jim Crow laws were coming into effect, and the freed slaves and their descendants were being pushed into a different kind of servitude.

The hour, the spot, are here at last
    Their purpose, cause and hope we know,
Our duty is to hold on fast
    To all the vows we made before.

To such as yield to our demand
    For freedom here and everywhere,
In homes of safety let them stand
    And all their household comforts spare.

Those who refuse us or resist,
    Be as it may by words or arms,
Enroll their names on death's black list
    To meet their dooms at war's alarms.

The blood that must be shed to-night
    Can never stain the name we bear,
We fight for God's own holy right
    Which is to all mankind so dear.

Virginia robbed it from a race
    For over two sad hundred years,
Abused and kept it in disgrace
    Regardless of entreating tears.

Those ancient tears rejoice to see
    This retributive night's advance,
While Negro blood to you, to me,
    Is crying aloud for vengeance.

Around us stand with cheering hand
    The ghost of every Negro dead,
Each blesses the freedom we demand,
    Each bids us press with zeal ahead.

Angels rejoice with gladness, too,
    While round the throne on high they stand,
To see poor mortal men pursue
    The common foe of God and man.

Though we are few in numbers now
    We trust the promise Jesus made,
That where a few for good shall bow
    His spirit will be there to aid.

The saints are singing music sweet
    All around the heavenly strand,
To see us here as Christians meet
    To help and save our brother man.

Oh! Saviour, Angels, Saints, look on
    While we the fathers will obey,
Befriend and comfort them that mourn
    And in the dust their burdens lay.

We open war at once to-night
    And liberty for all proclaim,
We'll lead from darkness unto light
    The weak, the poor, the blind and lame.

Before to-morrow's sun displays
    Its golden colors in the East,
We'll wake slaveholders in amaze
    To breakfast on a bloody feast.

My brothers what a holy war
    In which we all will soon engage,
It will assert free equal law
    Against the tyrants of the age.

The broken heart, the tearful eyes
    The cheerless face none sought to please,
Will ere the morning sun arise
    Have symptoms of a time of ease.

The runaways in forest wilds
    And children sold to foreign shore,
Will soon return with happy smiles
    To see their parents, friends, once more.

The screws, the lashes and the hounds
   Shall no more glut off Negro blood,
Our forward march, our bugle sounds,
   Will scatter them as by a flood.

Husband and wife, daughters and son,
   Forever more shall ne'er be sold,
Together they shall live as one
Till choice or Heaven breaks the fold.

The fertile earth shall no more yield
   Her fruits for unrequited toil,
The riches of the harvest field
   Must be for him who tills the soil.

Ye children all of Africa
   "Possess your soul" and weep no more,
This night will force America
   To grant you all you asked of yore.

The laws of God your rights ordain
   We are the instruments they send—
To cut your way, to break your chain,
   And ages long of troubles end.

STEPHEN VINCENT BENÉT (1898–1943)

John Brown's Prayer

From: John Brown's Body

Another part of Benét's epic narrative poem, John Brown's Body. *John Brown and four of his sons murdered five Kansas pro-slavery men living on the banks of the Pottawatomie River. Brown declared that he was an instrument in the hand of God. Benét places biblical images from Revelation—the breaking of the seals, the opening of the door, the beasts around the throne of God—in Brown's mouth. Brown did indeed believe that he was God's chosen weapon against slavery. But Benét also tries to have Brown show contrition for the murders in Kansas, and no evidence exists to show that Brown felt contrite about anything he had done.*

Omnipotent and steadfast God,
Who, in Thy mercy, hath
Upheaved in me Jehovah's rod
And his chastising wrath,

For fifty-nine unsparing years
Thy Grace hath worked apart
To mould a man of iron tears
With a bullet for a heart.

Yet, since this body may be weak
With all it has to bear,
Once more, before Thy thunders speak,
Almighty, hear my prayer.

I saw Thee when Thou did display
The black man and his lord
To bid me free the one, and slay
The other with the sword.

I heard Thee when Thou bade me spurn
Destruction from my hand
And, though all Kansas bleed and burn,
It was at Thy command.

I hear the rolling of the wheels,
The chariots of war!
I hear the breaking of the seals
And the opening of the door!

The glorious beasts with many eyes
Exult before the Crowned.
The buried saints arise, arise
Like incense from the ground!

Before them march the martyr-kings,
In bloody sunsets drest,
O, Kansas, bleeding Kansas,
You will not let me rest!

I hear your sighing corn again,
I smell your prairie-sky,
And I remember five dead men
By Pottawattomie.

Lord God it was a work of Thine,
And how might I refrain?
But Kansas, bleeding Kansas,
I hear her in her pain.

Her corn is rustling in the ground,
An arrow in my flesh.
And all night long I staunch a wound
That ever bleeds afresh.

Get up, get up, my hardy sons,
From this time forth we are
No longer men, but pikes and guns
In God's advancing war.

And if we live, we free the slave,
And if we die, we die.
But God has digged His saints a grave
Beyond the western sky.

Oh, fairer than the bugle-call
Its walls of jasper shine!
And Joshua's sword is on the wall
With space beside for mine.

And should the Philistine defend
His strength against our blows,
The God who doth not spare His friend,
Will not forget His foes.

Rukeyser's complex poem,
published in 1940, set John
Brown's fanaticism for justice
against the fierce injustice of his
world. She wrote when Hitler
seemed invincible and the United
States hesitated before the terror of
a new World War. Brown may
have been crazy but no crazier
than the slave-holders who
provoked the war.

MURIEL RUKEYSER (1913–1980)

The Soul and Body of John Brown

"Multitudes, multitudes in the valley of decision!"
JOEL III:14

His life is in the body of the living.
When they hanged him the first time, his image leaped
into the blackened air. His grave was the floating faces
of the crowd, and he refusing them release
rose open-eyed in autumn, a fanatic
beacon of fierceness leaping to meet them there,
match the white prophets of the storm,
the streaming meteors of the war.

Dreaming Ezekiel, threaten me alive!

Voices: Why don't you rip up that guitar?
Or must we listen to those blistering strings?

The trial of heroes follows their execution. The striding
wind of nations with new rain, new lightning,
destroyed in magnificent noon shining straight down
the fiery pines. Brown wanted freedom. Could not himself be free
until more grace reached a corroded world. Our guilt his own.

John Brown

Under the hooded century drops the trap—
There in October's fruition-fire three
tall images of him, Brown as he stood on the ground,
Brown as he stood on sudden air, Brown
standing to our fatal topmost hills
faded through dying altitudes, and low
through faces living under the dregs of the air,
deprived childhood and thwarted youth and change:
      fantastic sweetness gone to rags
      and incorruptible anger blurred by age.

Compel the steps of lovers, watch them lie silvery
attractive in naked embrace over the brilliant gorge,
and open them to love: enlarge their welcome
to sharp-faced countrysides, vicious familiar windows
whose lopped-off worlds say *I am promise*, holding
stopgap slogans of a thin season's offering,
false initials, blind address, dummy name—
enemies who reply in smiles; mild slavers; moderate whores.
There is another gorge to remember, where soldiers give
terrible answers of lechery after death.
Brown said at last, with a living look,
"I designed to have done the same thing
again on a larger scale." Brown sees his tree
grow in the land to leap these mountains.
Not mountains, but men and women sleeping.

      O my scene! my mother!
      America who offers many births.

Over the tier of barriers, compel the connected steps
past the attacks of sympathy, past black capitals,
to arrive with horizon sharpness, marching
in quick embrace toward people
faltering among hills among the symptoms of ice,
small lights of the shifting winter, the rapid snow-blue stars.
This must be done by armies. Nothing is free.
Brown refuses to speak direct again,
     "If I tell them the truth,
       they will say I speak in symbols."

White landscapes emphasize his nakedness
reflected in counties of naked who shiver at fires,
their backs to the hands that unroll worlds around them.
They go down the valleys. They shamble in the streets,
Blind to the sun-storming image in their eyes.
They dread the surface of their victim life,
lying helpless and savage in shade parks,
      asking the towers only what beggars dare:
       food, fire, water, and air.

Spring: the great hieroglyph: the mighty, whose first hour
collects the winter invalids, whose cloudless
pastures train swarms of mutable apple-trees
to blond delusions of light, the touch of whiter
more memorable breasts each evening, the resistant
male shoulders riding under sold terrible eyes.
The soldier-face persists, the victorious head
asks, kissing those breasts, more miracles—
Untarnished hair! Set them free! "Without the snap of a gun—"
More failures—but the season is a garden after sickness;

Then the song begins,
"The clearing of the sky
brings fulness to heroes—
Call Death out of the city
and ring the summer in."

Whether they sleep alone. Whether they understand darkness
of mine or tunnel or store. Whether they lay branches
with skill to entice their visions out of fire.
Whether she lie awake, whether he walk in guilt
down padded corridors, leaving no fingerprints.
Whether he weaken searching for power in papers,
or shut out every fantasy but the fragile eyelid to
      commemorate delight . . .
      They believe in their dreams.

They more and more, secretly, tell their dreams.
They listen oftener for certain words, look deeper
in faces for features of one remembered image.
They almost forget the face. They cannot miss the look.
It waits until faces have gathered darkness,
and country guitars a wide and subtle music.
It rouses love. It has mastered its origin:
      Death was its method. It will surpass its
      furious birth when it is known again.

      Dreaming Ezekiel, threaten me alive!

Greengrown with sun on it. All the living summer.
They tell their dreams on the cool hill reclining
after a twilight daytime painting machines on the sky,

---

the spite of tractors and the toothless cannon.
Slaves under factories deal out identical
gestures of reaching—cathedral-color-rose
resumes the bricks as the brick walls lean
away from the windows, blank in bellwavering air,
a slave's mechanical cat's-claw reaping sky.
The cities of horror are down. These are called born,
and Hungry Hill is a farm again.

       I know your face, deepdrowned
       prophet, and seablown eyes.

Darkflowing peoples. A tall tree, prophet, fallen,
your arms in their flesh laid on the mountains, all
your branches in the scattered valleys down.
Your boughs lie broken in channels of the land,
dim anniversaries written on many clouds.
There is no partial help. Lost in the face of a child,
lost in the factory repetitions, lost
on the steel plateaus, in a ghost distorted.
Calling More Life. In all the harm calling.
Pointing disaster of death and lifting up the bone,
heroic drug and the intoxication gone.

       I see your mouth calling
       before the words arrive.

Buzz of guitars repeat it in streamy
summernoon song, the whitelight of the meaning
changed to demand. More life, challenging
this hatred, this Hallelloo—risk it upon yourselves.

Free all the dangers of promise, clear the image
of freedom for the body of the world.
After the tree is fallen and has become the land,
when the hand in the earth declined rises and touches and
after the walls go down and all the faces turn,
the diamond shoals of eyes demanding life
deep in the prophet eyes, a wish to be again
threatened alive, in agonies of decision
part of our nation of our fanatic sun.

WILLIAM VAUGHN MOODY (1869–1910) ✨

An Ode in Time of Hesitation

(After seeing at Boston the statue of Robert Gould Shaw, killed while storming Fort Wagner, July 18, 1863, at the head of the first enlisted Negro regiment, the Fifty-fourth Massachusetts)

Moody taught English for a time at Harvard and then at the University of Chicago. This poem was inspired by the Boston monument in high relief by Augustus Saint-Gaudens of Colonel Robert Gould Shaw and black soldiers of the 54th Massachusetts Infantry. Despite its idealism, the poem illustrates the common attitude of white superiority over the "slow minds" of Shaw's black troops. Even so, this poem—using Shaw's idealism as an example—protests against the American imperialists who, after the quick victory in the Spanish-American War of 1898, wanted to take over the former Spanish colonies.

I   Before the solemn bronze Saint Gaudens made
      To thrill the heedless passer's heart with awe,
      And set here in the city's talk and trade
      To the good memory of Robert Shaw,
      This bright March morn I stand,
      And hear the distant spring come up the land;
      Knowing that what I hear is not unheard
      Of this boy soldier and his negro band,
      For all their gaze is fixed so stern ahead,
      For all the fatal rhythm of their tread.
      The land they died to save from death and shame
      Trembles and waits, hearing the spring's great name,
      And by her pangs these resolute ghosts are stirred.

II   Through street and mall the tides of people go
      Heedless; the trees upon the Common show
      No hint of green; but to my listening heart
      The still earth doth impart

Assurance of her jubilant emprise,
And it is clear to my long-searching eyes
That love at last has might upon the skies.
The ice is runneled on the little pond;
A telltale patter drips from off the trees;
The air is touched with southland spiceries,
As if but yesterday it tossed the frond
Of pendant mosses where the live-oaks grow
Beyond Virginia and the Carolines,
Or had its will among the fruits and vines
Of aromatic isles asleep beyond
Florida and the Gulf of Mexico.

III   Soon shall the Cape Ann children shout in glee,
Spying the arbutus, spring's dear recluse;
Hill lads at dawn shall hearken the wild goose
Go honking northward over Tennessee;
West from Oswego to Sault Sainte-Marie,
And on to where the Pictured Rocks are hung,
And yonder where, gigantic, wilful, young,
Chicago sitteth at the northwest gates,
With restless violent hands and casual tongue
Moulding her mighty fates,
The Lakes shall robe them in ethereal sheen;
And like a larger sea, the vital green
Of springing wheat shall vastly be outflung
Over Dakota and the prairie states.
By desert people immemorial
On Arizona's mesas shall be done
Dim rites unto the thunder and the sun;
Nor shall the primal gods lack sacrifice

More splendid, when the white Sierras call
Unto the Rockies straightway to arise
And dance before the unveiled ark of the year,
Sounding their windy cedars as for shawms,
Unrolling rivers clear
For flutter of broad phylacteries;
While Shasta signals to Alaskan seas
That watch old sluggish glaciers downward creep
To fling their icebergs thundering from the steep,
And Mariposa through the purple calms
Gazes at far Hawaii crowned with palms
Where East and West are met, —
A rich seal on the ocean's bosom set
To say that East and West are twain,
With different loss and gain:
The Lord hath sundered them; let them be sundered yet.

IV   Alas! what sounds are these that come
Sullenly over the Pacific seas, —
Sounds of ignoble battle, striking dumb
The season's half-awakened ecstasies?
Must I be humble, then,
Now when my heart hath need of pride?
Wild love falls on me from these sculptured men;
By loving much the land for which they died
I would be justified.
My spirit was away on pinions wide
To soothe in praise of her its passionate mood
And ease it of its ache of gratitude.
Too sorely heavy is the debt they lay
On me and the companions of my day.

I would remember now
My country's goodliness, make sweet her name.
Alas! what shade art thou
Of sorrow or of blame
Liftest the lyric leafage from her brow,
And pointest a slow finger at her shame?

V   Lies! lies! It cannot be! The wars we wage
Are noble, and our battles still are won
By justice for us, ere we lift the gage.
We have not sold our loftiest heritage.
The proud republic hath not stooped to cheat
And scramble in the market-place of war;
Her forehead weareth yet its solemn star.
Here is her witness: this, her perfect son,
This delicate and proud New England soul
Who leads despisèd men, with just-unshackled feet,
Up the large ways where death and glory meet,
To show all peoples that our shame is done,
That once more we are clean and spirit-whole.

VI   Crouched in the sea fog on the moaning sand
All night he lay, speaking some simple word
From hour to hour to the slow minds that heard,
Holding each poor life gently in his hand
And breathing on the base rejected clay
Till each dark face shone mystical and grand
Against the breaking day;
And lo, the shard the potter cast away
Was grown a fiery chalice crystal-fine
Fulfilled of the divine

Great wine of battle wrath by God's ring-finger stirred.
Then upward, where the shadowy bastion loomed
Huge on the mountain in the wet sea light,
Whence now, and now, infernal flowerage bloomed,
Bloomed, burst, and scattered down its deadly seed,—
They swept, and died like freemen on the height,
Like freemen, and like men of noble breed;
And when the battle fell away at night
By hasty and contemptuous hands were thrust
Obscurely in a common grave with him
The fair-haired keeper of their love and trust.
Now limb doth mingle with dissolvèd limb
In nature's busy old democracy
To flush the mountain laurel when she blows
Sweet by the southern sea,
And heart with crumbled heart climbs in the rose:—
The untaught hearts with the high heart that knew
This mountain fortress for no earthly hold
Of temporal quarrel, but the bastion old
Of spiritual wrong,
Built by an unjust nation sheer and strong,
Expugnable but by a nation's rue
And bowing down before that equal shrine
By all men held divine,
Whereof his band and he were the most holy sign.

VII O bitter, bitter shade!
Wilt thou not put the scorn
And instant tragic question from thine eye?
Do thy dark brows yet crave
That swift and angry stave—

Unmeet for this desirous morn—
That I have striven, striven to evade?
Gazing on him, must I not deem they err
Whose careless lips in street and shop aver
As common tidings, deeds to make his cheek
Flush from the bronze, and his dead throat to speak?
Surely some elder singer would arise,
Whose harp hath leave to threaten and to mourn
Above this people when they go astray.
Is Whitman, the strong spirit, overworn?
Has Whittier put his yearning wrath away?
I will not and I dare not yet believe!
Though furtively the sunlight seems to grieve,
And the spring-laden breeze
Out of the gladdening west is sinister
With sounds of nameless battle overseas;
Though when we turn and question in suspense
If these things be indeed after these ways,
And what things are to follow after these,
Our fluent men of place and consequence
Fumble and fill their mouths with hollow phrase,
Or for the end-all of deep arguments
Intone their dull commercial liturgies—
I dare not yet believe! My ears are shut!
I will not hear the thin satiric praise
And muffled laughter of our enemies,
Bidding us never sheathe our valiant sword
Till we have changed our birthright for a gourd
Of wild pulse stolen from a barbarian's hut;
Showing how wise it is to cast away
The symbols of our spiritual sway,

That so our hands with better ease
May wield the driver's whip and grasp the jailer's keys.

VIII   Was it for this our fathers kept the law?
This crown shall crown their struggle and their ruth?
Are we the eagle nation Milton saw
Mewing its mighty youth,
Soon to possess the mountain winds of truth,
And be a swift familiar of the sun
Where aye before God's face his trumpets run?
Or have we but the talons and the maw,
And for the abject likeness of our heart
Shall some less lordly bird be set apart? —
Some gross-billed wader where the swamps are fat?
Some gorger in the sun? Some prowler with the bat?

IX   Ah no!
We have not fallen so.
We are our fathers' sons: let those who lead us know!
'Twas only yesterday sick Cuba's cry
Came up the tropic wind, "Now help us, for we die!"
Then Alabama heard,
And rising, pale, to Maine and Idaho
Shouted a burning word.
Proud state with proud impassioned state conferred,
And at the lifting of a hand sprang forth,
East, west, and south, and north,
Beautiful armies. Oh, by the sweet blood and young
Shed on the awful hill slope at San Juan,
By the unforgotten names of eager boys
Who might have tasted girls' love and been stung

With the old mystic joys

And starry griefs, now the spring nights come on,

But that the heart of youth is generous, —

We charge you, ye who lead us,

Breathe on their chivalry no hint of stain!

Turn not their new-world victories to gain!

One least leaf plucked for chaffer from the bays

Of their dear praise,

One jot of their pure conquest put to hire,

The implacable republic will require;

With clamor, in the glare and gaze of noon,

Or subtly, coming as a thief at night,

But surely, very surely, slow or soon

That insult deep we deeply will requite.

Tempt not our weakness, our cupidity!

For save we let the island men go free,

Those baffled and dislaureled ghosts

Will curse us from the lamentable coasts

Where walk the frustrate dead.

The cup of trembling shall be drainèd quite,

Eaten the sour bread of astonishment,

With ashes of the hearth shall be made white

Our hair, and wailing shall be in the tent;

Then on your guiltier head

Shall our intolerable self-disdain

Wreak suddenly its anger and its pain;

For manifest in that disastrous light

We shall discern the right

And do it tardily. —O ye who lead,

Take heed!

Blindness we may forgive, but baseness we will smite.

Snapshots of War ❧

A sentimental poem, effective because of the reality it evokes of a widow's only son enlisting in the Confederate Army. This is another poem reflecting the democratic quality of a war fought not by the wealthy and the professional classes but by simple people moved by patriotism on both sides.

UNKNOWN ✺

Enlisted Today

I know the sun shines, and the lilacs are blowing,
    And summer sends kisses by beautiful May—
Oh! to see all the treasures the spring is bestowing,
    And think my boy Willie enlisted today,

It seems but a day since at twilight, low humming,
    I rocked him to sleep with his cheek upon mine,
While Robby, the four-year old, watched for the coming
    Of father, adown the street's indistinct line.

It is many a year since my Harry departed,
    To come back no more in the twilight or dawn:
And Robby grew weary of watching, and started
    Alone on the journey his father had gone.

It is many a year—and this afternoon sitting
    At Robby's old window, I heard the band play,
And suddenly ceased dreaming over my knitting,
    To recollect Willie is twenty today.

D. W. C. Arnold, private in the Union army

And that, standing beside him this soft May-day morning,
  And the sun making gold of his wreathed cigar smoke,
I saw in his sweet eyes and lips a faint warning,
  And choked down the tears when he eagerly spoke:

"Dear mother, you know how these Northmen are crowing,
  They would trample the rights of the South in the dust,
The boys are all fire; and they wish I were going—"
  He stopped, but his eyes said, "Oh, say if I must!"

I smiled on the boy, though my heart it seemed breaking,
  My eyes filled with tears, so I turned them away,
And answered him, "Willie, 'tis well you are waking—
  Go, act as you father would bid you, today!"

I sit in the window, and see the flags flying,
  And drearily list to the roll of the drum,
And smother the pain in my heart that is lying
  And bid all the fears in my bosom be dumb.

I shall sit in the window when summer is lying
  Out over the fields, and the honey-bee's hum
Lulls the rose at the porch from her tremulous sighing,
  And watch for the face of my darling to come.

And if he should fall—his young life he has given
  For freedom's sweet sake; and for me, I will pray
Once more with my Harry and Robby in Heaven
  To meet the dear boy that enlisted today.

HERMAN MELVILLE (1819–1891)

The March into Virginia

Ending in the First Battle of Manassas
(July, 1861)

*This poem is a Federal counterpart
to the Confederate "Enlisted
Today." As Melville notes here,
confident and green young Union
soldiers broke ranks to pick berries
on their way to being routed and
slaughtered by Confederates at the
first battle of Bull Run, called
Manassas by Southerners.
Moloch was an ancient god of the
Canaanites to whom children were
sacrificed (I Kings 11:7; II Kings
23:10). At the second battle of
Manassas in August 1862,
Federal forces were again routed
and slaughtered by Confederates.*

Did all the lets and bars appear
   To every just or larger end,
Whence should come the trust and cheer?
   Youth must its ignorant impulse lend—
Age finds place in the rear.
   All wars are boyish, and are fought by boys,
The champions and enthusiasts of the state:
   Turbid ardors and vain joys
    Not barrenly abate—
Stimulants to the power mature,
   Preparatives of fate.

Who here forecasteth the event?
What heart but spurns at precedent
And warnings of the wise,
Contemned foreclosures of surprise?
The banners play, the bugles call,
The air is blue and prodigal.
   No berrying party, pleasure-wooed,

Ruins of Henry House, first battle of Bull Run

No picnic party in the May,
Ever went less loth than they
   Into that leafy neighborhood.
In Bacchic glee they file toward Fate,
Moloch's uninitiate;
Expectancy, and glad surmise
Of battle's unknown mysteries.
All they feel is this: 'tis glory,
A rapture sharp, though transitory,
Yet lasting in belaureled story.
So they gayly go to fight,
Chatting left and laughing right.

But some who this blithe mood present,
   As on in lightsome files they fare,
Shall die experienced ere three days are spent—
   Perish, enlightened by the vollied glare;
Or shame survive, and, like to adamant,
   The throe of Second Manassas share.

The Cumberland *was a wooden
ship, a sloop with twenty-four
guns, rammed and sunk by the
Confederate ironclad* Merrimac *at
Hampton Roads, Virginia, on
Saturday, March 8, 1862. Union
sailors on the Cumberland fought
until the last, enduring fearsome
casualties. When the ship sank,
the main mast with the American
flag still flying remained above
water, waving in the breeze.*

HENRY WADSWORTH LONGFELLOW (1802–1887) ✍

The Cumberland

At anchor in Hampton Roads we lay,
    On board of the *Cumberland* sloop-of-war;
And at times from the fortress across the bay
        The alarum of drums swept past,
        Or a bugle-blast
    From the camp on the shore.

Then far away to the south uprose
    A little feather of snow-white smoke,
And we knew that the iron ship of our foes
        Was steadily steering its course
        To try the force
    Of our ribs of oak.

Down upon us heavily runs,
    Silent and sullen, the floating fort;
Then comes a puff of smoke from her guns,
        And leaps the terrible death,

With fiery breath,
From each open port.

We are not idle, but send her straight
Defiance back in a full broadside!
As hail rebounds from a roof of slate,
Rebounds our heavier hail
From each iron scale
Of the monster's hide.

"Strike your flag!" the rebel cries,
In his arrogant old plantation strain.
"Never!" our gallant Morris replies:
"It is better to sink than to yield!"
And the whole air pealed
With the cheers of our men.

Then like a kraken huge and black,
She crushed our ribs in her iron grasp!
Down went the *Cumberland* all awrack,
With a sudden shudder of death,
And the cannon's breath
For her dying gasp.

Next morn, as the sun rose over the bay,
Still floated our flag at the mainmast-head.
Lord, how beautiful was thy day!
Every waft of the air
Was a whisper of prayer,
Or a dirge for the dead.

Ho! brave hearts that went down in the seas!
  Ye are at peace in the troubled stream.
Ho! brave land! with hearts like these,
    Thy flag, that is rent in twain,
    Shall be one again,
  And without a seam.

HERMAN MELVILLE (1819–1891) ❧

A Dirge for McPherson

Killed in front of Atlanta
(July, 1864)

Thirty-five-year-old James McPherson commanded the Federal Army of the Tennessee in July 1864 during the advance on Atlanta. Riding into a party of Confederates by accident during the battle for a place called Bald Hill, he was ordered to surrender. He turned his horse and galloped away, only to be shot in the back and killed—the only commander of a Union army to die in battle during the war.

Arms reversed and banners craped—
   Muffled drums;
Snowy horses sable-draped—
   McPherson comes.

    But, tell us, shall we know him more,
    Lost-Mountain and lone Kenesaw?

Brave the sword upon the pall—
   A gleam in gloom;
So a bright name lighteth all
   McPherson's doom.

Bear him through the chapel-door—
   Let priest in stole
Pace before the warrior
   Who led. Bell—toll!

Battlefield of Atlanta, Georgia, where General James McPherson was killed

Lay him down within the nave,
  The Lesson read—
Man is noble, man is brave,
  But man's—a weed.

Take him up again and wend
  Graveward, nor weep:
There's a trumpet that shall rend
  This Soldier's sleep.

Pass the ropes the coffin round,
  And let descend;
Prayer and volley—let it sound
  McPherson's end.

  True fame is his, for life is o'er—
  Sarpedon of the mighty war.

A poem about faith, debating whether God's Providence controls the course of events. In the end, the answer is God's answer to Job: Human wisdom cannot penetrate the ways of God, but He remains in charge of the universe.

HERMAN MELVILLE (1819–1891) ✍

The Conflict of Convictions

On starry heights
   A bugle wails the long recall;
Derision stirs the deep abyss,
   Heaven's ominous silence over all.
Return, return, O eager Hope,
   And face man's latter fall.
Events, they make the dreamers quail;
Satan's old age is strong and hale,
A disciplined captain, gray in skill,
And Raphael a white enthusiast still;
Dashed aims, at which Christ's martyrs pale,
Shall Mammon's slaves fulfill?

   (Dismantle the fort,
   Cut down the fleet—
   Battle no more shall be!
   While the fields for fight in æons to come
   Congeal beneath the sea.)

Chaplain conducting Mass for the 69th New York Militia, Fort Corcoran

The terrors of truth and dart of death
  To faith alike are vain;
Though comets, gone a thousand years,
  Return again,
Patient she stands—she can no more—
And waits, nor heeds she waxes hoar.

      (At a stony gate,
      A statue of stone,
      Weed overgrown—
      Long 'twill wait!)

But God His former mind retains,
  Confirms his old decree;
The generations are inured to pains,
  And strong Necessity
Surges, and heaps Time's strand with wrecks.
  The People spread like a weedy grass,
  The thing they will they bring to pass,
And prosper to the apoplex.
The rout it herds around the heart,
  The ghost is yielded in the gloom;
Kings wag their heads—Now save thyself
  Who wouldst rebuild the world in bloom.

      (Tide-mark
      And top of the ages' strife,
      Verge where they called the world to come,
      The last advance of life—
      Ha ha, the rust on the Iron Dome!)

Nay, but revere the hid event;
   In the cloud a sword is girded on,
I mark a twinkling in the tent
   Of Michael the warrior one.
Senior wisdom suits not now,
The light is on the youthful brow.

   (Ay, in caves the miner see:
   His forehead bears a blinking light;
   Darkness so he feebly braves
   A meagre wight!)

But He who rules is old—is old;
Ah! faith is warm, but heaven with age is cold.

   (Ho ho, ho ho,
   The cloistered doubt
   Of olden times
   Is blurted out!)

The Ancient of Days forever is young,
   Forever the scheme of Nature thrives;
I know a wind in purpose strong—
   It spins *against* the way it drives.
What if the gulfs their slimed foundations bare?
So deep must the stones be hurled
Whereon the throes of ages rear
The final empire and the happier world.

   (The poor old Past,
   The Future's slave,

She drudged through pain and crime
To bring about the blissful Prime,
Then—perished. There's a grave!)

   Power unanointed may come—
Dominion (unsought by the free)
   And the Iron Dome,
Stronger for stress and strain,
Fling her huge shadow athwart the main;
But the Founders' dream shall flee.
Age after age shall be
As age after age has been,
(From man's changeless heart their way they win);
And death be busy with all who strive—
Death, with silent negative.

      YEA AND NAY—
      EACH HATH HIS SAY;
      BUT GOD HE KEEPS THE MIDDLE WAY.
      NONE WAS BY
      WHEN HE SPREAD THE SKY;
      WISDOM IS VAIN, AND PROPHESY.

HERMAN MELVILLE (1819–1891) ❧

The College Colonel

*A poem somewhat in opposition to
"The Conflict of Convictions."
The young colonel has been to war
where he has been in the final
terrible battles in northern Virginia,
and he has prematurely aged.
Above all the other horrors is the
discovery of a darker truth,
perhaps that none of this has any
ultimate meaning.*

He rides at their head;
   A crutch by his saddle just slants in view,
One slung arm is in splints, you see,
   Yet he guides his strong steed—how coldly too.

He brings his regiment home—
   Not as they filed two years before,
But a remnant half-tattered, and battered, and worn,
Like castaway sailors, who—stunned
     By the surf's loud roar,
   Their mates dragged back and seen no more—
Again and again breast the surge,
   And at last crawl, spent, to shore.

A still rigidity and pale—
   An Indian aloofness lones his brow;
He has lived a thousand years
Compressed in battle's pains and prayers,
   Marches and watches slow.

There are welcoming shouts, and flags;
　　Old men off hat to the Boy,
Wreaths from gay balconies fall at his feet,
　　But to *him*—there comes alloy.

It is not that a leg is lost,
　　It is not that an arm is maimed,
It is not that the fever has racked—
　　Self he has long disclaimed.

But all through the Seven Days' Fight,
　　And deep in the Wilderness grim,
And in the field-hospital tent,
　　And Petersburg crater, and dim
Lean brooding in Libby, there came—
　　Ah heaven!—what *truth* to him.

HERMAN MELVILLE (1819–1891) ❧

The House-Top

A Night Piece
(July 1863)

No sleep. The sultriness pervades the air
And binds the brain—a dense oppression, such
As tawny tigers feel in matted shades,
Vexing their blood and making apt for ravage.
Beneath the stars the roofy desert spreads
Vacant as Libya. All is hushed near by.
Yet fitfully from far breaks a mixed surf
Of muffled sound, the Atheist roar of riot.
Yonder, where parching Sirius set in drought,
Balefully glares red Arson—there—and there.
The Town is taken by its rats—ship-rats
And rats of the wharves. All civil charms
And priestly spells which late held hearts in awe—
Fear-bound, subjected to a better sway
Than sway of self; these like a dream dissolve
And man rebounds whole æons back in nature.
Hail to the low dull rumble, dull and dead,
And ponderous drag that jars the wall.
Wise Draco comes, deep in the midnight roll

This bitter poem is Melville's reaction to the draft riots in New York in July 1863, when the lower classes of the city erupted in protest to the draft and looted and burned much of Manhattan. Combat troops moved into the city and suppressed the riot with bloodshed. As might be expected from a poem inspired on a roof-top, stars and constellations—including Draco the Dragon, a legendary avenger—play a prominent part. Melville asks whether human beings are good enough to govern themselves; Lincoln would declare a few months later at Gettysburg that yes, they are.

Of black artillery; he comes, though late;
In code corroborating Calvin's creed
And cynic tyrannies of honest kings;
He comes, nor parlies; and the Town, redeemed,
Gives thanks devout; nor, being thankful, heeds
The grimy slur on the Republic's faith implied,
Which holds that Man is naturally good,
And—more—is Nature's Roman, never to be scourged.

WALT WHITMAN (1819–1892) 🖎

As I Lay with My Head in Your Lap Camerado

A poem with much in common with "Dover Beach," by the skeptical English poet Matthew Arnold, which was not published until 1867. In a world of desperate confusion without ultimate meaning, the best one can hope for is loyal love, with a companion on the senseless journey.

As I lay with my head in your lap camerado,

The confession I made I resume, what I said to you and the open air I resume,

I know I am restless and make others so,

I know my words are weapons full of danger, full of death,

For I confront peace, security, and all the settled laws, to unsettle them,

I am more resolute because all have denied me than I could ever have been had all accepted me,

I heed not and have never heeded either experience, cautions, majorities, nor ridicule,

And the threat of what is call'd hell is little or nothing to me,

And the lure of what is call'd heaven is little or nothing to me;

Dear camerado! I confess I have urged you onward with me, and still urge you, without the least idea what is our destination,

Or whether we shall be victorious, or utterly quell'd and defeated.

Emory Eugene King, private in the 4th Michigan Infantry

Whitman here looks at the dead
without mentioning which side or
sides they are on—an old man, a
boy, and a man in the fullness of
life, in whose corpse he sees the
Christ suffering for all humankind.

WALT WHITMAN (1819–1892) 🖎

A Sight in Camp in the Daybreak Gray and Dim

A sight in camp in the daybreak gray and dim,
As from my tent I emerge so early sleepless,
As slow I walk in the cool fresh air the path near by the hospital tent,
Three forms I see on stretchers lying, brought out there untended lying,
Over each the blanket spread, ample brownish woolen blanket,
Gray and heavy blanket, folding, covering all.

Curious I halt and silent stand,
Then with light fingers I from the face of the nearest the first just lift the blanket;
Who are you elderly man so gaunt and grim, with well-gray'd hair, and flesh all sunken
   about the eyes?
Who are you my dear comrade?

Then to the second I step—and who are you my child and darling?
Who are you sweet boy with cheeks yet blooming?

Then to the third—a face nor child nor old, very calm, as of beautiful yellow-white ivory;
Young man I think I know you— I think this face is the face of the Christ himself,
Dead and divine and brother of all, and here again he lies.

Winter quarters: Soldiers in front of their wooden hut, "Pine Cottage"

WALT WHITMAN (1819–1892) 🖈

Give Me the Splendid Silent Sun

A poem contrasting the love of silent nature with the manifold tumult of the metropolis, here New York, with all the excitement of a population tense with war. In the end the gregarious Whitman chooses crowds over solitude. The poem reflects the mood of many who found in the lethal passions of war the greatest moments of their lives.

I   Give me the splendid silent sun with all his beams full-dazzling,
Give me juicy autumnal fruit ripe and red from the orchard,
Give me a field where the unmow'd grass grows,
Give me an arbor, give me the trellis'd grape,
Give me fresh corn and wheat, give me serene-moving animals teaching content,
Give me nights perfectly quiet as on high plateaus west of the Mississippi, and I looking up
    at the stars,
Give me odorous at sunrise a garden of beautiful flowers where I can walk undisturb'd,
Give me for marriage a sweet-breath'd woman of whom I should never tire,
Give me a perfect child, give me away aside from the noise of the world a rural domestic life,
Give me to warble spontaneous songs recluse by myself, for my own ears only,
Give me solitude, give me Nature, give me again O Nature your primal sanities!

These demanding to have them, (tired with ceaseless excitement, and rack'd by the
    war-strife,)
These to procure incessantly asking, rising in cries from my heart,
While yet incessantly asking still I adhere to my city,
Day upon day and year upon year O city, walking your streets,
Where you hold me enchain'd a certain time refusing to give me up,

Yet giving to make me glutted, enrich'd of soul, you give me forever faces;

(O I see what I sought to escape, confronting, reversing my cries,

I see my own soul trampling down what it ask'd for.)

II Keep your splendid silent sun,

Keep your woods O Nature, and the quiet places by the woods,

Keep your fields of clover and timothy, and your corn-fields and orchards,

Keep the blossoming buckwheat fields where the Ninth-month bees hum;

Give me faces and streets— give me these phantoms incessant and endless along the trottoirs!

Give me interminable eyes—give me women—give me comrades and lovers by the thousand!

Let me see new ones every day—let me hold new ones by the hand every day!

Give me such shows—give me the streets of Manhattan!

Give me Broadway, with the soldiers marching—give me the sound of the trumpets and
    drums!

(The soldiers in companies or regiments—some starting away, flush'd and reckless,

Some, their time up, returning with thinn'd ranks, young, yet very old, worn, marching,
    noticing nothing;)

Give me the shores and wharves heavy-fringed with black ships!

O such for me! O an intense life, full to repletion and varied!

The life of the theatre, bar-room, huge hotel, for me!

The saloon of the steamer! the crowded excursion for me! the torchlight procession!

The dense brigade bound for the war, with high piled military wagons following;

People, endless, streaming, with strong voices, passions, pageants,

Manhattan streets with their powerful throbs, with beating drums as now,

The endless and noisy chorus, the rustle and clank of muskets, (even the sight of the
    wounded,)

Manhattan crowds, with their turbulent musical chorus!

Manhattan faces and eyes forever for me.

A poem expressing the terrible thrill of war, whose drums beat down every resistance and conquer the world of work and emotion to absorb everything into the mighty passions of conflict.

WALT WHITMAN (1819–1892) ❧

Beat! Beat! Drums!

Beat! beat! drums!—blow! bugles! blow!

Through the windows—through doors—burst like a ruthless force,

Into the solemn church, and scatter the congregation,

Into the school where the scholar is studying;

Leave not the bridegroom quiet—no happiness must he have now with his bride,

Nor the peaceful farmer any peace, ploughing his field or gathering his grain;

So fierce you whirr and pound you drums—so shrill you bugles blow.

Beat! beat! drums!—blow! bugles! blow!

Over the traffic of cities—over the rumble of wheels in the streets;

Are beds prepared for sleepers at night in the houses? no sleepers must sleep in those beds;

No bargainers' bargains by day—no brokers or speculators—would they continue?

Would the talkers be talking? would the singer attempt to sing?

Would the lawyer rise in the court to state his case before the judge?

Then rattle quicker, heavier drums—you bugles wilder blow.

Beat! beat! drums!—blow! bugles! blow!

Make no parley—stop for no expostulation;

Mind not the timid—mind not the weeper or prayer;

The Drummer Boy of Shiloh, John L. Clem, aged 10

Mind not the old man beseeching the young man;

Let not the child's voice be heard, nor the mother's entreaties;

Make even the trestles to shake the dead, where they lie awaiting the hearses,

So strong you thump, O terrible drums — so loud you bugles blow.

A snapshot of momentary repose as horses stop to drink while fighting men loll in the saddles. Whitman, whose poetry does not take either the Federal or the Confederate side, is here absorbed with colors. The red, white, and blue guidons could be Union or Confederate.

WALT WHITMAN (1819–1892) ❦

Cavalry Crossing a Ford

A line in long array, where they wind betwixt green islands;

They take a serpentine course—their arms flash in the sun—hark to the musical clank;

Behold the silvery river—in it the splashing horses, loitering, stop to drink;

Behold the brown-faced men—each group, each person, a picture—the negligent rest on the saddles;

Some emerge on the opposite bank—others are just entering the ford—while,

Scarlet, and blue, and snowy white,

The guidon flags flutter gaily in the wind.

WALT WHITMAN (1819–1892) ❧

Bivouac on a Mountain Side

A snapshot of war that impresses Whitman because of its contrasts: the ephemeral campfires symbolic of the brevity of life and the passing of the scene he observes, and overhead the eternal stars that will endure when all this momentous human activity has passed utterly away.

I see before me now a traveling army halting,

Below a fertile valley spread, with barns and the orchards of summer,

Behind, the terraced sides of a mountain, abrupt, in places rising high,

Broken, with rocks, with clinging cedars, with tall shapes dingily seen,

The numerous camp-fires scatter'd near and far, some away up on the mountain,

The shadowy forms of men and horses, looming, large-sized, flickering,

And over all the sky—the sky! far, far out of reach, studded, breaking out, the eternal stars.

Pioneers Camp, Lookout Mountain, Tennessee

WALT WHITMAN (1819–1892)

The Artilleryman's Vision

All this is imagined since Whitman never saw combat. But no poem in this collection better expresses the nostalgia for the war once it was over, the remembered excitement that brought thousands of men on both sides together for reunions with their comrades as long as they lived. Probably no better description of combat emerged from the Civil War — certainly not in poetry.

While my wife at my side lies slumbering, and the wars are over long,

And my head on the pillow rests at home, and the vacant midnight passes,

And through the stillness, through the dark, I hear, just hear, the breath of my infant,

There in the room as I wake from sleep this vision presses upon me;

The engagement opens there and then in fantasy unreal,

The skirmishers begin, they crawl cautiously ahead, I hear the irregular snap! snap!

I hear the sounds of the different missiles, the short *t-h-t! t-h-t!* of the rifle-balls,

I see the shells exploding leaving small white clouds, I hear the great shells shrieking as they
    pass,

The grape like the hum and whirr of wind through the trees, (tumultuous now the contest
    rages,)

All the scenes at the batteries rise in detail before me again,

The crashing and smoking, the pride of the men in their pieces,

The chief-gunner ranges and sights his piece and selects a fuse of the right time,

After firing I see him lean aside and look eagerly off to note the effect;

Elsewhere I hear the cry of a regiment charging, (the young colonel leads himself this time
    with brandish'd sword,)

I see the gaps cut by the enemy's volleys, (quickly fill'd up, no delay,)

I breathe the suffocating smoke, then the flat clouds hover low concealing all;

Now a strange lull for a few seconds, not a shot fired on either side,

Then resumed the chaos louder than ever, with eager calls and orders of officers,

While from some distant part of the field the wind wafts to my ears a shout of applause, (some special success,)

And ever the sound of the cannon far or near, (rousing even in dreams a devilish exultation and all the old mad joy in the depths of my soul,)

And ever the hastening of infantry shifting positions, batteries, cavalry, moving hither and thither,

(The falling, dying, I heed not, the wounded dripping and red I heed not, some to the rear are hobbling,)

Grime, heat, rush, aide-de-camps galloping by or on a full run,

With the patter of small arms, the warning *s-s-t* of the rifles, (these in my vision I hear or see,)

And bombs bursting in air, and at night the vari-color'd rockets.

*A poem pulsating with the thrill of
excitement at the spectacle of war,
a thrill Whitman could not suppress
despite the horror of it all.*

WALT WHITMAN (1819–1892)

An Army Corps on the March

With its cloud of skirmishers in advance,

With now the sound of a single shot snapping like a whip, and now an irregular volley,

The swarming ranks press on and on, the dense brigades press on,

Glittering dimly, toiling under the sun—the dust-cover'd men,

In columns rise and fall to the undulations of the ground,

With artillery interspers'd—the wheels rumble, the horses sweat,

As the army corps advances.

Engineer Camp, 8th New York Militia

WALT WHITMAN (1819–1892)

Come Up from the Fields Father

Come up from the fields father, here's a letter from our Pete,
And come to the front door mother, here's a letter from thy dear son.

Lo, 'tis autumn,
Lo, where the trees, deeper green, yellower and redder,
Cool and sweeten Ohio's villages with leaves fluttering in the moderate wind,
Where apples ripe in the orchards hang and grapes on the trellis'd vines,
(Smell you the smell of the grapes on the vines?
Smell you the buckwheat where the bees were lately buzzing?)

Above all, lo, the sky so calm, so transparent after the rain, and with wondrous clouds,
Below too, all calm, all vital and beautiful, and the farm prospers well.

Down in the fields all prospers well,
But now from the fields come father, come at the daughter's call,
And come to the entry mother, to the front door come right away.

Fast as she can she hurries, something ominous, her steps trembling,
She does not tarry to smooth her hair nor adjust her cap.

Open the envelope quickly,
O this is not our son's writing, yet his name is sign'd,
O a strange hand writes for our dear son, O stricken mother's soul!
All swims before her eyes, flashes with black, she catches the main words only,
Sentences broken, *gunshot wound in the breast, cavalry skirmish, taken to hospital,*
At present low, but will soon be better.

Ah now the single figure to me,
Amid all teeming and wealthy Ohio with all its cities and farms,
Sickly white in the face and dull in the head, very faint,
By the jamb of a door leans.

Grieve not so, dear mother, (the just-grown daughter speaks through her sobs,
The little sisters huddle around speechless and dismay'd),
See, dearest mother, the letter says Pete will soon be better.

Alas poor boy, he will never be better, (nor may-be needs to be better, that brave and
    simple soul,)
While they stand at home at the door he is dead already,
The only son is dead.

But the mother needs to be better,
She with thin form presently drest in black,
By day her meals untouch'd, then at night fitfully sleeping, often waking,
In the midnight waking, weeping, longing with one deep longing,
O that she might withdraw unnoticed, silent from life escape and withdraw,
To follow, to seek, to be with her dear dead son.

UNKNOWN 🖎

Hospital Duties

A poem depicting the role of women as nurses in the war. Many women on both sides volunteered to work in the makeshift hospitals where, as one wrote in her diary, they kneeled in blood and water all day long by the wounded and dying. This poem calls for an end of class consciousness in the emergency and extols the Providence of God.

Fold away all your bright-tinted dresses,
    Turn the key on your jewels today,
And the wealth of your tendril-like tresses
    Braid back in a serious way;
No more delicate gloves, no more laces,
    No more trifling in boudoir or bower,
But come with your souls in your faces
    To meet the stern wants of the hour.

Look around! By the torchlight unsteady
    The dead and the dying seem one—
What! trembling and paling already,
    Before your dear mission's begun?
These wounds are more precious than ghastly—
    Time presses her lips to each scar,
While she chants of that glory which vastly
    Transcends all the horrors of war.

Surgeons of Harwood Hospital, Washington, D.C.

Pause here by this bedside. How mellow
   The light showers down on that brow!
Such a brave, brawny visage, poor fellow!
   Some homestead is missing him now.
Some wife shades her eyes in the clearing,
   Some mother sits moaning distressed,
While the loved one lies faint but unfearing,
   With the enemy's ball in his breast.

Here's another—a lad—a mere stripling,
   Picked up in the field almost dead,
With the blood through his sunny hair rippling
   From the horrible gash in the head.
They say he was first in the action;
   Gay-hearted, quick-headed, and witty:
He fought till he dropped with exhaustion
   At the gates of our fair Southern city.

Fought and fell 'neath the guns of that city,
   With a spirit transcending his years—
Lift him up in your large-hearted pity,
   And wet his pale lips with your tears.
Touch him gently; most sacred the duty
   Of dressing that poor shattered hand!
God spare him to rise in his beauty,
   And battle once more for his land!

Pass on! it is useless to linger
   While others are calling your care;
There is need for your delicate finger,
   For your womanly sympathy there.

There are sick ones athirst for caressing,
    There are dying ones raving at home,
There are wounds to be bound with a blessing,
    And shrouds to make ready for some.

They have gathered about you the harvest
    Of death in its ghastliest view;
The nearest as well as the furthest
    Is there with the traitor and true.
And crowned with your beautiful patience,
    Made sunny with love at the heart,
You must balsam the wounds of the nations,
    Nor falter nor shrink from your part.

And the lips of the mother will bless you,
    And angels, sweet-visaged and pale,
And the little ones run to caress you,
    And the wives and the sisters cry hail!
But e'en if you drop down unheeded,
    What matter? God's ways are the best;
You have poured out your life where 'twas needed,
    And He will take care of the rest.

THOMAS BUCHANAN READ (1822–1872) ❧

Sheridan's Ride

This is one of the great old chestnuts of American literature, included in elementary school textbooks at least until the 1950s. The poem commemorates a battle at Cedar Creek south of Winchester, Virginia, on October 19, 1864. General Philip Sheridan was returning to his camp from Washington when he heard the firing and galloped toward it on his horse, Rienzi. He rallied his fleeing troops and reorganized them and crushed the Confederates before nightfall. He then continued laying waste the Shenandoah Valley.

Up from the South, at break of day,
Bringing to Winchester fresh dismay,
The affrighted air with a shudder bore,
Like a herald in haste, to the chieftain's door,
The terrible grumble, and rumble, and roar,
Telling the battle was on once more,
    And Sheridan twenty miles away.

And wider still those billows of war
Thundered along the horizon's bar;
And louder yet into Winchester rolled
The roar of that red sea uncontrolled,
Making the blood of the listener cold,
As he thought of the stake in that fiery fray,
    With Sheridan twenty miles away.

But there is a road from Winchester town,
A good, broad highway leading down;
And there, through the flush of the morning light,

A steed as black as the steeds of night
Was seen to pass, as with eagle flight;
As if he knew the terrible need,
He stretched away with the utmost speed;
Hills rose and fell, but his heart was gay,
　With Sheridan fifteen miles away.

Still sprang from those swift hoofs, thundering South,
The dust, like smoke from the cannon's mouth;
Or the trail of a comet, sweeping faster and faster,
Foreboding to traitors the doom of disaster,
The heart of the steed and the heart of the master
Were beating like prisoners assaulting their walls,
Impatient to be where the battlefield calls;
Every nerve of the charger was strained to full play,
　With Sheridan only ten miles away.

Under his spurning feet, the road
Like an arrowy Alpine river flowed,
And the landscape sped away behind
Like an ocean flying before the wind;
And the steed, like a barque fed with furnace ire,
Swept on, with his wild eye full of fire.
But, lo! he is nearing his heart's desire;
He is snuffing the smoke of the roaring fray,
　With Sheridan only five miles away.

The first that the general saw were the groups
Of stragglers, and then the retreating troops;
What was done? what to do? A glance told him both.
Then striking his spurs, with a terrible oath,

He dashed down the line 'mid a storm of huzzas,
And the wave of retreat checked its course there, because
The sight of the master compelled it to pause.
With foam and with dust the black charger was gray;
By the flash of his eye and the red nostril's play,
He seemed to the whole great army to say,
"I have brought you Sheridan all the way
    From Winchester down to save the day!"

Hurrah! hurrah for Sheridan!
Hurrah! hurrah for horse and man!
And when their statues are placed on high,
Under the dome of the Union sky,
The American soldier's Temple of Fame,
There, with the glorious general's name,
Be it said, in letters both bold and bright,
"Here is the steed that saved the day,
By carrying Sheridan into the fight,
    From Winchester, twenty miles away!"

*Melville's poem treats the same
event memorialized by Thomas
Buchanan Read, adding touches
beyond Read's mediocre powers.
He praises Sheridan's horse and
makes a classical pun on the name
"Philip," which in Greek means
"lover of horses." He puns,
too, on the name of the inept
Confederate commander,
Jubal Early. In the end he
ponders the deaths of those in
a victorious cause.*

HERMAN MELVILLE (1819–1891) ❦

Sheridan at Cedar Creek
(October, 1864)

Shoe the steed with silver
   That bore him to the fray,
When he heard the guns at dawning—
    Miles away;
When he heard them calling, calling—
    Mount! nor stay:
      Quick, or all is lost;
      They've surprised and stormed the post,
      They push your routed host—
Gallop! retrieve the day.

House the horse in ermine—
   For the foam-flake blew
White through the red October;
   He thundered into view;
They cheered him in the looming,
   Horseman and horse they knew.
      The turn of the tide began,
      The rally of bugles ran,

Union General Philip H. Sheridan

He swung his hat in the van;
The electric hoof-spark flew.

Wreathe the steed and lead him—
  For the charge he led
Touched and turned the cypress
  Into amaranths for the head
Of Philip, king of riders,
  Who raised them from the dead.
      The camp (at dawning lost),
      By eve, recovered—forced,
      Rang with laughter of the host
  At belated Early fled.

Shroud the horse in sable—
  For the mounds they heap!
There is firing in the Valley,
  And yet no strife they keep;
It is the parting volley,
  It is the pathos deep.
      There is glory for the brave
      Who lead, and nobly save,
      But no knowledge in the grave
  Where the nameless followers sleep.

JAMES MADISON BELL (1826–1902) 🦅

Though Tennyson the Poet King
From: "A Poem Entitled the Day and the War"

The poem commemorates the exploits of three regiments of black troops, known as the "African Brigade," at Milliken's Bend, just north of Vicksburg. On June 7, 1863, Confederates attacked Federal troops there and in savage fighting were repulsed. Federal forces suffered 652 casualties; 566 of these were from the African Brigade.

Though Tennyson, the poet king,
　　Has sung of Balaklava's charge,
Until his thund'ring cannons ring
　　From England's center to her marge,
The pleasing duty still remains
To sing a people from their chains —
To sing what none have yet assay'd,
The wonders of the Black Brigade.
The war had raged some twenty moons,
Ere they in columns or platoons,
To win them censure or applause,
Were marshal'd in the Union cause —
Prejudged of slavish cowardice,
While many a taunt and foul device
Came weekly forth with Harper's sheet,
To feed that base, infernal cheat.

But how they would themselves demean,
Has since most gloriously been seen.

'Twas seen at Milliken's dread bend!
Where e'en the Furies seemed to lend
To dark Secession all their aid,
To crush the Union Black Brigade.

The war waxed hot, and bullets flew
   Like San Francisco's summer sand,
But they were there to dare and do,
   E'en to the last, to save the land.
And when the leaders of their corps
   Grew wild with fear, and quit the field,
The dark remembrance of their scars
   Before them rose, they could not yield:
And, sounding o'er the battle din,
   They heard their standard-bearer cry—
"Rally! and prove that ye are men!
   Rally! and let us do or die!
For war, nor death, shall boast a shade
To daunt the Union Black Brigade!"

And thus he played the hero's part,
   Till on the ramparts of the foe
A score of bullets pierced his heart,
   He sank within the trench below.
His comrades saw, and fired with rage,
Each sought his man, him to engage
In single combat. Ah! 'twas then
The Black Brigade proved they were men!
For ne'er did Swiss! or Russ! or knight!
   Against such fearful odds arrayed,

With more persistent valor fight,
 Than did the Union Black Brigade!

As five to one, so stood their foes,
When that defiant shout arose,
And 'long their closing columns ran,
Commanding each to choose his man!
And ere the sound had died away,
Full many a ranting rebel lay
Gasping piteously for breath —
Struggling with the pangs of death,
From bayonet thrust or shining blade,
Plunged to the hilt by the Black Brigade.
And thus they fought, and won a name —
None brighter on the scroll of Fame;
For out of one full corps of men,
But one remained unwounded, when
The dreadful fray had fully past —
All killed or wounded but the last!

And though they fell, as has been seen,
Each slept his lifeless foes between,
And marked the course and paved the way
To ushering in a better day.
Let Balaklava's cannons roar,
 And Tennyson his hosts parade,
But ne'er was seen and never more
 The equals of the Black Brigade!

Then nerve thy heart, gird on thy sword,
For dark Oppression's ruthless horde

And thy tried friends are in the field—
Say which shall triumph, which shall yield?
Shall they that heed not man nor God—
Vile monsters of the *gory rod*—
Dark forgers of the *rack* and *chain:*
Shall *they* prevail—and Thraldom's reign,
With all his dark unnumber'd ills,
Become eternal as the hills?
No! by the blood of freemen slain,
On hot-contested field and main,
And by the mingled sweat and tears,
Extorted through these many years
From Afric's patient sons of toil—
Weak victims of a braggart's spoil—
This bastard plant, the Upas tree,
Shall not supplant our liberty!

WILL HENRY THOMPSON (1848–1918) ❧

The High Tide at Gettysburg

A cloud possessed the hollow field,
The gathering battle's smoky shield.
Athwart the gloom the lightning flashed,
And through the cloud some horsemen dashed,
And from the heights the thunder pealed.

Then at the brief command of Lee
Moved out that matchless infantry,
With Pickett leading grandly down,
To rush against the roaring crown
Of those dread heights of destiny.

Far heard above the angry guns
A cry across the tumult runs,—
The voice that rang through Shiloh's woods
And Chickamauga's solitudes,
The fierce South cheering on her sons!

The poem commemorates Pickett's Charge (more properly called Longstreet's Assault) on the third day at Gettysburg. Thompson makes much of Tennessee and Virginia, but more soldiers from North Carolina took part in Pickett's Charge than from any other Confederate state, including Virginia. Obviously "North Carolina" is less manageable in poetry than on the battlefield. A reader might also wrongly assume from this poem that the battle of Chickamauga, fought in September 1863, came before the battle of Gettysburg, fought in July.

Ah, how the withering tempest blew
Against the front of Pettigrew!
A Khamsin wind that scorched and singed
Like that infernal flame that fringed
The British squares at Waterloo!

A thousand fell where Kemper led;
A thousand died where Garnett bled;
In blinding flame and strangling smoke
The remnant through the batteries broke
And crossed the works with Armistead.

"Once more in Glory's van with me!"
Virginia cried to Tennessee;
"We two together, come what may,
Shall stand upon these works to-day!"
(The reddest day in history.)

Brave Tennessee! In reckless way
Virginia heard her comrade say:
"Close round this rent and riddled rag!"
What time she sat her battle flag
Amid the guns of Doubleday.

But who shall break the guards that wait
Before the awful face of Fate?
The tattered standards of the South
Were shriveled at the cannon's mouth,
And all her hope were desolate.

In vain the Tennesseean set
His breast against the bayonet!
In vain Virginia charged and raged,
A tigress in her wrath uncaged,
Till all the hill was red and wet!

Above the bayonets, mixed and crossed,
Men saw a gray, gigantic ghost
Receding through the battle cloud,
And heard across the tempest loud
The death cry of a nation lost!

The brave went down! Without disgrace
They leaped to Ruin's red embrace.
They only heard Fame's thunders wake,
And saw the dazzling sunburst break
In smiles on Glory's bloody face!

They fell, who lifted up a hand
And bade the sun in heaven to stand!
They smote and fell, who set the bars
Against the progress of the stars,
And stayed the march of Motherland!

They stood, who saw the future come
On through the fight's delirium!
They smote and stood, who held the hope
Of nations on that slippery slope
Amid the cheers of Christendom.

God lives! He forged the iron will
That clutched and held that trembling hill.
God lives and reigns! He built and lent
The heights for Freedom's battlement
Where floats her flag in triumph still!

Fold up the banners! Smelt the guns!
Love rules. Her gentler purpose runs.
A mighty mother turns in tears
The pages of her battle years,
Lamenting all her fallen sons!

EDGAR LEE MASTERS (1869–1950) ❧

The Battle of Gettysburg

This rhyming doggerel is much inferior to Spoon River Anthology, *the volume of poetry that made its author famous. Masters here contrasts Southern nobility with Northern industrial power and still gives the outcome of the battle to Tyche, the goddess of luck. In the end he meditates on the stillness that comes after battle.*

I   'Twas a battle of States:
'Twas Georgia, Alabama,
And North Carolina;
'Twas South Carolina
And Tennessee.
But Virginia starred the drama
To make the South free
From the board of trade, the bank, the factory.
'Twas a battle of States
With New York for the banks,
With sixty-eight regiments of steel in ranks.
'Twas a masque of the Fates
Traveling with tents,
With machine Massachusetts with eighteen regiments;
'Twas a butchery of hates
With Ohio of oil with thirteen regiments,
Standing by Connecticut of mouse-traps and clocks
With five bloody regiments,
Having there for mates

Illinois, Vermont full of merchant ire,
Hiding in the rocks,
With Maine, Minnesota and New Hampshire
Behind the stone-wall, the ditch and the fence
With Wisconsin, Rhode Island and Michigan,
Regiments, regiments, regiments,
A hundred and forty foot-regiments,
And thirty-eight cavalries
And four score batteries,
Something altogether like ninety thousand men,
With four hundred cannon, and a full commissary
All lined up by the Gettysburg Cemetery,
Led by Humphreys, Reynolds and Hays
Favored by Fate, whom to favor betrays;
Led by Hancock battle-keyed;
Led by Birney, Crawford, and Gibbon,
Led by Meade;
Leaders and led of all those regiments
Believing it was treason they were fighting there;
Believing that to conquer Robert E. Lee
Was to save the Union, and to make the people free;
Believing they were acting for Providence,
And helping the white man, the pioneer,
And ending the bondsman and slavery;
Not ending the farm, but giving it aid;
Not giving the hip-lock to ships and trade.
Nor was it of any captain seen,
Neither of Humphreys, Hancock, Meade,
That the one-eyed genius of the machine
Was sprawling on the rocks of the battle scene,
Was stalking the orchards as he gazed and glowered,

Over the Ridges and the July meadow,
Throwing his giant and viewless shadow
On fields and hills as he paused and towered,
Taking a one-eyed reconnaissance,
Of those enemy regiments.

II   'Twas the Loki of luck, the treacherous Tyche,
She with the rudder who guides amiss,
She with a ball for token and toy
Which rolls out of hand for Nemesis,
Who staged the battle and gave the crown
Of victory at Gettysburg town.
Else never had Stephen Pomeroy,
Climbed over mountains for seventeen miles,
Rode horseback for the latter half
Of the way to reach the telegraph,
And send the word over Pennsylvania
That Lee was coming, and scatter the news,
That the army of Lee was coming for cattle,
For horses, clothing and shoes,
For food, for Harrisburg gold in the banks;
Tramping, all flushed with the victory
At Fredericksburg, with unconquerable ranks
Coming to win another battle
Under the iron audacity
Of Virginia commanded by Lee.

'Twas Tyche that kept the historic clown
From fighting the battle at Cashtown,
And saved the Muses the shamefulness
Of the Cashtown address.

'Twas Tyche that kept Jeb Stuart squandering
Precious time with circuitous wandering,
And let Longstreet hang with long complaining
Talk on Lee, and logic straining,
And thereby lose the day.
'Twas Tyche that sent Meade to Culp's Hill,
Where his troops dug in and fortified
The rocks from which to watch and kill.
And it was Tyche satire-eyed
Who chose George Pickett to make the charge,
Since Pickett owed to Lincoln all
His West Point training.
But it was blindness breathed like mist
Upon those armies ranged in wrath
Which brought them by a fateful path,
And led them to the bloody marge,
And made them mad-men for a cause,
For freedoms and for laws
Which never did exist.
Their wills heroical,
Their spirits mystical,
Their courage, loyalty,
Their dreams of liberty,
Their vision of a people who had sinned;
Their very souls were used and blown
As odors of blossoms leveled prone
By an unregarding wind.

III   First there was the thunder of the guns!
And Culp's Hill answers to the thunder of the guns;
And the woodlands echo to the thunder of the guns.

And the crows rise and scatter
With the thunder of the guns;
And the crackles soar and chatter
With the thunder of the guns.
For the battle commences behind the stone fences,
There are racing cattle, as the roar and rattle
Of the ridges and the hills reverberate the battle.
There are whinnying horses, as they pile up the corses
By the wagons and caissons.
White clouds look down
On these hell-fire passions;
White clouds look down
On Seminary Ridge,
On Cemetery Ridge,
Olympian, cool, white clouds,
Calm as eternity
Look down on spire and bridge,
Look down
On Gettysburg town;
Look down on Lee and Meade.
And the open eye of the sun,
And the cloud eye-lids that shadow
Stay not to see what will be done,
Nor to count those soon to be lying dead
By ridges, orchards and meadow.

IV   'Twas Tyche that led Lee's men to believe
     That the cannonade had shattered the lines,
     That the thunder of the guns had battered the lines
     Of Meade in Cemetery Ridge;

And now it was time to achieve,
Time to fight, time for vengeance wines,
Time to charge from Seminary Ridge.
And from the wood and orchards poured
That impetuous horde
Of men in gray, in butternut,
In motley regimentals, in rags,
Waving their battle-flags!
And forth they streamed
With bayonets which gleamed
Under the crucible hot
July sun.
One line comes forth, another one,
All steady and well aligned,
And all with equal tread
And all with fearless mind,
Come forth, advance file after file
From the woods, and cross that mile
Of meadow-land to Cemetery Ridge
Whose guns were double-charged with lead.

And soon these men of Pickett saw
The Union line two miles in length
With bayonets and batteries
Behind the rocks in strength
Of cannon and musketries.
And Pickett's men began to draw
The long-range guns upon them,
And bursting shells upon them,
And grape-shot and grenading

And Round Top's enfilading;

But on they went,

Regiment after regiment.

Till at last the Union infantry

Rose from the fences, rocks and rails

And poured their musketry

On Pickett's men, whose will no more avails,

No more, since now the cannon double-shotted

Are let go in their faces,

And thousands, blown in air, are blotted

From the scene in empty spaces,

Toward the blue of the sky, where the white cloud races.

Still on they went, scattered like chaff

To be beat back by rammer and staff

As they scaled the walls around oak trees

And perished, vanished paid the cost

Of the battle lost.

V   The peach orchard, the oak trees,

The graves of those long dead,

The pastures where the cattle fed,

The old farm houses in the meadow,

The rocks in Culp Hill's shadow,

The old bridges and wooded ridges,

Waited through many years for these

To come to them for this event,

Fulfilling their fated destinies

By the road of Emmitsburg,

Near Gettysburg,

Where perished Pickett's regiment.

None passing this spot for many a year

Saw in oak trees and in peach trees
The demon of luring sorceries,
As a place where thousands in wonderment
Should suddenly see the implacable Fear
Under a summer sky,
With white clouds drifting high.

VI   Then the grackles returned,
And the crows flew over the field,
Trodden, bloodied and burned,
Back and forth to the quiet woods.
And the cattle broods
Browsed as the sun went down
Behind the hills of Gettysburg town.
And Nature took these solitudes
For hers again, and starred the sky
With stars which twinkled on meadow and hill.
They glimmered in many a soldier's eye,
Who stared and lay so still.

PAUL LAURENCE DUNBAR (1872–1906) ❧

The Colored Soldiers

Dunbar was a black poet and novelist who in his brief life turned often to the Civil War for inspiration against the Jim Crow laws that segregated the South after Reconstruction. Black troops began to be enlisted in 1862. By the end of the war almost ten percent of the Union Army was black. Twenty-one black soldiers won the Congressional Medal of Honor. Fort Pillow, above Memphis, was taken by Nathan Bedford Forrest's Confederates on April 12, 1864. Black Federal soldiers who tried to surrender were massacred.

If the muse were mine to tempt it
   And my feeble voice were strong,
If my tongue were trained to measures,
   I would sing a stirring song.
I would sing a song heroic
   Of those noble sons of Ham,
Of the gallant colored soldiers
   Who fought for Uncle Sam!

In the early days you scorned them,
   And with many a flip and flout,
Said "these battles are the white man's
   And the whites will fight them out."
Up the hills you fought and faltered,
   In the vales you strove and bled,
While your ears still heard the thunder
   Of the foes' increasing tread.

107th United States "Colored" Infantry guard and guardhouse, Fort Corcoran

Then distress fell on the nation
    And the flag was dropping low;
Should the dust pollute your banner?
    No! the nation shouted, No!
So when war, in savage triumph,
    Spread abroad his funeral pall—
Then you called the colored soldiers,
    And they answered to your call.

And like hounds unleashed and eager
    For the life blood of the prey,
Sprung they forth and bore them bravely
    In the thickest of the fray.
And where'er the fight was hottest—
    Where the bullets fastest fell,
There they pressed unblanched and fearless
    At the very mouth of hell.

Ah, they rallied to the standard
    To uphold it by their might,
None were stronger in the labors,
    None were braver in the fight.
At Forts Donelson and Henry
    On the plains of Olustee,
They were foremost in the fight
    Of the battles of the free.

And at Pillow! God have mercy
    On the deeds committed there,
And the souls of those poor victims
    Sent to Thee without a prayer.

Let the fullness of thy pity
　　O'er the hot wrought spirits sway,
Of the gallant colored soldier
　　Who fell fighting on that day!

Yes, the Blacks enjoy their freedom
　　And they won it dearly, too;
For the life blood of their thousands
　　Did the southern fields bedew.
In the darkness of their bondage,
　　In their depths of slavery's night;
Their muskets flashed the dawning
　　And they fought their way to light.

They were comrades then and brothers,
　　Are they more or less to-day?
They were good to stop a bullet
　　And to front the fearful fray.
They were citizens and soldiers,
　　When rebellion raised its head;
And the traits that made them worthy—
　　Ah! those virtues are not dead.

They have shared your nightly vigils,
　　They have shared your daily toil;
And their blood with yours commingling
　　Has made rich the Southern soil.
They have slept and marched and suffered
　　'Neath the same dark skies as you,
They have met as fierce a foeman
　　And have been as brave and true.

And their deeds shall find a record,
    In the registry of Fame;
For their blood has cleansed completely
    Every blot of Slavery's shame.
So all honor and all glory
    To those noble Sons of Ham—
To the gallant colored soldiers,
    Who fought for Uncle Sam!

Dunbar's use of dialect was
common in writing about blacks
at the time. This poem loosely
describes some time in the summer
of 1862, when the Congress had
authorized the use of freed slaves
as soldiers in the Union Army.
The masters in the poem would
have joined the Confederates a
year before.

PAUL LAURENCE DUNBAR (1872–1906)

When Dey 'Listed Colored Soldiers

Dey was talkin' in de cabin, dey was talkin' in de hall;
But I listened kin' o' keerless, not a-t'inkin' 'bout it all;
An' on Sunday, too, I noticed, dey was whisp'rin' mighty much,
Stan'in' all erroun' de roadside w'en dey let us out o' chu'ch.
But I did n't t'ink erbout it 'twell de middle of de week,
An' my 'Lias come to see me, an' somehow he could n't speak.
Den I seed all in a minute whut he'd come to see me for; —
Dey had 'listed colo'ed sojers an' my 'Lias gwine to wah.

Oh, I hugged him, an' I kissed him, an' I baiged him not to go;
But he tol' me dat his conscience, hit was callin' to him so,
An' he could n't baih to lingah w'en he had a chanst to fight
For de freedom dey had gin him an' de glory of de right.
So he kissed me, an' he lef' me, w'en I'd p'omised to be true;
An' dey put a knapsack on him, an' a coat all colo'ed blue.
So I gin him pap's ol' Bible f'om de bottom of de draw', —
W'en dey 'listed colo'ed sojers an' my 'Lias went to wah.

But I t'ought of all de weary miles dat he would have to tramp,
An' I could n't be contented w'en dey tuk him to de camp.
W'y my hea't nigh broke wid grievin' 'twell I seed him on de street;
Den I felt lak I could go an' th'ow my body at his feet.
For his buttons was a-shinin', an' his face was shinin', too,
An' he looked so strong an' mighty in his coat o' sojer blue,
Dat I hollahed, "Step up, manny," dough my th'oat was so' an' raw, —
W'en dey 'listed colo'ed sojers an' my 'Lias went to wah.

Ol' Mis' cried w'en mastah lef' huh, young Miss mou'ned huh brothah Ned,
An' I did n't know dey feelin's is de ve'y wo'ds dey said
W'en I tol' 'em I was so'y. Dey had done gin up dey all;
But dey only seemed mo' proudah dat dey men had hyeahed de call.
Bofe my mastahs went in gray suits, an' I loved de Yankee blue,
But I t'ought dat I could sorrer for de losin' of 'em too;
But I could n't, for I did n't know de ha'f o' whut I saw,
'Twell dey 'listed colo'ed sojers an' my 'Lias went to wah.

Mastah Jack come home all sickly; he was broke for life, dey said;
An' dey lef' my po' young mastah some'r's on de roadside, — dead.
W'en de women cried an' mou'ned 'em, I could feel it thoo an' thoo,
For I had a loved un fightin' in de way o' dangah, too.
Den dey tol' me dey had laid him some'r's way down souf to res',
Wid de flag dat he had fit for shinin' daih acrost his breas'.
Well, I cried, but den I reckon dat's whut Gawd had called him for,
W'en dey 'listed colo'ed sojers an' my 'Lias went to wah.

*A difficult poem, the "Event"
seemingly a suicide. The old
Confederate veteran who has
known death in war is as
bewildered as the child about why
a younger man—the old man's
son, the boy's father?—would
choose to die. The poem depends
on our knowledge that the end of
the war brought rejoicing to those
who survived it only to discover
that death remained when the war
was done.*

ROBERT PENN WARREN (1905–1989) ❧

A Confederate Veteran Tries to Explain the Event

"But why did he do it, Grandpa?" I said
to the old man sitting under the cedar,
who had come a long way to that place, and that time
when that younger man lay down in the hay

to arrange himself. And now the old man
lifted his head to stare at me.
"It's one of those things," he said, and stopped.
"What things?" I said. And he said: "Son—

"son, one of those things you never know."
"But there must be a *why*," I said. Then he
said: "Folks—yes, folks, they up and die."
"But, Grandpa—" I said. And he: "They die."

Said: "Yes, by God, and I've seen 'em die.
I've seen 'em die and I've seen 'em dead.

Inside the Confederate lines, 1865, Petersburg, Virginia

I've seen 'em die hot and seen 'em die cold.
Hot lead and cold steel—" The words, they stopped.

The mouth closed up. The eyes looked away.
Beyond the lawn where the fennel throve,
beyond the fence where the whitewash peeled,
beyond the cedars along the lane,

the eyes fixed. The land, in sunlight,
swam, with the meadow the color of rust,
and distance the blue of Time, and nothing—
oh, nothing—would ever happen, and

in the silence my breath did not happen. But
the eyes, they happened, they found me, I
stood there and waited. "Dying," he said,
"hell, dying's a thing any fool can do."

"But what made him do it?" I said, again.
Then wished I hadn't, for he stared at me.
He stared at me as though I weren't there,
or as though I were dead, or had never been born,

and I felt like dandelion fuzz blown away,
or a word you'd once heard but never could spell,
or only an empty hole in the air.
From the cedar shade his eyes burned red.

Darker than shade, his mouth opened then.
Spit was pink on his lips, I saw the tongue move

beyond the old teeth, in the dark of his head.
It moved in that dark. Then, "Son—" the tongue said.

"For some folks the world gets too much," it said.
In that dark, the tongue moved. "For some folks," it said.

A modernist poem, an eloquent
series of snapshots, the poet's mind
flitting from subject to subject, as
minds do, without the imposition of
any narrative order on his
thoughts. Great leaders in war
know how to manage men, and the
men die in achieving the goals the
leaders set. Olson hints that the
leaders wanted power — as Jay
Gould did when he tried to corner
the gold market after the war — and
the ordinary soldier pays the price.

CHARLES OLSON (1910–1970) 🖋

Anecdotes of the Late War

I   the lethargic vs violence as alternatives of each other for los americanos
        & U S Grant (at Shiloh, as ex.) had the gall to stay
        inside a lethargy until it let him down into either
        vice (Galena, or, as president) or
        a virtue of such a movement as, example,
        Vicksburg

        say that he struck, going down, either
        morass or
        rock — and when it was rock, he was

        — this wld seem to be the power in the principle —

        able to comprehend the movement of mass of men, the
        transposition of the
        Mississippi (Or
        continents, example,
        somebody else than:
        grant

John Wilkes Booth

better, that is, that a man stay lethargic than
blow somebody's face off—off,
the face of, blow
the earth

II   that (like the man sd) Booth
killing Lincoln is the melodrama right with
the drama: Mister Christ and
Broadway

        Or going out to Bull Run looking for
Waterloo. the
diorama. And having to get the fastidious hell home
that afternoon
as fast as the carriage horses
can't make it (Lee Highway
littered with broken
elegances

        Reverse of
sic transit gloria, the
Latin American whom the cab driver told me
he picked up at Union Station had
one word of english—link-
cone. And drove him
straight to the monument, the man
went up the stairs and fell down on his knees
where he could see the statue and stayed there
in the attitude of prayer

III   whoop,
went the bird
in the tree the day
the fellow
fell down
in the thicket

whoop, was the bird's
lay as the fellow lay

and I picked up a minie ball
(the way
it can be
again
of an afternoon,

or with the French girl Brandy Station
was
thick grass
and the gray house and back of it

yes mam the movement
of horses, as
—I repeat—
the bird.

IV   West Point it wasn't. Nor New England. Nor
those cavalry
flauntlets

As the Mexican War was
filibusterers
in the West,
and cadets
before Chapultepec: the elevator

goink down
from waterloo,
the Civil War

was the basement. Only nobody
except butternut
and his fellow on the other side
wanted to believe it, they all wanted

what Jay Gould got

(and Joe Blow got swap
in the side of the head

V   Now you take this Forrest, Nathan Bedford Forrest. He stalks the Western
theater of operations as something the English, to this day, think Lee
wouldn't have surpassed had anybody dared to give this Memphis slave-
trader the width of men and field to command which he only had as
first Grand Wizard of the Ku Klux Klan. And didn't use, Forrest
could already avoid the temptation of the Filibuster, he had applied
first principles in the War.

What I'd wanted to say was,
that he's a man so locked in the act of himself

(right up to after Davis had been taken
and no last movie scene to the way he was still
cutting tracks behind U.S. Army units, a very

exact and busy man.

I also have to voice this impression of him to give, if it
does, the sense of how he was:

he's like a man his tongue was cut out,
before even Shiloh showed him
an extraordinary executive
of men horses and goods

VI   Two things still aren't brought in to give context to the War: (I), that
you don't get Grant except as you find what he was that Geo Washington
also comes alive at only if you realize he was to real estate—

and I mean land
when land was as oil steel and what, now?

Managing men, wasn't it, when men suddenly what was Grant's

because of the industrial revolution

were what the guys who died then were

For the first time,
like that, the sprawled fellow Devil's Glen, natural
resource.

The older half of it—(2)—that each one of them,

Butternut,

and Yankee Doodle,

weren't as different as North and South, farmer and factory etc.

They were—for the first time—enough of them.

                                        Plus railroad tracks
                                        to be moved around as
utility

                    The leaders,   Grant Sherman Forrest not
                    Jeb Stuart
and themselves

the birth of

the recent   And Lincoln

likewise   (after Christ

Link-cone

VII   You take it
       from there

VIII   What he said was, in that instance
I got there first
with the most men

Grant didn't hurry.
He just had the most.

More of the latter died.

RANDALL JARRELL (1914–1965)

A Description of Some Confederate Soldiers

The torn hillside with its crooked hands
Where Tom lay beneath the banks of light
Grows shadier, and through its shades
The sun looks seldomer. The laurels are faded.

Ah, how it blazed! the splintered leaves
Burned against your forehead, and your tongue
Grew thick with wisdom; till you laughed, and fled
Like a shadow from that senseless shape.

Then that pale life—scars on the tree—
Where, listlessly, among the mushrooms of your hill,
You stared at your comrades—fatal waxworks!—
And saw, pale, virtuous, half-concealed,

Hovering over each leafy and swollen cheek,
The blue transparency of a smile.
This was the last of that furious speech—
The lustre, the wreathing of the shade.

Strewn like sweat, like dropped jewels,
They lay there; their ringed mouths gaped
Like wounds about to speak, their eyes
Shrank back from those curved faces,

Staring, coagulated with light.
Tell how you were hunted by cunning death,
That night when, stumbling, soaked with blood,
You sank there with open mouth

Until the hunters came, and kneeling there
Lifted you, and saw covering your face
That greedy and imperishable arrogance. . . .
Man's choice, and man's magnificence

Grow monstrous, and unclouded by
The empty measure of his breath.
How can the grave hold, a statue name
Blood dried in that intolerable glare?

They stand like shattered and untopped columns,
The barbarous foliage of an age
Necessity instructed and destroyed.
There is no hesitation in those eyes.

A modern poem about a father
gone South to fetch the body of a
son who fell in battle fighting for
the Union. The boy had been
killed on January 15, 1865, in the
fighting for Fort Fisher, on the
coast of North Carolina and held
by the Confederates.

ELEANOR ROSS TAYLOR (1920–) ✥

A Few Days in the South in February

A Hospitality for S. K. Wightman, 1865
(Based on Mr. Wightman's account of his pilgrimage to
North Carolina, reprinted from family papers in American
Heritage, *February 1963)*

I   One ship, one only
      One sentry
      One grave marked

      An old man seeking a battlefield,
      I march on the land of the enemy
      For my son.
      Who will know where he fell?
      How take him, taken by the enemy?
      How wrest him, young and strong
      From war, from peace?

      Your Christmas letter descended
      Like a Parrot shell and near
      Annihilated this home-starved soldier. . . .
      Six days before!
      Climbing the parapet, a minie ball.
      His comrade's flask implored declining lips.

The battlefield stretches south.
Is it salt-marsh birds—
Or dead soldiers whistling?
Nightmare or real madness?
I stumble over dead grass locked in ice.

This alien wind blows sand
Not southern; arctic sand peppers
My flowing eyes and face.
I hear my wild voice singing hymns;
Feel tears like death-throes shake me,
Then breath gives out and I sit down to rest.
The salt wind roughs sand-wounds.
The eye calls, *Edward*. . . .
Answer, only those wind-borne birds.
Expanse of sea and marsh.
Expanse of dunes.

I hail the single soldier strolling near.
We two meet in an empty world.
   (Surely the bounds of fate,
    A grim tale's magic.)
"Graves from the battle of January 15?"
"On that knoll, sir."

   Surely the bounds of our lives.
   Are fixed by our Creator.
   One marked, one only,
   The pine-stave written on in lampblack.
   My trembling spectacles give time for magic:

Sergt Major
3rd NYV
E. K. Wightman

The darling of his sisters, mother
His steady eye, good sense
His quiet dreams
It seems I may spend out my years
Beside the spot.

I walk away,
Return and weep again.

Again I try to go on with my plan,
Set out for General Terry's—
Come back to him.

Three times I leave and
Stay to mourn.
    So, thanking God for His
    Mercy and goodness to me—
    Only one grave marked.
    Surely the bounds of our lives

II   Take up the body now?
     Only a pine coffin? Ah.
     At some future time. . . .
     With one of lead. . . .
         Gentlemen, I must say
         Without intending to offend that
         (If it be not counter to God's will)

I will never leave Federal Point
Without Edward's body.

"If we had salt and rosin. . . .
"Things unsettled. . . ."
   Only to wait,
   Thanking God for His mercy and goodness:
   One ship, one only.
   One sentry,
   One grave marked.

   On the sealing of coffins. . . .
Salt in supply.
Tentcloth, none. No pitch nor rosin.

III   (Surely the bounds of fate,
    A grim tale's magic)
      No pitch no rosin
    Here near the tidewater is a knoll of sand.
    I loiter,
    Led by—the devil despair?
    Godmother in disguise?
    The hand of God?
      Take this fragment of a pickax
      And look there near the tidewater.
        Hans, or Abraham, obey.

      To my astonishment. . . .
      A barrel of rosin
      There buried in the sand.
        Tears, thanking, etc.

I take the load upon my back
Struggling through deep sand
    (Especially as . . . not at that time
    In good health and not for years
    Subject to so great exposure)

Near nightfall, greatly fatigued,
I drift into a German fairy tale:
    Pity the sorrows of a poor old man
    Whose trembling limbs have borne him to your door. . . .

    "Orderly, take your horse and another;
    "Go with this gentleman to the Point."

    And so aboard the *Montauk* for the night.

IV   Needing what you don't want is hell.
    A need for pitch, for sealing-black. . . .
    Again stand at the magic spot
    The Cape Fear's tide,
    Conjure a barrel grounded in the shallows
    Delightful as the ark in Pharaoh's flags
    Delightful as the babe to Levi's house,
    This coffin-gift.

    The tide gone out, the barrel turns to staves—
    Staves thick-pitched inside.
      Thanking God, etc. . . .
    Beside the joiner's bench
    I steady planks, his bed,

Give from my hand the separate coffin nails,
    Thanking God,

V   A tent-cloth, a detail of men,
    A hollow in the sand, a fire,
    Pitch and a little rosin in a pot.
    It bubbles smackingly.
    We frost the coffin and pitch tight the box,
    Swab black the tent-cloth.

    Unbidden blue coats straggle round
    To meet my son.
    I watch each salt of sand
    On each gross shovel
    Each inch to forty-eight,
    Down to the end of miracles.

    He lies half-turned,
    His braided collar up
    Against the elements (now chiefly earth)
    Cape folded over face.
        Face . . . speeding from face to skull.
    (*The teeth appeared very prominent.*)

    What has your plum-pudding to do with me?
    Ah, my friends, thus it was with the captain
    In ancient times, when afar off he gazed
    At the smoking ruins
    Of the beloved city of his birth
    Burned by a barbarous enemy.

In enemy land
Who mourns burned cities?
—Ruin!
Consider the holes made by the ball.
The hands, you judge, are very like. . . .
   ("Ah, can ye doubt?" asks one rough man,
   "For sure now, he greatly resembles ye")
Face, white and swollen;
Eyes, somehow injured.
The wreck of our anticipations
His love for me. . . .
His Virgil parody. . . .
"A favorite with the men"

   A puzzle, one set out so late
   Has overshot into eternity
   And left me plodding on.

At last I let them.
They wind the cloth about him.
And I, mounting, whip to Fort Lamb
Driven by the hammers.

Some days are pages ragtorn from hell.
Yet on this cruellest day night came.
Aboard the *Montauk*, water-rocked,
I slept, slept peacefully,
As if we two
Slept in our beds at home.

VI   His corpse recaptured from the enemy,
       I brought him back where he was born
       To that address his letters came.
          (*"To all—Dear Father Mother Fred*
             Abbie and Jim Chas
                Mary Ell and
                   Babies")

       To services appropriately grave.
       There lie in peace till Morning.
       The sent-out child lies harvested.
       The stone doves peck.

       My watch ticks in my waistcoat.
       My *News* waits by the window.
       Snow falls
          I believe that the bounds of our lives
          Are fixed by our Creator
          And we cannot pass them.
          The Lord gives and the Lord takes away
          Blessed be the name of the Lord.

*A snapshot poem of Richmond
in the 1960s, conveying nostalgia
and the changes that turn the once-
present past to strangeness. Edgar
Allan Poe (1809–1849) was
born in Boston but grew up
in Richmond.*

JOHN UPDIKE (1932–) ❦

Richmond

The shadows in his eye sockets like shades
upon a bearded hippie, Stonewall Jackson
stares down Monument Avenue toward where Lee
sits on an even higher horse. The cause
was lost but lingers in the faintly defiant
dignity of the pale-gray, Doric dollhouse
from whence Jeff Davis, conscientious Satan,
directed our second rebellion: a damn good try.

Brick graciousness prevails; across the James
wood houses hold black pensioners, and Poe's
ghost haunts a set of scattered tombs, *musei*
exposing to Northern visitors his quills,
a model of his muddy city, and
an etching of, wry-necked in death, Virginia.

Ruins of Galligo Mills, April 1865, Richmond, Virginia

*A modernist poem, filled with
images the reader must translate
into meaning. A blue sky rent by a
column [a military column?] of
light from the setting sun, and a
gray [?] mare falling, losing her
rider on a downhill slope that
becomes precipitous. Is this the
South descending to its doom in
the war?*

SUZANNE RHODENBAUGH (1944–) ❦

The Civil War

A column of lemon sky lit one hill.
Heaven to earth it divided the blue
and all the movement was downward.

Slimming runnels foraged
for a streambed in the bracken.
Rills of dirt slid down.

She picked her way downhill.
Burrs and stalks in the undergrowth
pricked and rasped her fetlocks.

Rocks dislodged tumbled.
As the declivity steepened
they fell headlong.

The mare without her rider
lay down in the valley of the valley.

A vivid depiction by a modern poet of how casual violent death can seem in the familiar circumstances of a rural world, the kind of world whence most soldiers in both armies came.

JANE KENYON (1947–)

Gettysburg, July 1, 1863

The young man, hardly more
than a boy, who fired the shot
had looked at him with an air
not of anger but of concentration,
as if he were surveying a road,
or feeding a length of wood into a saw:
it had to be done just so.

The bullet passed through
his upper chest, below the collarbone.
The pain was not what he might
have feared. Strangely exhilarated
he staggered out of the pasture
and into a grove of trees.

He pressed and pressed
the wound, trying to stanch
the blood, but he could only press
what he could reach, and he could

Union and Confederate dead, Gettysburg battlefield

not reach his back, where the bullet
had exited.

            He lay on the earth
smelling the leaves and mosses,
musty and damp and cool
after the blaze of open afternoon.
How good the earth smelled,
as it had when he was a boy
hiding from his father —
intent on strapping him for doing
his chores late one time too many.

A cowbird razzed from a rail fence.
It isn't mockery, he thought,
no malice in it . . . just a noise.
Stray bullets nicked the oaks
overhead. Leaves and splinters fell.

Someone near him groaned.
But it was his own voice he heard.
His fingers and feet tingled,
the roof of his mouth,
and the bridge of his nose . . .

He became dry, dry, and thought
of Christ, who said, *I thirst*.
His man-smell—the smell of his hair
and skin, his sweat, the salt smell
of his cock and the little ferny hairs
that two women had known—

left him, and a sharp, almost sweet
smell began to rise from his open mouth
in the warm shade of the oaks.
A streak of sun climbed the rough
trunk of a tree, but he did not
see it with his open eye.

ANDREW HUDGINS (1951–) 🦅

Serenades in Virginia
(Summer, 1863)

An imagined collection of snapshot verses, mixed with one battle scene, focusing on the trivial details of daily life, the whole tending to reduce the drama of the war to the soldier's experience of variety and routine, all against a background of possible sudden death. Many soldiers carried books with them to war. Victor Hugo's Les Misérables *in English translation was a great favorite of soldiers in the Confederate Army of Northern Virginia. They called themselves "Lee's Miserables." Hudgins is writing in the persona of Sidney Lanier, poet and Confederate soldier.*

I   When we heard of a lady who
was said to be a stunning beauty,
we went to serenade her charms.
We were denied by summer rain—
a gully washer that got in my flute
before I played a single bar.
With Clifford's extra guitar string,
we tied a note to her doorknob, and left.

Next week, we were invited back
for meals that made the table bow:
Virginia ham, stuffed eggs, roast hens,
and mounds of biscuits I sopped full
of honey then ate with a spoon
when they collapsed. Our gracious hosts
insisted that we spend the night.
We did. A pleasant yellow slave
brought us mint juleps as we rose.

II   To stop our signal flags, the Yanks
sent several hundred men. But we
smelled out their trap and answered it
with such firepower they did not,
thank God, perceive we numbered less
than twenty men. Across two miles
of sumac and a second growth of pine,
which we relinquished inch by inch,
we poured great quantities of lead
into their ranks and watched their lines
collapse. It seemed almost a lark.

But I see clear in memory
what I ignored back then: the dull
inhuman thud of lead on flesh,
the buckling of a shot man's knees,
the outward fling of arms, and the
short arc a head inscribes before
it hits the ground. The war, my God,
had been over for two long years
before I understood that they,
the Yanks we killed, were human too.

III   (*To His Father*)
But in the rush and scrabble of the raid
we lost *Aurora Leigh*, *Les Misérables*,
volumes of Shelley, Coleridge, and Keats,
and one by Heine. Secure at any price
the works of Uhland, Schelling, Tieck.
Because my flute was in my haversack,
it wasn't lost. I'm well. Don't fear for me.

IV   Miss Hankins was a handsome girl.
Not pretty—handsome. Her forehead was
too broad, her lips too thin, for pretty.
But she was full of life, possessed
a mind that almost rivaled mine,
and had a solemn faith—in me.
One night as we sat in the swing,
I made, for her, a rendering
of Heine's "Du bist wie eine Blume."

And when it landed on my hand
I brushed a firefly off and said,
"Fly thou away and know that once
in midst of summer greenness thou
didst light upon a poet's hand."
And Ginna Hankins never cracked a smile.
A girl like that's beyond compare—
a pearl! a ruby! After the war
I asked her to become my wife.
She said she couldn't leave her brothers
without a woman in the house.
Within a month I was engaged
to Mary Day. I couldn't wait.
To this day we still correspond.

V   (*To W. A. Hopson*)
I should have answered long ago.
But I've indulged myself so thoroughly
in chills and fever, I've had scant time
for food and drink. Or correspondence.

Miss H. is here. She presses me
to send her warmest sentiments
and say she's humbly satisfied
that your one friend in Franklin of her sex
is cross-eyed, dull, and otherwise
devoid of grace, because, she adds,
you'll have less call to tarry there.
It's true. Speed back. We need your bass
to add a bottom to our sing-alongs.

VI   When Cliff and I discuss the war,
we talk of lovely women, serenades,
the moonlit dashes on the beach,
the brushes of our force with theirs,
with whom we clashed with more élan
and consequence. We had enough
hair's-breadth escapes to keep our spirits high.
What a godforsaken war it would have been
if we'd run short of decent horses!

But there are many things we don't recall.
Like Hopson, who, at Gettysburg,
had one heel sliced off by a minié ball.
He sings as deeply as he ever did
but does it leaning slightly to the left.

ANDREW HUDGINS (1951–) 🕊

Burial Detail

*An imagined scene that had its
counterpart in reality during the
war itself. The poem expresses the
mystery of bodies that become
mere stuff after life has left them. It
calls to mind the kinship all living
things have with death and the only
temporary way by which the
consciousness of death can be
averted.*

Between each layer of tattered, broken flesh
we spread, like frosting, a layer of lime,
and then we spread it extra thick on top
as though we were building a giant torte.
The lime has something to do with cholera
and aids, I think, the chemistry of decay
when slathered between the ranks of sour dead.
I know what we did; I'm not sure why.
The colonel had to ask us twice for volunteers;
the second time, I went. I don't know why.
Even in August heat I cannot sleep
unless I have a sheet across my shoulders.
I guess we owe our species something.
We stacked the flaccid meat all afternoon,
and then night fell so black and absolute
it was as if the day had never been,
was something impossible we'd made up
to comfort ourselves in our long work.
And even in the pitch-black, pointless dark

we stacked the men and spread the lime
as we had done all day. Though not as neat.

They were supposed to be checked thoroughly.
I didn't look; I didn't sift their pockets.
A lot of things got buried that shouldn't have been.
I tossed men unexamined in the trench.
But out of the corner of my eyes
I kept seeing faces I thought I knew.
At first they were the faces of anonymous men
I may have seen in camp or on the field.
Later, as I grew tired, exhausted, sick,
I saw they were my mother, father, kin
whom I had never seen but recognized
by features I knew in different combinations
on the shifting, similar faces of my cousins,
and even, once, a face that looked like mine.
But when I stopped to stare at them
I found the soft, unfocused eyes of strangers
and let them drop into the common grave.

Then, my knees gave. I dropped my shovel
and pitched, face first, into the half-filled trench.
I woke almost immediately, and stood
on someone's chest while tired hands pulled me out.
It's funny: standing there, I didn't feel
the mud-wet suck of death beneath my feet
as I had felt it often enough before
when we made forced marches through Virginia rain.
That is to say, the dead man's spongy chest
was firmer than the roads that led us—

and him—into the Wilderness.
For six or seven days I had to hear
a lot of stupid jokes about that faint:
folks are dying to get in, that sort of thing.
I wasn't the only one to faint.
You'd think I would have fainted for my father,
for some especially mutilated boy,
for Clifford or my mother. Not for myself.

In the hot inexhaustible work of the night
a good wind blowing from a distant storm
was heaven, more so because the bodies needed
to be wet, to ripen in moisture and lime,
to pitch and rock with tiny lives,
or whatever it takes to make them earth again.
Okay, I'm sorry for this, for getting worked up.
The thought that they might not decay
was enough to make my stomach heave.
Some men I've argued with seem to think
that they'll stay perfect, whole and sweet,
beneath the ground. It makes me shudder:
dead bodies in no way different from my own
except mine moves, and shudders in its moving.
I take great comfort in knowing I will rot
and that the chest I once stood on
is indistinguishable from other soil
and I will be indistinguishable from it.

But standing there, looking out of the grave,
eyes barely above the lip of earth, I saw
the most beautiful thing I've ever seen:

dawn on the field after the Wilderness.
The bodies, in dawn light, were simply forms;
the landscape seemed abstract, unreal.
It didn't look like corpses, trees, or sky,
but shapes on shapes against a field of gray
and in the distance a source of doubtful light,
itself still gray and close to darkness.
There were a thousand shades of gray,
with colors—some blue perhaps and maybe green—
trying to assert themselves against that gray.
In short, it looked like nothing human.
But the sun broke from the horizon soon enough
and we could see exactly what we'd done.

ANDREW HUDGINS (1951–) 🪶

A Soldier on the Marsh

The poem suggests the vivid intensity of ordinary sensations — the routine sights of a rural landscape, set against the knowledge that a war is going on and the speaker will have to return to it.

On leave, I sat on marsh grass, watched
bees tremble into new red blooms,
and thought of how, a boy, I'd put
my finger on the backs of bees.
Engrossed, they didn't notice me,
and I, careful, wouldn't touch them long,
a second or two, but long enough
to feel the hard hum of their wings.
I never got stung. Clifford did.
And Mother whipped me with a belt
for showing him my trick. He asked.
She was more dangerous than bees,
and danger was what fascinated me
so much I'd wait until a bee
crawled in a morning glory bloom.
I'd pinch the flower shut and shake
the bloom, loving the angry buzz,
the danger I had trapped. The war

has killed that stupid fascination—
"D-E-D, dead," as Father says.

Blue as blood hidden in the body,
storm winds tore at oak leaves, which raged
like green birds limed to whipping limbs.
Dead limbs dislodged. Pine cones and acorns
swept toward me as I shut my eyes,
lay underneath an oak, and listened.
They sounded like a giant's feet
approaching, blundering from the west.
A thick branch skittered through the limbs
and hit six inches from my head.
I lay there through the storm, got drenched,
took off my clothes, and draped them on
a redbud tree. As they dried, I,
nude, played my flute. I caught
the trills and cadence of the birds
and was rewarded when a far
wood thrush responded to my music,
not note for note, not harmony,
but just enough to let me know
I'd swayed, a little bit, her song.

As I reached for my clothes, sunset
—red as blood liberated from the body—
fell over me, and, from the redbud tree,
a clumsy panicked bird, a cardinal,
exploded. One wingtip brushed my chest
an inch below the nipple, and,
in that red light off blood-red things

—blooms, bird—my whole white body turned
to flame, an *ignis fatuus*,
will-o'-the-wisp, a brief, bright light
that flickers on the marsh and means
delusion, which is my greatest gift.

Near home, the fields were bright with fire.
A farmer burning off his land
had walked the border of the marsh,
plunging a torch into the underbrush.
But where a dozen fires converged
I found a bright green tulip tree.
Leaves quivered in the winds that whipped
across the closing fires, then flared,
like torches, one by one, before
flames even touched them. Inside
the green wood, hot sap chortled, sang,
until the branches blew apart
like overheated cannon. The tree
was opening itself to fire.
I watched. I stood and watched as it
was blasted in the burning air.
The trunk collapsed, broke into embers.
Their tiny lights sprawled constellations
across the smoldering black earth.
As they consumed themselves, went dark,
the true stars came out, one beyond the next,
and in redbuds beyond burnt ground
a bobwhite sang its stupid, cheerful name.

Pantheon ❧

A stark poem conveying the image of John Brown, hanged at Charles Town, Virginia (later West Virginia). Melville has him looking South, towards the Shenandoah River and its great, fertile valley, where so much of the war took place. A meteor or a comet (the words were often interchangeable in this time) was taken to be a portent of disaster.

HERMAN MELVILLE (1819–1891) ❦

The Portent

Hanging from the beam,
　　Slowly swaying (such the law),
Gaunt the shadow on your green,
　　Shenandoah!
The cut is on the crown
(Lo, John Brown),
And the stabs shall heal no more.

Hidden in the cap
　　Is the anguish none can draw;
So your future veils its face,
　　Shenandoah!
But the streaming beard is shown
(Weird John Brown),
The meteor of the war.

FRANCIS ORRERY TICKNOR (1822–1874) 🐦

Little Giffen

This poem was probably inspired by the battle of Shiloh in south-western Tennessee on April 6, 1862. Albert Sidney Johnston, perhaps the most able Confederate commander, was killed just after he had successfully urged a reluctant Tennessee regiment to charge into a peach orchard held by Federal troops. The poem would vindicate Tennesseans at one of the bloodiest battles of the war.

Out of the focal and foremost fire,
Out of the hospital walls as dire,
Smitten of grape-shot and gangrene
(Eighteenth battle, and he sixteen!)
Specter! such as you seldom see,
Little Giffen, of Tennessee!

"Take him—and welcome!" the surgeons said;
"Little the doctor can help the dead!"
So we took him and brought him where
The balm was sweet on the summer air;
And we laid him down on a wholesome bed—
Utter Lazarus, heel to head!

And we watched the war with bated breath—
Skeleton Boy against skeleton Death.
Months of torture, how many such!
Weary weeks of the stick and crutch;

And still a glint in the steel-blue eye
Told of a spirit that wouldn't die,

And didn't. Nay, more! in death's despite
The crippled skeleton learned to write.
"Dear Mother," at first, of course; and then
"Dear Captain," inquiring about "the men."
Captain's answer: "Of eighty-and-five,
Giffen and I are left alive."

Word of gloom from the war one day:
"Johnston's pressed at the front, they say!"
Little Giffen was up and away;
A tear—his first—as he bade good-by,
Dimmed the glint of his steel-blue eye.
"I'll write, if spared!" There was news of the fight;
But none of Giffen—he did not write.

I sometimes fancy that, were I king
Of the princely Knights of the Golden Ring,
With the song of the minstrel in mine ear,
And the tender legend that trembles here,
I'd give the best, on his bended knee,
The whitest soul of my chivalry,
For Little Giffen, of Tennessee.

GEORGE MOSES HORTON (1797?–1883?) 🐦

General Grant — the Hero of the War

A romantic bit of doggerel that stumbles over an occasional compound fracture of the meter. Not much poetry was written about Grant. His own laconic style of both life and prose was the antithesis of melodrama, and he was singularly lacking in the charismatic qualities that might have made him beloved.

Brave Grant, thou hero of the war,
Thou art the emblem of the morning star,
Transpiring from the East to banish fear,
Revolving o'er a servile Hemisphere,
At large thou hast sustained the chief command
And at whose order all must rise and stand,
To hold position in the field is thine,
To sink in darkness or to rise and shine.

Thou art the leader of the Fed'ral band,
To send them at thy pleasure through the land,
Whose martial soldiers never did recoil
Nor fail in any place to take the spoil,
Thus organized was all the army firm,
And led unwavering to their lawful term,
Never repulsed or made to shrink with fear,
Advancing in their cause so truly dear.

Union General Ulysses S. Grant at Cold Harbor

The love of Union burned in every heart,
Which led them true and faithful from the start,
Whether upon water or on land,
They all obeyed their marshal's strict command,
By him the regiments were all surveyed,
His trumpet voice was by the whole obeyed,
His order right was every line to form,
And all be well prepared to front the storm.

Ye Southern gentlemen must grant him praise,
Nor on the flag of Union fail to gaze;
Ye ladies of the South forego the prize,
Our chief commander here to recognize,
From him the stream of general orders flow,
And every chief on him some praise bestow,
The well-known victor of the mighty cause
Demands from every voice a loud applause.

What more has great Napoleon ever done,
Though many battles in his course he won?
What more has Alexander e'er achieved,
Who left depopulated cities grieved?
To him we dedicate the whole in song,
The verses from our pen to him belong,
To him the Union banners are unfurled,
The star of peace the standard of the world.

JAMES RUSSELL LOWELL (1819–1891) ❦

Memoriae Positum R. G. Shaw

I   Beneath the trees,
    My lifelong friends in this dear spot,
    Sad now for eyes that see them not,
     I hear the autumnal breeze
  Wake the dry leaves to sigh for gladness gone,
  Whispering vague omens of oblivion,
     Hear, restless as the seas,
  Time's grim feet rustling through the withered grace
  Of many a spreading realm and strong-stemmed race,
     Even as my own through these.

    Why make we moan
    For loss that doth enrich us yet
    With upward yearnings of regret?
     Bleaker than unmossed stone
  Our lives were but for this immortal gain
  Of unstilled longing and inspiring pain!
     As thrills of long-hushed tone
  Live in the viol, so our souls grow fine

With keen vibrations from the touch divine
        Of noble natures gone.

        'T were indiscreet
    To vex the shy and sacred grief
    With harsh obtrusions of relief;
        Yet, Verse, with noiseless feet,
Go whisper: "*This* death hath far choicer ends
Than slowly to impearl in hearts of friends;
        These obsequies 't is meet
Not to seclude in closets of the heart,
But, church-like, with wide doorways, to impart
        Even to the heedless street."

II   Brave, good, and true,
    I see him stand before me now,
    And read again on that young brow,
        Where every hope was new,
How sweet were life! Yet, by the mouth firm-set,
And look made up for Duty's utmost debt,
        I could divine he knew
That death within the sulphurous hostile lines,
In the mere wreck of nobly-pitched designs,
        Plucks heart's-ease, and not rue.

        Happy their end
    Who vanish down life's evening stream
    Placid as swans that drift in dream
        Round the next river-bend!
Happy long life, with honor at the close,
Friends' painless tears, the softened thought of foes!

And yet, like him, to spend
All at a gush, keeping our first faith sure
From mid-life's doubt and eld's contentment poor,
What more could Fortune send?

Right in the van,
On the red rampart's slippery swell,
With heart that beat a charge, he fell
Foeward, as fits a man;
But the high soul burns on to light men's feet
Where death for noble ends makes dying sweet;
His life her crescent's span
Orbs full with share in their undarkening days
Who ever climbed the battailous steeps of praise
Since valor's praise began.

III   His life's expense
Hath won him coeternal youth
With the immaculate prime of Truth;
While we, who make pretence
At living on, and wake and eat and sleep,
And life's stale trick by repetition keep,
Our fickle permanence
(A poor leaf-shadow on a brook, whose play
Of busy idlesse ceases with our day)
Is the mere cheat of sense.

We bide our chance,
Unhappy, and make terms with Fate
A little more to let us wait;
He leads for aye the advance,

Hope's forlorn-hopes that plant the desperate good
For nobler Earths and days of manlier mood;
    Our wall of circumstance
  Cleared at a bound, he flashes o'er the fight,
  A saintly shape of fame, to cheer the right
    And steel each wavering glance.

    I write of one,
  While with dim eyes I think of three;
  Who weeps not others fair and brave as he?
    Ah, when the fight is won,
Dear Land, whom triflers now make bold to scorn,
(Thee! from whose forehead Earth awaits her morn,)
    How nobler shall the sun
Flame in thy sky, how braver breathe thy air,
That thou bred'st children who for thee could dare
    And die as thine have done!

JULIA WARD HOWE (1819–1910) ❦

Robert E. Lee

A gallant foeman in the fight,
　A brother when the fight was o'er,
The hand that led the host with might
　The blessed torch of learning bore.

No shriek of shells nor roll of drums,
　No challenge fierce, resounding far,
When reconciling Wisdom comes
　To heal the cruel wounds of war.

Thought may the minds of men divide,
　Love makes the heart of nations one,
And so, the soldier grave beside,
　We honor thee, Virginia's son.

Confederate General Robert E. Lee

ABRAM JOSEPH RYAN (1839–1894) ❦

The Sword of Robert Lee

Forth from its scabbard, pure and bright,
   Flashed the sword of Lee!
Far in the front of the deadly fight,
High o'er the brave in the cause of Right
Its stainless sheen, like a beacon light,
   Led us to Victory!

Out of its scabbard, where, full long,
   It slumbered peacefully,
Roused from its rest by the battle's song,
Shielding the feeble, smiting the strong,
Guarding the right, avenging the wrong,
   Gleamed the sword of Lee!

Forth from its scabbard, high in air
   Beneath Virginia's sky—
And they who saw it gleaming there,
And knew who bore it, knelt to swear

That where that sword led they would dare
   To follow—and to die!

Out of its scabbard! Never hand
   Waved sword from stain as free,
Nor purer sword led braver band,
Nor braver bled for a brighter land,
Nor brighter land had a cause so grand,
   Nor cause a chief like Lee!

Forth from its scabbard! How we prayed
   That sword might victor be;
And when our triumph was delayed,
And many a heart grew sore afraid,
We still hoped on while gleamed the blade
   Of noble Robert Lee!

Forth from its scabbard all in vain
   Bright flashed the sword of Lee;
'Tis shrouded now in its sheath again,
Its sleeps the sleep of our noble slain,
Defeated, yet without stain,
   Proudly and peacefully!

David Glasgow Farragut was an East Tennessean, 60 years old when the war began. In April 1862 he ran a flotilla of warships up the Mississippi, past the forts guarding New Orleans, and captured the city. In August 1864 in an act of similar daring, he captured Forts Gaines and Morgan guarding Mobile Bay. This poem commemorates this latter action.

WILLIAM TUCKEY MEREDITH (b. 1839) 🖋

Farragut, Farragut

Farragut, Farragut,
   Old Heart of Oak,
Daring Dave Farragut,
   Thunderbolt stroke,
Watches the hoary mist
   Lift from the bay,
Till his flag, glory-kissed,
   Greets the young day.

Far, by gray Morgan's walls,
   Looms the black fleet.
Hark, deck to rampart calls
   With the drums' beat!
Buoy your chains overboard,
   While the steam hums;
Men! to the battlement,
   Farragut comes.

Admiral David G. Farragut

See, as the hurricane
   Hurtles in wrath
Squadrons of clouds amain
   Back from its path!
Back to the parapet,
   To the guns' lips,
Thunderbolt Farragut
   Hurls the black ships.

Now through the battle's roar
   Clear the boy sings,
"By the mark fathoms four,"
   While his lead swings.
Steady the wheelmen five
   "Nor' by east keep her,"
"Steady," but two alive:
   How the shells sweep her!

Lashed to the mast that sways
   Over red decks,
Over the flame that plays
   Round the torn wrecks,
Over the dying lips
   Framed for a cheer,
Farragut leads his ships,
   Guides the line clear.

On by heights cannon-browed,
   While the spars quiver;
Onward still flames the cloud
   Where the hulks shiver.

See, yon fort's star is set,
   Storm and fire past.
Cheer him, lads,—Farragut,
   Lashed to the mast!

Oh! while Atlantic's breast
   Bears a white sail,
While the Gulf's towering crest
   Tops a green vale;
Men thy bold deeds shall tell,
   Old Heart of Oak,
Daring Dave Farragut,
   Thunderbolt stroke!

A narrative, anti-war poem by a
popular poet and novelist of Ohio
who, after the war, lived for a time
in the South. The event can be
precisely dated. In July 1863,
while the battle of Gettysburg was
going on, Confederate raider John
Hunt Morgan, a Kentuckian, led
a cavalry force into Ohio. He was
pursued by troops from Michigan
and captured. He spent four
months in the Ohio state prison
before breaking out and rejoining
the Confederate forces.

CONSTANCE FENIMORE WOOLSON (1840–1894)

Kentucky Belle

Summer of 'sixty-three, sir, and Conrad was gone away—
Gone to the county town, sir, to sell our first load of hay.
We lived in the log house yonder, poor as ever you've seen;
Roschen there was a baby, and I was only nineteen.

Conrad, he took the oxen, but he left Kentucky Belle;
How much we thought of Kentuck, I couldn't begin to tell—
Came from the Bluegrass country; my father gave her to me
When I rode north with Conrad, away from the Tennessee.

Conrad lived in Ohio—a German he is, you know—
The house stood in broad cornfields, stretching on, row after row;
The old folks made me welcome; they were kind as kind could be;
But I kept longing, longing, for the hills of Tennessee.

O, for a sight of water, the shadowed slope of a hill!
Clouds that hang on the summit, a wind that never is still!
But the level land went stretching away to meet the sky—
Never a rise, from north to south, to rest the weary eye!

From east to west, no river to shine out under the moon,
Nothing to make a shadow in the yellow afternoon;
Only the breathless sunshine, as I looked out, all forlorn,
Only the "rustle, rustle," as I walked among the corn.

When I fell sick with pining we didn't wait any more,
But moved away from the cornlands out to this river shore—
The Tuscarawas it's called, sir—off there's a hill, you see—
And now I've grown to like it next best to the Tennessee.

I was at work that morning. Someone came riding like mad
Over the bridge and up the road—Farmer Rouf's little lad.
Bareback he rode; he had no hat; he hardly stopped to say,
"Morgan's men are coming, Fraü, they're galloping on this way.

"I'm sent to warn the neighbors. He isn't a mile behind;
He sweeps up all the horses—every horse that he can find;
Morgan, Morgan the raider, and Morgan's terrible men,
With bowie knives and pistols, are galloping up the glen."

The lad rode down the valley, and I stood still at the door—
The baby laughed and prattled, playing with spools on the floor;
Kentuck was out in the pasture; Conrad, my man, was gone;
Near, near Morgan's men were galloping, galloping on!

Sudden I picked up baby and ran to the pasture bar:
"Kentuck!" I called; "Kentucky!" She knew me ever so far!
I led her down the gully that turns off there to the right,
And tied her to the bushes; her head was just out of sight.

As I ran back to the log house at once there came a sound—
The ring of hoofs, galloping hoofs, trembling over the ground,
Coming into the turnpike out from the White-Woman Glen—
Morgan, Morgan the raider, and Morgan's terrible men.

As near they drew and nearer my heart beat fast in alarm;
But still I stood in the doorway, with baby on my arm.
They came; they passed; with spur and whip in haste they sped along;
Morgan, Morgan the raider, and his band six hundred strong.

Weary they looked and jaded, riding through night and through day;
Pushing on east to the river, many long miles away,
To the border strip where Virginia runs up into the west,
And for the Upper Ohio before they could stop to rest.

On like the wind they hurried, and Morgan rode in advance;
Bright were his eyes like live coals, as he gave me a sideways glance;
And I was just breathing freely, after my choking pain,
When the last one of the troopers suddenly drew his rein.

Frightened I was to death, sir; I scarce dared look in his face,
As he asked for a drink of water and glanced around the place;
I gave him a cup, and he smiled— 'twas only a boy, you see,
Faint and worn, with dim blue eyes; and he'd sailed on the Tennessee.

Only sixteen he was, sir—a fond mother's only son—
Off and away with Morgan before his life had begun!
The damp drops stood on his temples; drawn was the boyish mouth;
And I thought me of the mother waiting down in the South!

O, pluck was he to the backbone and clear grit through and through;
Boasted and bragged like a trooper; but the big words wouldn't do;
The boy was dying, sir, dying, as plain as plain could be,
Worn out by his ride with Morgan up from the Tennessee.

But, when I told the laddie that I too was from the South,
Water came in his dim eyes and quivers around his mouth.
"Do you know the Bluegrass country?" he wistful began to say,
Then swayed like a willow sapling and fainted dead away.

I had him into the log house, and worked and brought him to;
I fed him and coaxed him, as I thought his mother'd do;
And, when the lad got better, and the noise in his head was gone,
Morgan's men were miles away, galloping, galloping on.

"O, I must go," he muttered; "I must be up and away!
Morgan, Morgan is waiting for me! O, what will Morgan say?"
But I heard a sound of tramping and kept him back from the door —
The ringing sound of horses' hoofs that I had heard before.

And on, on came the soldiers — the Michigan cavalry —
And fast they rode, and black they looked galloping rapidly;
They had followed hard on Morgan's track; they had followed day and night;
But of Morgan and Morgan's raiders they had never caught a sight.

And rich Ohio sat startled through all those summer days,
For strange, wild men were galloping over her broad highways;
Now here, now there, now seen, now gone, now north, now east, now west,
Through river valleys and corn-land farms, sweeping away her best.

A bold ride and a long ride! But they were taken at last.
They almost reached the river by galloping hard and fast;
But the boys in blue were upon them ere ever they gained the ford,
And Morgan, Morgan the raider, laid down his terrible sword.

Well, I kept the boy till evening—kept him against his will—
But he was too weak to follow, and sat there pale and still;
When it was cool and dusky—you'll wonder to hear me tell—
But I stole down to that gully and brought up Kentucky Belle.

I kissed the star on her forehead—my pretty, gentle lass—
But I knew that she'd be happy back in the old Bluegrass;
A suit of clothes of Conrad's, with all the money I had,
And Kentuck, pretty Kentuck, I gave to the worn-out lad.

I guided him to the southward as well as I knew how;
The boy rode off with many thanks, and many a backward bow;
And then the glow it faded, and my heart began to swell,
As down the glen away she went, my lost Kentucky Belle!

When Conrad came in the evening the moon was shining high;
Baby and I were both crying—I couldn't tell him why—
But a battered suit of rebel gray was hanging on the wall,
And a thin old horse with drooping head stood in Kentucky's stall.

Well, he was kind, and never once said a hard word to me;
He knew I couldn't help it—'twas all for the Tennessee;
But, after the war was over, just think what came to pass—
A letter, sir; and the two were safe back in the old Bluegrass.

The lad had got across the border, riding Kentucky Belle;

And Kentuck she was thriving, and fat, and hearty, and well;

He cared for her, and kept her, nor touched her with whip or spur:

Ah! we've had many horses, but never a horse like her!

*Johnston took a bullet in the leg at
Shiloh on April 6, 1862, and died
of a severed artery because no one
knew how to apply the tourniquet
he carried in his pocket against
just such an emergency. He was
thought to be the most capable
general on the Southern side, and
only after his death did Robert E.
Lee come to prominence. Here
Johnston seems only an excuse
for the poet to extol the
reunited nation.*

KATE BROWNLEE SHERWOOD (1841–1914) ❧

Albert Sidney Johnston

I hear again the tread of war go thundering through the land,
And Puritan and Cavalier are clinching neck and hand,
Round Shiloh church the furious foes have met to thrust and slay,
Where erst the peaceful sons of Christ were wont to kneel and pray.

The wrestling of the ages shakes the hills of Tennessee,
With all their echoing mounts a-throb with war's wild minstrelsy;
A galaxy of stars new-born round the shield of Mars,
And set against the Stars and Stripes the flashing Stars and Bars.

'Twas Albert Sidney Johnston led the columns of the Gray,
Like Hector on the plains of Troy his presence fired the fray;
And dashing horse and gleaming sword spake out his royal will
As on the slopes of Shiloh field the blasts of war blew shrill.

"Down with the base invaders," the Gray shout forth the cry,
"Death to presumptuous rebels," the Blue ring out reply;
All day the conflict rages and yet again all day,
Though Grant is on the Union side he cannot stem nor stay.

Confederate General Albert Sidney Johnston

They are a royal race of men, these brothers face to face,
Their fury speaking through their guns, their frenzy in their pace;
The sweeping onset of the Gray bears down the sturdy Blue,
Though Sherman and his legions are heroes through and through.

Though Prentiss and his gallant men are forcing scaur and crag,
They fall like sheaves before the scythes of Hardee and of Bragg;
Ah, who shall tell the victor's tale when all the strife is past,
When man and man in one great mould the men who strive are cast.

As when the Trojan hero came from that fair city's gates,
With tossing mane and flaming crest to scorn the scowling fates,
His legions gather round him and madly charge and cheer,
And fill the besieging armies with wild disheveled fear.

Then bares his breast unto the dart the daring spearsman sends,
And dying hears his cheering foes, the wailing of his friends,
So Albert Sidney Johnston, the chief of belt and scar,
Lay down to die at Shiloh and turned the scales of war.

Now five and twenty years are gone, and lo, today they come,
The Blue and Gray in proud array with throbbing fife and drum;
But not as rivals, not as foes, as brothers reconciled,
To twine love's fragrant roses where the thorns of hate grew wild.

They tell the hero of three wars, the lion-hearted man,
Who wore his valor like a star—uncrowned American;
Above his heart serene and still the folded Stars and Bars,
Above his head like mother-wings the sheltering Stripes and Stars.

Aye, five and twenty years, and lo, the manhood of the South
Has held its valor stanch and strong as at the cannon's mouth,
With patient heart and silent tongue has kept its true parole,
And in the conquests born of peace has crowned its battle roll.

But ever while we sing of war, of courage tried and true,
Of heroes wed to gallant deeds, or be it Gray or Blue,
Then Albert Sidney Johnston's name shall flash before our sight
Like some resplendent meteor across the sombre night.

America, thy sons are knit with sinews wrought of steel,
They will not bend, they will not break, beneath the tyrant's heel;
But in the white-hot flame of love, to silken cobwebs spun,
They whirl the engines of the world, all keeping time as one.

Today they stand abreast and strong, who stood as foes of yore,
The world leaps up to bless their feet, heaven scatters blessings o'er;
Their robes are wrought of gleaming gold, their wings are freedom's own,
The tramping of their conquering hosts shakes pinnacle and throne.

Oh, veterans of the Blue and Gray, who fought on Shiloh field,
The purposes of God are true, His judgment stands revealed;
The pangs of war have rent the veil, and lo, His high decree;
One heart, one hope, one destiny, one flag from sea to sea.

*This poem commemorates an
incident of May 6, 1864, during
the battle of the Wilderness. At
a desperate moment for the
Confederates, a Texas brigade
moved into battle, and Lee, sitting
his horse Traveler and urging the
Texans forward with his hat, was
so carried away with his own
enthusiasm that he rode towards the
guns with them. The troops cried
out, "Lee to the Rear," and
Longstreet led him back to relative
safety. Thompson, editor of the
Southern Literary Messenger
after the war, became one of the
most passionate writers about the
Lost Cause and its knights.*

JOHN REUBEN THOMPSON (1823–1873)

Lee to the Rear

Dawn of a pleasant morning in May,
Broke through the Wilderness cool and gray;
While perched in the tallest tree-tops, the birds
Were carolling Mendelssohn's "Songs without Words."

Far from the haunts of men remote,
The brook brawled on with a liquid note;
And Nature, all tranquil and lovely, wore
The smile of the spring, as in Eden of yore.

Little by little, as daylight increased,
And deepened the roseate flush in the East—
Little by little did morning reveal
Two long glittering lines of steel;

Where two hundred thousand bayonets gleam,
Tipped with the light of the earliest beam,
And the faces are sullen and grim to see
In the hostile armies of Grant and Lee.

Confederate General Robert E. Lee

All of a sudden, ere rose the sun,
Pealed on the silence the opening gun—
A little white puff of smoke there came,
And anon the valley was wreathed in flame.

Down on the left of the Rebel lines,
Where a breastwork stands in a copse of pines,
Before the Rebels their ranks can form,
The Yankees have carried the place by storm.

Stars and Stripes on the salient wave,
Where many a hero has found a grave,
And the gallant Confederates strive in vain
The ground they have drenched with their blood to regain.

Yet louder the thunder of battle roared
Yet a deadlier fire on the columns poured;
Slaughter infernal rode with Despair,
Furies twain, through the murky air.

Not far off, in the saddle there sat
A gray-bearded man in a black slouched hat;
Not much moved by the fire was he,
Calm and resolute Robert Lee.

Quick and watchful he kept his eye
On the bold Rebel brigades close by,
Reserves that were standing (and dying) at ease,
While the tempest of wrath toppled over the trees.

For still with their loud, deep, bull-dog bay,
The Yankee batteries blazed away,
And with every murderous second that sped
A dozen brave fellows, alas! fell dead.

The grand old gray-beard rode to the space
Where Death and his victims stood face to face,
And silently waved his old slouched hat —
A world of meaning there was in that!

"Follow me! Steady! We'll save the day!"
This was what he seemed to say;
And to the light of his glorious eye
The bold brigades thus made reply:

"We'll go forward, but you must go back" —
And they moved not an inch in the perilous track:
"Go to the rear, and we'll send them to hell!"
And the sound of the battle was lost in their yell.

Turning his bridle, Robert Lee
Rode to the rear. Like waves of the sea,
Bursting the dikes in their overflow,
Madly his veterans dashed on the foe.

And backward in terror that foe was driven,
Their banners rent and their columns riven,
Wherever the tide of battle rolled
Over the Wilderness, wood and wold.

Sunset out of a crimson sky
Streamed o'er a field of ruddier dye,
And the brook ran on with a purple stain,
From the blood of ten thousand foemen slain.

Seasons have passed since that day and year —
Again o'er its pebbles the brook runs clear,
And the field in a richer green is drest
Where the dead of a terrible conflict rest.

Hushed is the roll of the Rebel drum,
The sabres are sheathed, and the cannon are dumb;
And Fate, with his pitiless band, has furled
The flag that once challenged the gaze of the world;

But the fame of the Wilderness fight abides;
And down into history grandly rides,
Calm and unmoved as in battle he sat,
The gray-bearded man in the black slouched hat.

JOHN REUBEN THOMPSON (1823–1873) 🜲

Obsequies of Stuart
(May 12, 1864)

A companion poem to "Lee to the
Rear." James Ewell Brown
("Jeb") Stuart was one of the most
dashing cavalry commanders of the
Confederacy. He was shot in the
side at fighting at Yellow Tavern
near Richmond on May 12 and
died that evening. Although he had
been in the thick of many battles,
he had never been wounded before
taking the shot that killed him.
This is not a good poem, but it
may be better than Randall's
"Maryland, My Maryland" and
James Russell Lowell's "Ode
Recited at the Harvard
Commemoration."

We could not pause, while yet the noontide air
   Shook with the cannonade's incessant pealing,
The funeral pageant fitly to prepare—
   A nation's grief revealing.

The smoke, above the glimmering woodland wide
   That skirts our southward border in its beauty,
Marked where our heroes stood and fought and died
   For love and faith and duty.

And still, what time the doubtful strife went on,
   We might not find expression for our sorrow;
We could but lay our dear dumb warrior down,
   And gird us for the morrow.

One weary year agone, when came a lull
   With victory in the conflict's stormy closes,
When the glad Spring, all flushed and beautiful,
   First mocked us with her roses,

Confederate cavalry commander J. E. B. ("Jeb") Stuart

With dirge and bell and minute-gun, we paid
    Some few poor rites—an inexpressive token
Of a great people's pain—to Jackson's shade,
    In agony unspoken.

No wailing trumpet and no tolling bell,
    No cannon, save the battle's boom receding,
When Stuart to the grave we bore, might tell,
    With hearts all crushed and bleeding.

The crisis suited not with pomp, and she
    Whose anguish bears the seal of consecration
Had wished his Christian obsequies should be
    Thus void of ostentation.

Only the maidens came, sweet flowers to twine
    Above his form so still and cold and painless,
Whose deeds upon our brightest records shine,
    Whose life and sword were stainless.

They well remembered how he loved to dash
    Into the fight, festooned from summer bowers;
How like a fountain's spray his sabre's flash
    Leaped from a mass of flowers.

And so we carried to his place of rest
    All that of our great Paladin was mortal:
The cross, and not the sabre, on his breast,
    That opes the heavenly portal.

No more of tribute might to us remain:
 But there will still come a time when Freedom's martyrs
A richer guerdon of renown shall gain
 Than gleams in stars and garters.

I hear from out that sunlit land which lies
 Beyond these clouds that gather darkly o'er us,
The happy sounds of industry arise
 In swelling peaceful chorus.

And mingling with these sounds, the glad acclaim
 Of millions undisturbed by war's afflictions,
Crowning each martyr's never-dying name
 With grateful benedictions.

In some fair future garden of delights,
 Where flowers shall bloom and song-birds sweetly warble,
Art shall erect the statues of our knights
 In living bronze and marble.

And none of all that bright heroic throng
 Shall wear to far-off time a semblance grander,
Shall still be decked with fresher wreaths of song,
 Than this beloved commander.

The Spanish legend tells us of the Cid,
 That after death he rode, erect, sedately,
Along his lines, even as in life he did,
 In presence yet more stately;

And thus our Stuart, at this moment, seems
   To ride out of our dark and troubled story
Into the region of romance and dreams,
   A realm of light and glory;

And sometimes, when the silver bugles blow,
   That ghostly form, in battle reappearing,
Shall lead his horsemen headlong on the foe,
   In victory careering!

Captain William Latané, a
Confederate cavalry officer under
"Jeb" Stuart, died in June 1862,
in a skirmish near Hanover Court
House, Virginia. He was buried
at a plantation near the place
where he fell. He was the only
Confederate killed in a daring
hundred-mile ride led by Stuart
around the entire Army of the
Potomac. Thompson promptly
ground out this poem and made
the young officer one of the
Confederacy's great heroes.
The poem moved William D.
Washington to paint an impressive
tableau of the funeral showing
women, children, and various
slaves in appropriate grief for the
fallen martyr.

JOHN REUBEN THOMPSON (1823–1873) ❦

The Burial of Latané

The combat raged not long, but our's the day;
   And through the hosts that compassed us around
Our little band rode proudly on its way,
   Leaving one gallant comrade, glory-crowned,
Unburied on the field he died to gain,
Single of all his men amid the hostile slain.

One moment on the battle's edge he stood,
   Hope's halo like a helmet round his hair,
The next beheld him, dabbled in his blood,
   Prostrate in death, and yet in death how fair!
Even thus he passed through the red gate of strife,
From earthly crowns and palms to an immortal life.

A brother bore his body from the field
   And gave it unto stranger's hands that closed
The calm, blue eyes on earth forever sealed,
   And tenderly the slender limbs composed:

Strangers, yet sisters, who with Mary's love,
Sat by the open tomb and weeping looked above.

A little child strewed roses on his bier,
    Pale roses, not more stainless than his soul.
Nor yet more fragrant than his life sincere
    That blossomed with good actions, brief, but whole:
The aged matron and the faithful slave
Approached with reverent feet the hero's lowly grave.

No man of God might say the burial rite
    Above the "rebel"—thus declared the foe
That blanched before him in the deadly fight,
    But woman's voice, in accents soft and low,
Trembling with pity, touched with pathos, read
Over his hallowed dust the ritual for the dead.

" 'Tis sown in weakness, it is raised in power,"
    Softly the promise floated on the air,
And the sweet breathings of the sunset hour
    Came back responsive to the mourner's prayer;
Gently they laid him underneath the sod,
And left him with his fame, his country, and his God.

Let us not weep for him whose deeds endure,
    So young, so brave, so beautiful, he died;
As he had wished to die; the past is sure,
    Whatever yet of sorrow may betide
Those who still linger by the stormy shore,
Change cannot harm him now nor fortune touch him more.

And when Virginia, leaning on her spear,
    Victrix et vidua, the conflict done,
Shall raise her mailed hand to wipe the tear
    That starts as she recalls each martyred son,
No prouder memory her breast shall sway,
Than thine, our early-lost, lamented Latané.

JOHN WILLIAMSON PALMER (1825–1906)

Stonewall Jackson's Way

A heroic poem showing Jackson as one of us, an ordinary-looking man with a quirky religious fanaticism and yet with a charismatic power to lead men in battle. In life Jackson was quarrelsome, secretive, and more eccentric than most. But he was an aggressive and dauntless fighter.

Come, stack arms, men. Pile on the rails,
   Stir up the camp-fire bright;
No matter if the canteen fails,
   We'll make a roaring night.
Here Shenandoah brawls along,
   There burly Blue Ridge echoes strong
To swell the brigade's rousing song
   Of "Stonewall Jackson's way."

We see him now—the old slouched hat
   Cocked o'er his eye askew—
The shrewd, dry smile—the speech so pat—
   So calm, so blunt, so true.
The "Blue-Light Elder" knowns 'em well—
   Says he, "That's Banks; he's fond of shell—
Lord save his soul! we'll give him" well,
   That's "Stonewall Jackson's way."

Confederate General Stonewall Jackson

Silence! ground arms! kneel all! caps off!
　　Old Blue Light's going to pray;
Strangle the fool that dares to scoff;
　　Attention; it's his way!
Appealing from his native sod,
　　In forma pauperis to God—
"Lay bare thine arm; stretch forth thy rod;
　　Amen." That's "Stonewall's way."

He's in the saddle now! Fall in!
　　Steady, the whole brigade!
Hill's at the ford, cut off! He'll win
　　His way out, ball and blade.
What matter if our shoes are worn?
　　What matter if our feet are torn?
"Quick step—we're with him ere the dawn!"
　　That's "Stonewall Jackson's way."

The sun's bright glances rout the mists
　　Of morning, and, by George!
There's Longstreet struggling in the lists,
　　Hemmed in an ugly gorge—
Pope and his Yankees whipped before—
　　"Bayonet and grape!" hear Stonewall roar,
"Charge, Stuart! Pay off Ashby's score
　　In Stonewall Jackson's way."

Ah, maiden! wait and watch and yearn
　　For news of Stonewall's band!
Ah, widow! read with eyes that burn
　　That ring upon thy hand!

Ah, wife! sew on, pray on, hope on,
Thy life shall not be all forlorn—
The foe had better ne'er been born,
That gets in Stonewall's way.

BRET HARTE (1836–1902) 🕊

John Burns of Gettysburg

John Burns was a 72-year-old cobbler in Gettysburg when the battle came. He picked up his rifle, joined the 150th Pennsylvania Infantry, and blasted away at the Confederates. He was wounded in action, returned to his home when Lee had retreated, and then was lionized by the Union press all over the country.

Have you heard the story that gossips tell
Of Burns of Gettysburg? No? Ah, well:
Brief is the glory that hero earns,
Briefer the story of poor John Burns.
He was the fellow who won renown, —
The only man who didn't back down
When the rebels rode through his native town;
But held his own in the fight next day,
When all his townsfolk ran away.
That was in July, sixty-three, —
The very day that General Lee,
Flower of Southern chivalry,
Baffled and beaten, backward reeled
From a stubborn Meade and a barren field.

I might tell how, but the day before,
John Burns stood at his cottage door,
Looking down the village street,
Where, in the shade of his peaceful vine,

John Burns (with wife) and cottage, Gettysburg, Pennsylvania

He heard the low of his gathered kine,
And felt their breath with incense sweet;
Or I might say, when the sunset burned
The old farm gable, he thought it turned
The milk that fell like a babbling flood
Into the milk-pail, red as blood;
Or how he fancied the hum of bees
Were bullets buzzing among the trees.
But all such fanciful thoughts as these
Were strange to a practical man like Burns,
Who minded only his own concerns,
Troubled no more by fancies fine
Than one of his calm-eyed, long-tailed kine, —
Quite old-fashioned and matter-of-fact,
Slow to argue, but quick to act.
That was the reason, as some folk say,
He fought so well on that terrible day.

And it was terrible. On the right
Raged for hours the heady fight,
Thundered the battery's double bass, —
Difficult music for men to face;
While on the left, — where now the graves
Undulate like the living waves
That all the day unceasing swept
Up to the pits the rebels kept, —
Round-shot ploughed the upland glades,
Sown with bullets, reaped with blades;
Shattered fences here and there,
Tossed their splinters in the air;
The very trees were stripped and bare;

The barns that once held yellow grain
Were heaped with harvests of the slain;
The cattle bellowed on the plain,
The turkeys screamed with might and main,
And brooding barn-fowl left their rest
With strange shells bursting in each nest.

Just where the tide of battle turns,
Erect and lonely, stood old John Burns.
How do you think the man was dressed?
He wore an ancient, long buff vest,
Yellow as saffron,—but his best;
And buttoned over his manly breast
Was a bright blue coat with a rolling collar,
And large gilt buttons,—size of a dollar,—
With tails that the country-folk called "swaller."
He wore a broad-brimmed, bell-crowned hat,
White as the locks on which it sat.
Never had such a sight been seen
For forty years on the village green,
Since old John Burns was a country beau,
And went to the "quiltings" long ago.

Close at his elbows all that day,
Veterans of the Peninsula,
Sunburnt and bearded, charged away;
And striplings, downy of lip and chin,—
Clerks that the Home Guard mustered in,—
Glanced, as they passed, at the hat he wore,
Then at the rifle his right hand bore;
And hailed him, from out their youthful lore,

With scraps of a slangy repertoire:
"How are you, White Hat?" "Put her through!"
"Your head's level!" and "Bully for you!"
Called him "Daddy,"—begged he'd disclose
The name of the tailor who made his clothes,
And what was the value he set on those;
While Burns, unmindful of jeer and scoff,
Stood there picking the rebels off,—
With his long brown rifle, and bell-crowned hat,
And the swallow-tails they were laughing at.

'Twas but a moment, for that respect
Which clothes all courage their voices checked;
And something the wildest could understand
Spake in the old man's strong right hand,
And his corded throat, and the lurking frown
Of his eyebrows under his old bell-crown;
Until, as they gazed, there crept an awe
Through the ranks in whispers, and some men saw,
In the antique vestments and long white hair,
The Past of the Nation in battle there;
And some of the soldiers since declare
That the gleam of his old white hat afar,
Like the crested plume of the brave Navarre,
That day was their oriflamme of war.
Thus raged the battle. You know the rest;
How the rebels, beaten, and backward pressed,
Broke at the final charge and ran.
At which John Burns,—a practical man,—
Shouldered his rifle, unbent his brows,
And then went back to his bees and cows.

That is the story of old John Burns;
This is the moral the reader learns:
In fighting the battle, the question's whether
You'll show a hat that's white, or a feather.

JOHN GREENLEAF WHITTIER (1807–1892) 🐦

Barbara Frietchie

Up from the meadows rich with corn,
Clear in the cool September morn,

The clustered spires of Frederick stand
Green-walled by the hills of Maryland.

Round about them orchards sweep,
Apple and peach tree fruited deep,

Fair as the garden of the Lord
To the eyes of the famished Rebel horde,

On that pleasant morn of the early fall
When Lee marched over the mountain-wall;

Over the mountains winding down,
Horse and foot, into Frederick town.

With Stonewall Jackson safely dead, even a poet like Whittier, who had demonized the Confederacy, could afford to allow the fallen giant a tincture of nobility. The Barbara Frietchie story apparently grew out of an incident on September 10, 1862, when Lee's army was marching toward what became the battle of Antietam. A 95-year-old woman named Barbara Frietchie stood unmolested on the porch of her house in Frederick, Maryland, waving the Stars and Stripes as the Confederates marched by. The story gathered feathers until it reached Whittier, who made it fly into one of the great legends of the war. A great many women did, in fact, display the Stars and Stripes as the Confederates moved through Frederick.

Forty flags with their silver stars,
Forty flags with their crimson bars,

Flapped in the morning wind: the sun
Of noon looked down, and saw not one.

Up rose old Barbara Frietchie then,
Bowed with her fourscore years and ten;

Bravest of all in Frederick town,
She took up the flag the men hauled down;

In her attic window the staff she set,
To show that one heart was loyal yet.

Up the street came the rebel tread,
Stonewall Jackson riding ahead.

Under his slouched hat left and right
He glanced; the old flag met his sight.

"Halt!"—the dust-brown ranks stood fast.
"Fire!"—out blazed the rifle-blast.

It shivered the window, pane and sash;
It rent the banner with seam and gash.

Quick, as it fell, from the broken staff
Dame Barbara snatched the silken scarf.

She leaned far out on the window-sill,
And shook it forth with a royal will.

"Shoot, if you must, this old gray head,
But spare your country's flag," she said.

A shade of sadness, a blush of shame,
Over the face of the leader came;

The nobler nature within him stirred
To life at that woman's deed and word;

"Who touches a hair of yon gray head
Dies like a dog! March on!" he said.

All day long through Frederick street
Sounded the tread of marching feet:

All day long that free flag tossed
Over the heads of the Rebel host.

Ever its torn folds rose and fell
On the loyal winds that loved it well;

And through the hill-gaps sunset light
Shone over it with a warm good-night.

Barbara Frietchie's work is o'er,
And the Rebel rides on his raids no more.

Honor to her! and let a tear
Fall, for her sake, on Stonewall's bier.

Over Barbara Frietchie's grave,
Flag of Freedom and Union, wave!

Peace and order and beauty draw
Round thy symbol of light and law;

And ever the stars above look down
On thy stars below in Frederick town!

SIDNEY LANIER (1842–1881) ❧

The Dying Words of Stonewall Jackson

"Order A. P. Hill to prepare for battle."
"Tell Major Hawks to advance the Commissary train."
"Let us cross the river and rest in the shade."

On the night of May 2, after
heavy fighting all day long at
Chancellorsville, Stonewall
Jackson rode out with some fellow
officers to reconnoiter the Federal
position. Riding back to his own
lines in the moonlight, his party
was mistaken for Federal cavalry
by Confederate pickets. The
Confederates fired two volleys.
Jackson was hit. His left arm was
amputated, and he seemed to be
recovering. But he developed
pneumonia, and on May 10 he
died in a delirium, speaking words
Lanier uses as an epigraph to
this poem.

The stars of Night contain the glittering Day
And rain his glory down with sweeter grace
Upon the dark World's grand, enchanted face—
    All loth to turn away.

And so the Day, about to yield his breath,
Utters the stars unto the listening Night,
To stand for burning fare-thee-wells of light
    Said on the verge of death.

O hero-life that lit us like the sun!
O hero-words that glittered like the stars
And stood and shone above the gloomy wars
    When the hero-life was done!

The phantoms of a battle came to dwell
I' the fitful vision of his dying eyes—
Yet even in battle-dreams, he sends supplies
    To those he loved so well.

His army stands in battle-line arrayed:
His couriers fly: all's done: now God decide!
—And not till then saw he the Other Side
   Or would accept the shade.

Thou Land whose sun is gone, thy stars remain!
Still shine the words that miniature his deeds.
O thrice-beloved, where'er thy great heart bleeds,
   Solace hast thou for pain!

*This plaintive poem, written by
a black poet in the time of Jim
Crow segregation, reveres Shaw
but announces that the sacrifice
was all for nothing.*

PAUL LAURENCE DUNBAR (1872–1906)

Robert Gould Shaw

Why was it that the thunder voice of Fate
    Should call thee, studious, from the classic groves,
    Where calm-eyed Pallas with still footsteps roves,
And charge thee seek the turmoil of the State?
What bade thee hear the voice and rise elate,
    Leave home and kindred and thy spicy loaves,
    To lead th' unlettered and despised droves
To manhood's home and thunder at the gate?

Far better the slow blaze of Learning's light,
    The cool and quiet of her dearer fane,
Than this hot terror of a hopeless fight,
    This cold endurance of the final pain, —
Since thou and those who with thee died for right
    Have died, the Present teaches, but in vain!

Douglass (1817–1895) escaped
to the North from slavery and
became one of the greatest black
orators and writers of the nineteenth
century. He helped organize
both the 54th and the 55th
Massachusetts regiments, and
two of his sons served under
Robert Gould Shaw. This
poem commemorates
Douglass's death.

PAUL LAURENCE DUNBAR (1872–1906) ✍

Frederick Douglass

A hush is over all the teeming lists,
    And there is pause, a breath-space in the strife;
A spirit brave has passed beyond the mists
    And vapors that obscure the sun of life.
And Ethiopia, with bosom torn,
Laments the passing of her noblest born.

She weeps for him a mother's burning tears—
    She loved him with a mother's deepest love.
He was her champion thro' direful years,
    And held her weal all other ends above.
When Bondage held her bleeding in the dust,
He raised her up and whispered, "Hope and Trust."

For her his voice, a fearless clarion, rung
    That broke in warning on the ears of men;
For her the strong bow of his power he strung,
    And sent his arrows to the very den

Where grim Oppression held his bloody place
And gloated o'er the mis'ries of a race.

And he was no soft-tongued apologist;
    He spoke straightforward, fearlessly uncowed;
The sunlight of his truth dispelled the mist,
    And set in bold relief each dark-hued cloud;
To sin and crime he gave their proper hue,
And hurled at evil what was evil's due.

Through good and ill report he cleaved his way
    Right onward, with his face set toward the heights,
Nor feared to face the foeman's dread array, —
    The lash of scorn, the sting of petty spites.
He dared the lightning in the lightning's track,
And answered thunder with his thunder back.

PAUL LAURENCE DUNBAR (1872–1906) 〜

Douglass

Ah, Douglass, we have fall'n on evil days,
　Such days as thou, not even thou didst know,
　When thee, the eyes of that harsh long ago
Saw, salient, at the cross of devious ways,
And all the country heard thee with amaze.
　Not ended then, the passionate ebb and flow,
　The awful tide that battled to and fro;
We ride amid a tempest of dispraise.

Now, when the waves of swift dissension swarm,
　And Honor, the strong pilot, lieth stark,
Oh, for thy voice high-sounding o'er the storm,
　For thy strong arm to guide the shivering bark,
The blast-defying power of thy form,
　To give us comfort through the lonely dark.

ROBERT HAYDEN (1913–) 🌿

Frederick Douglass

A poem of aspiration and recollection. A black poet recognizes that black Americans have not yet been granted the true freedom that is their birthright and looks back to Douglass who stands at the source of black hope.

When it is finally ours, this freedom, this liberty, this beautiful
And terrible thing, needful to man as air,
usable as earth; when it belongs at last to our children,
when it is truly instinct, brain matter, diastole, systole,
reflex action; when it is finally won; when it is more
than the gaudy mumbo jumbo of politicians:
this man, this Douglass, this former slave, this Negro
beaten to his knees, exiled, visioning a world
where none is lonely, none hunted, alien,
this man, superb in love and logic, this man
shall be remembered. Oh, not with statues' rhetoric,
not with legends and poems and wreaths of bronze alone,
but with the lives grown out of his life, the lives
fleshing his dream of the beautiful, needful thing.

A strong poem honoring the black soldiers who fought for the Union. Port Hudson was a Confederate fortress on the Mississippi River in Louisiana, besieged by Federal troops at the same time Vicksburg was under siege by Grant. After Vicksburg fell in July 1863, the fall of Port Hudson soon followed. The African Brigade, celebrated by poet James Madison Bell fought in the Mississippi campaign.

PAUL LAURENCE DUNBAR (1872–1906)

The Unsung Heroes

A song for the unsung heroes who rose in the country's need,
When the life of the land was threatened by the slaver's cruel greed,
For the men who came from the cornfield, who came from the plough and the flail,
Who rallied round when they heard the sound of the mighty man of the rail.

They laid them down in the valleys, they laid them down in the wood,
And the world looked on at the work they did, and whispered, "It is good."
They fought their way on the hillside, they fought their way in the glen,
And God looked down on their sinews brown, and said, "I have made them men."

They went to the blue lines gladly, and the blue lines took them in,
And the men who saw their muskets' fire thought not of their dusky skin.
The gray lines rose and melted beneath their scathing showers,
And they said, " 'T is true, they have force to do, these old slave boys of ours."

Ah, Wagner saw their glory, and Pillow knew their blood,
That poured on a nation's altar, a sacrificial flood.
Port Hudson heard their war-cry that smote its smoke-filled air,
And the old free fires of their savage sires again were kindled there.

They laid them down where the rivers, the greening valleys gem.

And the song of the thund'rous cannon was their sole requiem,

And the great smoke wreath that mingled its hue with the dusky cloud,

Was the flag that furled o'er a saddened world, and the sheet that made their shroud.

Oh, Mighty God of the Battles Who held them in Thy hand,

Who gave them strength through the whole day's length, to fight for their native land,

They are lying dead on the hillsides, they are lying dead on the plain,

And we have not fire to smite the lyre and sing them one brief strain.

Give, Thou, some seer the power to sing them in their might,

The men who feared the master's whip, but did not fear the fight;

That he may tell of their virtues as minstrels did of old,

Till the pride of face and the hate of race grow obsolete and cold.

A song for the unsung heroes who stood the awful test,

When the humblest host that the land could boast went forth to meet the best;

A song for the unsung heroes who fell on the bloody sod,

Who fought their way from night to day and struggled up to God.

LANGSTON HUGHES (1902–1967) ✐

Frederick Douglass: 1817–1895

Douglass was someone who,
Had he walked with wary foot
And frightened tread,
From very indecision
Might be dead,
Might have lost his soul,
But instead decided to be bold
And capture every street
On which he set his feet,
To route each path
Toward freedom's goal,
To make each highway
Choose *his* compass' choice,
To all the world cried,
Hear my voice! . . .
Oh, to be a beast, a bird,
Anything but a slave! he said.

Frederick Douglass

Who would be free
Themselves must strike
The first blow, he said.

He died in 1895.
He is not dead.

One of many poems inspired by photographs of soldiers in the war.

PAUL HORGAN (1905–) 〜

Tintype of a Private of the Fifteenth Georgia Infantry

Lynx-eyed, cat-quiet, sleepy mild,
He could seem a wary child,
His tilted head a little turned
Like one who very early learned
Of unexpectedness in life.
But the blade within his knife
Is the razor temper in his bone
Which he never had to hone
To edge it ready for the kill.
Surely light-voiced, lounging still,
Southern-sweet at mouth and brow,
Once provoked, he'd show you how
In an instant he could spring
To be the death of anything.
The yellow gaze in his sighting eye
Will never flick when his bullets fly.

*In the poem, Lee is President of
Washington College, later named
Washington and Lee, in
Lexington, Virginia, in the
foothills of the Blue Ridge. He
ruminates on his life, especially
on his father, Henry Lee,
known as Light-Horse Harry,
Revolutionary War hero and
governor of Virginia, but towards
the end of his life imprisoned for
debt. Lee was leading his troops
towards the mountains when he
was intercepted by Grant's forces
and forced to surrender at
Appomattox; he reflects on
the irony that at last he is
in the mountains.*

DONALD DAVIDSON (1922–) ✍

Lee in the Mountains
(1865–1870)

Walking into the shadows, walking alone
Where the sun falls through the ruined boughs of locust
Up to the president's office. . . .

                                  Hearing the voices
Whisper, *Hush, it is General Lee!* And strangely
Hearing my own voice say, *Good morning, boys.*
(*Don't get up. You are early. It is long
Before the bell. You will have long to wait
On these cold steps. . . .*)

                              The young have time to wait
But soldiers' faces under their tossing flags
Lift no more by any road or field,
And I am spent with old wars and new sorrow.
Walking the rocky path, where steps decay
And the paint cracks and grass eats on the stone.
It is not General Lee, young men . . .
It is Robert Lee in a dark civilian suit who walks,
An outlaw fumbling for the latch, a voice
Commanding in a dream where no flag flies.

My father's house is taken and his hearth
Left to the candle-drippings where the ashes
Whirl at a chimney-breath on the cold stone.
I can hardly remember my father's look, I cannot
Answer his voice as he calls farewell in the misty
Mounting where riders gather at gates.
He was old then—I was a child—his hand
Held out for mine, some daybreak snatched away,
And he rode out, a broken man. Now let
His lone grave keep, surer than cypress roots,
The vow I made beside him. God too late
Unseals to certain eyes the drift
Of time and the hopes of men and a sacred cause.
The fortune of the Lees goes with the land
Whose sons will keep it still. My mother
Told me much. She sat among the candles,
Fingering the *Memoirs*, now so long unread.
And as my pen moves on across the page
Her voice comes back, a murmuring distillation
Of old Virginia times now faint and gone,
The hurt of all that was and cannot be.

Why did my father write? I know he saw
History clutched as a wraith out of blowing mist
Where tongues are loud, and a glut of little souls
Laps at the too much blood and the burning house
He would have his say, but I shall not have mine.
What I do is only a son's devoir
To a lost father. Let him only speak.
The rest must pass to men who never knew
(But on a written page) the strike of armies,

And never heard the long Confederate cry
Charge through the muzzling smoke or saw the bright
Eyes of the beardless boys go up to death.
It is Robert Lee who writes with his father's hand—
The rest must go unsaid and the lips be locked.

If all were told, as it cannot be told—
If all the dread opinion of the heart
Now could speak, now in the shame and torment
Lashing the bound and trampled States—

If a word were said, as it cannot be said—
I see clear waters run in Virginia's Valley
And in the house the weeping of young women
Rises no more. The waves of grain begin.
The Shenandoah is golden with a new grain.
The Blue Ridge, crowned with a haze of light,
Thunders no more. The horse is at plough. The rifle
Returns to the chimney crotch and the hunter's hand.
And nothing else than this? Was it for this
That on an April day we stacked our arms
Obedient to a soldier's trust? To lie
Ground by heels of little men,

Forever maimed, defeated, lost, impugned?
And was I then betrayed? Did I betray?
If it were said, as still it might be said—
If it were said, and a word should run like fire,
Like living fire into the roots of grass,
The sunken flag would kindle on wild hills,
The brooding hearts would waken, and the dream

Stir like a crippled phantom under the pines,
And this torn earth would quicken into shouting
Beneath the feet of ragged bands—

                         The pen
Turns to the waiting page, the sword
Bows to the rust that cankers and the silence.

Among these boys whose eyes lift up to mine
Within gray walls where droning wasps repeat
A hollow reveillé, I still must face,
Day after day, the courier with his summons
Once more to surrender, now to surrender all.
Without arms or men I stand, but with knowledge only
I face what long I saw, before others knew,
When Pickett's men streamed back, and I heard the tangled
Cry of the Wilderness wounded, bloody with doom.

The mountains, once I said, in the little room
At Richmond, by the huddled fire, but still
The President shook his head. The mountains wait,
I said, in the long beat and rattle of siege
At cratered Petersburg. Too late
We sought the mountains and those people came.
And Lee is in mountains now, beyond Appomattox,
Listening long for voices that never will speak
Again; hearing the hoofbeats come and go and fade
Without a stop, without a brown hand lifting
The tent-flap, or a bugle call at dawn,
Or ever on the long white road the flag
Of Jackson's quick brigades. I am alone,
Trapped, consenting, taken at last in mountains.

It is not the bugle now, or the long roll beating.
The simple stroke of a chapel bell forbids
The hurtling dream, recalls the lonely mind.
Young men, the God of your fathers is a just
And merciful God Who in this blood once shed
On your green altars measures out all days,
And measures out the grace
Whereby alone we live;
And in His might He waits,
Brooding within the certitude of time,
To bring this lost forsaken valor
And the fierce faith undying
And the love quenchless
To flower among the hills to which we cleave,
To fruit upon the mountains whither we flee,
Never forsaking, never denying
His children and His children's children forever
Unto all generations of the faithful heart.

Lincoln ❧

Bryant read this poem to an assembly of New Yorkers in Union Square on April 24, 1865, ten days after Lincoln was shot.

WILLIAM CULLEN BRYANT (1794–1878) ❧

The Death of Abraham Lincoln

Oh, slow to smite and swift to spare,
    Gentle and merciful and just!
Who, in the fear of God, didst bear
    The sword of power, a nation's trust.

In sorrow by thy bier we stand,
    Amid the awe that hushes all,
And speak the anguish of a land
    That shook with horror at thy fall.

Thy task is done; the bound are free;
    We bear thee to an honored grave,
Whose proudest monument shall be
    The broken fetters of the slave.

Pure was thy life; its bloody close
    Hath placed thee with the sons of light,
Among the noble host of those
    Who perished in the cause of Right.

Ford's Theatre chair in which President Lincoln was sitting when shot

HERMAN MELVILLE (1819–1891) ❧

The Martyr
*(Indicative of the Passion of the People
on the 15th Day of April, 1865)*

Good Friday was the day
  Of the prodigy and crime,
When they killed him in his pity,
  When they killed him in his prime
Of clemency and calm—
  When with yearning he was filled
  To redeem the evil-willed,
And, though conqueror, be kind;
  But they killed him in his kindness,
  In their madness and their blindness,
And they killed him from behind.

  There is sobbing of the strong,
  And a pall upon the land;
But the People in their weeping
  Bare the iron hand:
Beware the People weeping
  When they bare the iron hand.

He lieth in his blood—
   The father in his face;
They have killed him, the Forgiver—
   The Avenger takes his place,
The Avenger wisely stern,
     Who in righteousness shall do
     What the heavens call him to,
And the parricides remand;
   For they killed him in his kindness,
   In their madness and their blindness,
And his blood is on their hand.

    There is sobbing of the strong,
      And a pall upon the land;
    But the People in their weeping
      Bare the iron hand:
    Beware the People weeping
      When they bare the iron hand.

WALT WHITMAN (1819–1892)

When Lilacs Last in the Dooryard Bloom'd

From: "Memories of President Lincoln"

I   When lilacs last in the dooryard bloom'd
And the great star early droop'd in the western sky in the night,
I mourn'd, and yet shall mourn with ever-returning spring.

Ever-returning spring, trinity sure to me you bring,
Lilac blooming perennial and drooping star in the west,
And thought of him I love.

II   O powerful western fallen star!
O shades of night—O moody, tearful night!
O great star disappear'd—O the black murk that hides the star!
O cruel hands that hold me powerless—O helpless soul of me!
O harsh surrounding cloud that will not free my soul.

III   In the dooryard fronting an old farmhouse near the whitewash'd palings,
Stands the lilac-bush tall-growing with heart-shaped leaves of rich green,
With many a pointed blossom rising delicate, with the perfume strong I love,
With every leaf a miracle—and from this bush in the dooryard,

Walt Whitman

With delicate-color'd blossoms and heart-shaped leaves of rich green,
A sprig with its flower I break.

IV   In the swamp in secluded recesses,
A shy and hidden bird is warbling a song.
Solitary the thrush,
The hermit withdrawn to himself, avoiding the settlements,
Sings by himself a song.

Song of the bleeding throat,
Death's outlet song of life, (for well dear brother I know,
If thou wast not granted to sing thou would'st surely die.)

V   Over the breast of the spring, the land, amid cities,
Amid lanes and through old woods, where lately the violets peep'd from the ground, spotting
    the grey debris,
Amid the grass in the fields each side of the lanes, passing the endless grass,
Passing the yellow-spear'd wheat, every grain from its shroud in the dark-brown fields
    uprisen,
Passing the apple-tree blows of white and pink in the orchards,
Carrying a corpse to where it shall rest in the grave,
Night and day journeys a coffin.

VI   Coffin that passes through lanes and streets,
Through day and night with the great cloud darkening the land,
With the pomp of the inloop'd flags, with the cities draped in black,
With the show of the States themselves as of crape-veil'd women standing,
With processions long and winding and the flambeaus of the night,
With the countless torches lit, with the silent sea of faces and the unbared heads,
With the waiting depot, the arriving coffin, and the sombre faces,
With dirges through the night, with the thousand voices rising strong and solemn,

With the mournful voices of the dirges pour'd around the coffin,

The dim-lit churches and the shuddering organs—where amid these you journey,

With the tolling tolling bells' perpetual clang,

Here, coffin that slowly passes,

I give you my sprig of lilac.

VII   (Nor for you, for one alone,

Blossoms and branches green to coffins all I bring,

For fresh as the morning, thus would I chant a song for you, O sane and sacred death.

All over bouquets of roses,

O death, I cover you over with roses and early lilies,

But mostly and now the lilac that blooms the first,

Copious I break, I break the sprigs from the bushes,

With loaded arms I come, pouring for you,

For you and the coffins all of you, O death.)

VIII   O western orb sailing the heaven,

Now I know what you must have meant as a month since I walk'd,

As I walk'd in silence the transparent shadowy night,

As I saw you had something to tell as you bent to me night after night,

As you droop'd from the sky low down as if to my side, (while the other stars all look'd on,)

As we wander'd together the solemn night, (for something I know not what kept me from
    sleep,)

As the night advanced, and I saw on the rim of the west how full you were of woe,

As I stood on the rising ground in the breeze in the cool transparent night,

As I watch'd where you pass'd and was lost in the netherward black of the night,

As my soul in its trouble dissatisfied sank, as where you, sad orb,

Concluded, dropt in the night, and was gone.

IX   Sing on there in the swamp,
        O singer bashful and tender, I hear your notes, I hear your call,
        I hear, I come presently, I understand you,
        But a moment I linger, for the lustrous star has detain'd me,
        The star my departing comrade holds and detains me.

X   O how shall I warble myself for the dead one there I loved?
        And how shall I deck my song for the large sweet soul that has gone?
        And what shall my perfume be for the grave of him I love?

        Sea-winds blown from east and west,
        Blown from the Eastern sea and blown from the Western sea, till there on the prairies
            meeting,
        These and with these and the breath of my chant,
        I'll perfume the grave of him I love.

XI   O what shall I hang on the chamber walls?
        And what shall the pictures be that I hang on the walls,
        To adorn the burial-house of him I love?

        Pictures of growing spring and farms and homes,
        With the Fourth-month eve at sundown, and the grey smoke lucid and bright,
        With floods of yellow gold of the gorgeous, indolent, sinking sun, burning, expanding the air,
        With the fresh sweet herbage under foot, and the pale green leaves of the trees prolific,
        In the distance the flowing glaze, the breast of the river, with a wind-dapple here and there,
        With ranging hills on the banks, with many a line against the sky, and shadows,
        And the city at hand with dwellings so dense, and stacks of chimneys,
        And all the scenes of life and the workshops, and the workmen homeward returning.

XII   Lo, body and soul—this land,
        My own Manhattan with spires, and the sparkling and hurrying tides, and the ships,

The varied and ample land, the South and the North in the light, Ohio's shores and flashing
   Missouri,
And ever the far-spreading prairies cover'd with grass and corn.

Lo, the most excellent sun so calm and haughty,
The violet and purple morn with just-felt breezes,
The gentle soft-born measureless light,
The miracle spreading bathing all, the fulfill'd noon,
The coming eve delicious, the welcome night and the stars,
Over my cities shining all, enveloping man and land.

XIII Sing on, sing on you gray-brown bird,
Sing from the swamps, the recesses, pour your chant from the bushes,
Limitless out of the dusk, out of the cedars and pines.

Sing on dearest brother, warble your reedy song,
Loud human song, with voice of uttermost woe.

O liquid and free and tender!
O wild and loose to my soul—O wondrous singer!
You only I hear—yet the star holds me, (but will soon depart,)
Yet the lilac with mastering odor holds me.

XIV Now while I sat in the day and look'd forth,
In the close of the day with its light and the fields of spring, and the farmers preparing their
   crops,
In the large unconscious scenery of my land with its lakes and forests,
In the heavenly aerial beauty, (after the perturb'd winds and the storms,)
Under the arching heavens of the afternoon swift passing, and the voices of children and
   women,
The many-moving sea-tides, and I saw the ships how they sail'd,

And the summer approaching with richness, and the fields all busy with labor,
And the infinite separate houses, how they all went on, each with its meals and minutia of
  daily usages,
And the streets how their throbbings throbb'd, and the cities pent—lo, then and there,
Falling upon them all and among them all, enveloping me with the rest,
Appear'd the cloud, appear'd the long black trail;
And I knew death, its thought, and the sacred knowledge of death.

Then with the knowledge of death as walking one side of me,
And the thought of death close-walking the other side of me,
And I in the middle as with companions, and as holding the hands of companions,
I fled forth to the hiding receiving night that talks not,
Down to the shores of the water, the path by the swamp in the dimness,
To the solemn shadowy cedars and ghostly pines so still.

And the singer so shy to the rest receiv'd me,
The gray-brown bird I know receiv'd us comrades three,
And he sang the carol of death, and a verse for him I love.

From deep secluded recesses,
From the fragrant cedars and the ghostly pines so still,
Came the carol of the bird.

And the charm of the carol rapt me,
As I held as if by their hands my comrades in the night,
And the voice of my spirit tallied the song of the bird.

Come lovely and soothing death,
Undulate round the world, serenely arriving, arriving,
In the day, in the night, to all, to each,
Sooner or later delicate death.

Prais'd be the fathomless universe,
For life and joy, and for objects and knowledge curious,
And for love, sweet love—but praise! praise! praise!
For the sure-enwinding arms of cool-enfolding death.

Dark mother always gliding near with soft feet,
Have none chanted for thee a chant of fullest welcome?
Then I chant it for thee, I glorify thee above all,
I bring thee a song that when thou must indeed come, come unfalteringly.

Approach strong deliveress,
When it is so, when thou hast taken them I joyously sing the dead,
Lost in the loving floating ocean of thee,
Laved in the flood by thy bliss O death.

From me to thee glad serenades,
Dances for thee I propose saluting thee, adornments and feastings for thee,
And the sights of the open landscape and the high-spread sky are fitting,
And life and the fields, and the huge and thoughtful night.

The night in silence under many a star,
The ocean shore and the husky whispering wave whose voice I know,
And the soul turning to thee, O vast and well-veil'd death,
And the body gratefully nestling close to thee.

Over the tree-tops I float thee a song,
Over the rising and sinking waves, over the myriad fields and the prairies wide,
Over the dense-pack'd cities all and the teeming wharves and ways,
I float this carol with joy, with joy to thee O death.

XV   To the tally of my soul,
Loud and strong kept up the gray-brown bird,
With pure, deliberate notes spreading filling the night.

Loud in the pines and cedars dim,
Clear in the freshness moist and the swamp-perfume,
And I with my comrades there in the night.
While my sight that was bound in my eyes unclosed,
As to long panoramas of visions.

And I saw askant the armies,
I saw as in noiseless dreams hundreds of battle-flags,
Borne through the smoke of the battles and pierc'd with missiles I saw them,
And carried hither and yon through the smoke, and torn and bloody,
And at last but a few shreds left on the staffs, (and all in silence,)
And the staffs all splinter'd and broken.

I saw battle-corpses, myriads of them,
And the white skeletons of young men, I saw them,
I saw the debris and debris of all the slain soldiers of the war,
But I saw they were not as was thought,
They themselves were fully at rest, they suffer'd not,
The living remain'd and suffer'd, the mother suffer'd,
And the wife and the child and the musing comrade suffer'd,
And the armies that remained suffer'd.

XVI Passing the visions, passing the night,
Passing, unloosing the hold of my comrades' hands,
Passing the song of the hermit bird and the tallying song of my soul,
Victorious song, death's outlet song, yet varying ever-altering song,
As low and wailing, yet clear the notes, rising and falling, flooding the night,

Sadly sinking and fainting, as warning and warning, and yet again bursting with joy,
Covering the earth and filling the spread of the heaven,
As that powerful psalm in the night I heard from recesses,
Passing, I leave thee lilac with heart-shaped leaves,
I leave thee there in the dooryard, blooming, returning with spring.

I cease my song for thee,
From my gaze on thee in the west, fronting the west, communing with thee,
O comrade lustrous with silver face in the night.

Yet each to keep and all, retrievements out of the night,
The song, the wondrous chant of the gray-brown bird,
And the tallying chant, the echo arous'd in my soul,
With the lustrous and drooping star with the countenance full of woe,
With the holders holding my hand nearing the call of the bird,
Comrades mine and I in the midst, and their memory ever to keep, for the dead I loved so
    well,
For the sweetest, wisest soul of all my days and lands—and this for his dear sake,
Lilac and star and bird twined with the chant of my soul,
There in the fragrant pines and the cedars dusk and dim.

*The best known of Whitman's
poems about Lincoln's death,
but not the best of his poems on
the subject. Here he makes an
uncharacteristic and somewhat
half-hearted attempt at rhyme. The
mood is strikingly different from its
companion piece, "When Lilacs
Last in the Dooryard Bloom'd."
It seems almost as if after the
outpouring of a hymn to death the
poet lost his nerve before the
enormous loss of the greatest of
our Presidents.*

WALT WHITMAN (1819–1892) ❧

O Captain! My Captain!

From: "Memories of President Lincoln"

O Captain! my Captain! our fearful trip is done,
The ship has weather'd every rack, the prize we sought is won,
The port is near, the bells I hear, the people all exulting,
While follow eyes the steady keel, the vessel grim and daring;
    But O heart! heart! heart!
      O the bleeding drops of red,
        Where on the deck my Captain lies,
          Fallen cold and dead.

O Captain! my Captain! rise up and hear the bells;
Rise up—for you the flag is flung—for you the bugle trills,
For you bouquets and ribbon'd wreaths—for you the shores a-crowding,
For you they call, the swaying mass, their eager faces turning;
    Here Captain! dear father!
      This arm beneath your head!
        It is some dream that on the deck,
          You've fallen cold and dead.

Abraham Lincoln, President of the United States

My Captain does not answer, his lips are pale and still,
My father does not feel my arm, he has no pulse nor will,
The ship is anchor'd safe and sound, its voyage closed and done,
From fearful trip the victor ship comes in with object won;
    Exult O shores, and ring O bells!
      But I with mournful tread,
        Walk the deck my Captain lies,
          Fallen cold and dead.

EDWIN MARKHAM (1852–1940) 🖎

Lincoln, the Man of the People

Another poem about Lincoln the martyr, famous for its last two lines. This poem is much akin in spirit to Markham's "The Man with a Hoe." Lincoln was indeed of lowly origins, but he was also a well-to-do corporate lawyer at the time he engaged in the debates with Stephen Douglas that made him famous.

When the Norn Mother saw the Whirlwind Hour
Greatening and darkening as it hurried on,
She left the Heaven of Heroes and came down
To make a man to meet the mortal need.
She took the tried clay of the common road—
Clay warm yet with the genial heat of Earth,
Dasht through it all a strain of prophecy;
Tempered the heap with thrill of human tears;
Then mixt a laughter with the serious stuff.
Into the shape she breathed a flame to light
That tender, tragic, ever-changing face;
And laid on him a sense of the Mystic Powers,
Moving—all husht—behind the mortal vail.
Here was a man to hold against the world.
A man to match the mountains and the sea.

The color of the ground was in him, the red earth;
The smack and tang of elemental things;
The rectitude and patience of the cliff;

The good-will of the rain that loves all leaves;
The friendly welcome of the wayside well;
The courage of the bird that dares the sea;
The gladness of the wind that shakes the corn;
The pity of the snow that hides all scars;
The secrecy of streams that make their way
Under the mountain to the rifted rock;
The tolerance and equity of light
That gives as freely to the shrinking flower
As to the great oak flaring to the wind—
To the grave's low hill as to the Matterhorn
That shoulders out the sky. Sprung from the West,
He drank the valorous youth of a new world.
The strength of virgin forests braced his mind,
The hush of spacious prairies stilled his soul,
His words were oaks in acorns; and his thoughts
Were roots that firmly gript the granite truth.

Up from log cabin to the Capitol,
One fire was on his spirit, one resolve—
To send the keen ax to the root of wrong,
Clearing a free way for the feet of God,
The eyes of conscience testing every stroke,
To make his deed the measure of a man,
He built the rail-pile as he built the State,
Pouring his splendid strength through every blow:
The grip that swung the ax in Illinois
Was on the pen that set a people free.

So came the Captain with the mighty heart;
And when the judgment thunders split the house,

Wrenching the rafters from their ancient rest,
He held the ridgepole up, and spikt again
The rafters of the Home. He held his place—
Held the long purpose like a growing tree—
Held on through blame and faltered not at praise—
Held on in calm rough-hewn sublimity,
And when he fell in whirlwind, he went down
As when a lordly cedar, green with boughs,
Goes down with a great shout upon the hills,
And leaves a lonesome place against the sky.

EDGAR LEE MASTERS (1869–1950) ❧

Anne Rutledge
From: Spoon River Anthology

Out of me unworthy and unknown
The vibrations of deathless music;
"With malice toward none, with charity for all."
Out of me the forgiveness of millions toward millions,
And the beneficent face of a nation
Shining with justice and truth.
I am Anne Rutledge who sleep beneath these weeds,
Beloved in life of Abraham Lincoln,
Wedded to him, not through union,
But through separation.
Bloom forever, O Republic,
From the dust of my bosom!

Robinson, a lover of irony, takes
into account the ridicule heaped on
Lincoln during his life and recalls it
amid the sanctification of Lincoln
that took place at his death.

EDWIN ARLINGTON ROBINSON (1869–1935) ❧

The Master

(About Lincoln, supposed to have been written not long after the Civil War)

A flying word from here and there
Had sown the name at which we sneered,
But soon the name was everywhere,
To be reviled and then revered:
A presence to be loved and feared,
We cannot hide it, or deny
That we, the gentlemen who jeered,
May be forgotten by and by.

He same when days were perilous
And hearts of men were sore beguiled;
And having made his note of us,
He pondered and was reconciled.
Was ever master yet so mild
As he, and so untamable?
We doubted, even when he smiled,
Not knowing what he knew so well.

He knew that undeceiving fate
Would shame us whom he served unsought;
He knew that he must wince and wait—
The jest of those for whom he fought;
He knew devoutly what he thought
Of us and of our ridicule;
He knew that we must all be taught
Like little children in a school.

We gave a glamour to the task
That he encountered and saw through,
But little of us did he ask,
And little did we ever do.
And what appears if we review
The season when we railed and chaffed?
It is the face of one who knew
That we were learning while we laughed.

The face that in our vision feels
Again the venom that we flung,
Transfigured to the world reveals
The vigilance to which we clung.
Shrewd, hallowed, harassed, and among
The mysteries that are untold,
The face we see was never young,
Nor could it ever have been old.

For he, to whom we had applied
Our shopman's test of age and worth,
Was elemental when he died,
As he was ancient at his birth:

The saddest among kings of earth,
Bowed with a galling crown, this man
Met rancor with a cryptic mirth,
Laconic—and Olympian.

The love, the grandeur, and the fame
Are bounded by the world alone;
The calm, the smoldering, and the flame
Of awful patience were his own:
With him they are forever flown
Past all our fond self-shadowings,
Wherewith we cumber the Unknown
As with inept Icarian wings.

For we were not as other men:
'Twas ours to soar and his to see.
But we are coming down again,
And we shall come down pleasantly;
Nor shall we longer disagree
On what it is to be sublime,
But flourish in our perigee
And have one Titan at a time.

VACHEL LINDSAY (1879–1931)

Abraham Lincoln Walks at Midnight

It is portentous, and a thing of state
That here at midnight, in our little town
A mourning figure walks, and will not rest,
Near the old court-house pacing up and down,

Or by his homestead, or in shadowed yards
He lingers where his children used to play,
Or through the market, on the well-worn stones
He stalks until the dawn-stars burn away.

A bronzed, lank man! His suit of ancient black,
A famous high-top hat and plain worn shawl
Make him the quaint great figure that men love,
The prairie-lawyer, master of us all.

He cannot sleep upon his hillside now.
He is among us:—as in times before!
And we who toss and lie awake for long,
Breathe deep, and start, to see him pass the door.

His head is bowed. He thinks of men and kings.
Yea, when the sick world cries, how can he sleep?
Too many peasants fight, they know not why;
Too many homesteads in black terror weep.

The sins of all the war-lords burn his heart.
He sees the dreadnaughts scouring every main.
He carries on his shawl-wrapped shoulders now
The bitterness, the folly and the pain.

He cannot rest until a spirit-dawn
Shall come; — the shining hope of Europe free:
A league of sober folk, the workers' earth,
Bringing long peace to Cornland, Alp and Sea.

It breaks his heart that kings must murder still,
That all his hours of travail here for men
Seem yet in vain. And who will bring white peace
That he may sleep upon his hill again?

*A good poem, incorporating
the legend of Anne Rutledge.
Fletcher, a native of Arkansas,
won a Pulitzer Prize in 1938 for
his* Selected Poems. *He was one
of the Agrarians, and, like Allen
Tate, Robert Penn Warren, and
others, he opposed modern
urbanization and industry and
harked back to an age that he
imagined was more simple. The
tale of Anne Rutledge fitted the
nostalgia of the Agrarians.*

JOHN GOULD FLETCHER (1886–1950)

Lincoln

I Like a gaunt, scraggly pine
  Which lifts its head above the mournful sandhills;
  And patiently, through dull years of bitter silence,
  Untended and uncared for, begins to grow.

  Ungainly, laboring, huge,
  The wind of the north has twisted and gnarled its branches;
  Yet in the heat of midsummer days, when thunder-clouds ring the horizon,
  A nation of men shall rest beneath its shade.

  And it shall protect them all,
  Hold everyone safe there, watching aloof in silence;
  Until at last one mad stray bolt from the zenith
  Shall strike it in an instant down to earth.

II There was a darkness in this man; an immense and hollow darkness,
  Of which we may not speak, nor share with him, nor enter;
  A darkness through which strong roots stretched downwards into the earth
  Towards old things;

Mrs. Abraham Lincoln

Towards the herdman-kings who walked the earth and spoke with God,
Towards the wanderers who sought for they knew not what, and found their goal at last;
Towards the men who waited, only waited patiently when all seemed lost,
Many bitter winters of defeat;
Down to the granite of patience
These roots swept, knotted fibrous roots, prying, piercing, seeking,
And drew from the living rock and the living waters about it
The red sap to carry upwards to the sun.

Not proud, but humble,
Only to serve and pass on, to endure to the end through service;
For the ax is laid at the root of the trees, and all that bring not forth good fruit
Shall be cut down on the day to come and cast into the fire.

III   There is silence abroad in the land today,
And in the hearts of men, a deep and anxious silence;
And, because we are still at last, those bronze lips slowly open,
Those hollow and weary eyes take on a gleam of light.

Slowly a patient, firm-syllabled voice cuts through the endless silence
Like laboring oxen that drag a plow through the chaos of rude clay-fields:
"I went forward as the light goes forward in early spring,
But there were also many things which I left behind.

"Tombs that were quiet;
One, of a mother, whose brief light went out in the darkness,
One, of a loved one, the snow on whose grave is long-falling,
One, only of a child, but it was mine.

"Have you forgot your graves? Go, question them in anguish,
Listen long to their unstirred lips. From your hostages to silence,

Learn there is no life without death, no dawn without sunsetting,
No victory but to Him who has given all."

IV The clamor of cannon dies down, the furnace-mouth of the battle is silent.
The midwinter sun dips and descends, the earth takes on afresh its bright colors.
But he whom we mocked and obeyed not, he whom we scorned and mistrusted,
He has descended, like a god, to his rest.

Over the uproar of cities,
Over the million intricate threads of life wavering and crossing,
In the midst of problems we know not, tangling, perplexing, ensnaring,
Rises one white tomb alone.
Beam over it, stars.
Wrap it round, stripes—stripes red for the pain that he bore for you—
Enfold it forever, O flag, rent, soiled, but repaired through your anguish;
Long as you keep him there safe, the nations shall bow to your law.

Strew over him flowers:
Blue forget-me-nots from the north, and the bright pink arbutus
From the east, and from the west rich orange blossoms,
But from the heart of the land take the passion-flower;
Rayed, violet, dim,
With the nails that pierced, the cross that he bore and the circlet,
And beside it there lay also one lonely snow-white magnolia,
Bitter for remembrance of the healing which has passed.

CARL SANDBURG (1878–1967)

The Long Shadow of Lincoln
A Litany

Be sad, be cool, be kind,
Remembering those now dream-dust
Hallowed in the ruts and gullies,
Solemn bones under the smooth blue sea,
Faces war-blown in a falling rain.

Be a brother, if so can be,
To those beyond battle fatigue
Each in his own corner of earth
Or forty fathoms undersea
Beyond all boom of guns,
Beyond any bong of a great bell,
Each with a bosom and number,
Each with a pack of secrets,
Each with a personal dream and doorway,
And over them now the long endless winds
With the low healing song of time,
The hush and sleep murmur of time.
Make your wit a guard and cover.

President Lincoln and his generals at Antietam

Sing low, sing high, sing wide.
Let your laughter come free
Remembering looking toward peace:
"We must disenthrall ourselves."

Be a brother, if so can be,
To those thrown forward
For taking hard-won lines,
For holding hard-won points
And their reward so-so.
Little they care to talk about,
Their pay held in a mute calm,
High-spot memories going unspoken;
What they did being past words,
What they took being hard won.
Be sad, be kind, be cool.
Weep if you must,
And weep, open and shameless,
Before these altars.

There are wounds past words.
There are cripples less broken
Than many who walk whole.
There are dead youths
With wrists of silence
Who keep a vast music
Under their shut lips;
What they did being past words;
Their dreams, like their deaths,
Beyond any smooth and easy telling;
Having given till no more to give.

There is dust alive
With dreams of the Republic,
With dreams of the family of man
Flung wide on a shrinking globe;
With old timetables,
Old maps, old guideposts
Torn into shreds,
Shot into tatters,
Burnt in a fire wind,
Lost in the shambles,
Faded in rubble and ashes.

There is dust alive.
Out of a granite tomb,
Out of a bronze sarcophagus,
Loose from the stone and copper
Steps a white-smoke ghost,
Lifting an authoritative hand
In the name of dreams worth dying for,
In the name of men whose dust breathes
Of those dreams so worth dying for;
What they did being past words,
Beyond all smooth and easy telling.

Be sad, be kind, be cool,
Remembering, under God, a dream-dust
Hallowed in the ruts and gullies,
Solemn bones under the smooth blue sea,
Faces war-blown in a falling rain.

Sing low, sing high, sing wide.
Make your wit a guard and cover.
Let your laughter come free,
Like a help and a brace of comfort.

The earth laughs, the sun laughs
Over every wise harvest of man,
Over man looking toward peace
By the light of the hard old teaching:
"We must disenthrall ourselves."

LANGSTON HUGHES (1902–1967) 🕊

Lincoln Monument: Washington

Hughes was a modernist poet with a sharp eye for irony. He knew that blacks suffered all over America at the hands of whites who would profess undying love for Lincoln and his principles.

Let's go see Old Abe
Sitting in the marble and the moonlight,
Sitting lonely in the marble and the moonlight,
Quiet for ten thousand centuries, old Abe.
Quiet for a million, million years.

Quiet—

And yet a voice forever
Against the
Timeles walls
Of time—
Old Abe.

Aftermath ❧

JOHN GREENLEAF WHITTIER (1807–1892) ❧

The Battle Autumn of 1862

The flags of war like storm-birds fly,
   The charging trumpets blow,
Yet rolls no thunder in the sky,
   No earthquake strives below.

And, calm and patient, Nature keeps
   Her ancient promise well,
Though o'er her bloom and greenness sweeps
   The battle's breath of hell.

And still she walks in golden hours
   Through harvest-happy farms,
And still she wears her fruits and flowers
   Like jewels on her arms.

What mean the gladness of the plain,
   This joy of eve and morn,
The mirth that shakes the beard of grain
   And yellow locks of corn?

Oh, eyes may be full of tears,
    And hearts with hate are hot;
But even-paced come round the years,
    And Nature changes not.

She meets with smiles our bitter grief,
    With songs our groans of pain;
She mocks with tint of flower and leaf
    The war-field's crimson stain.

Still, in the cannon's pause, we hear
    Her sweet thanksgiving-psalm;
Too near to God for doubt or fear,
    She shares the eternal calm.

She knows the seed lies safe below
    The fires that blast and burn;
For all the tears of blood we sow
    She waits the rich return.

She sees with clearer eye than ours
    The good of suffering born—
The hearts that blossom like her flowers,
    And ripen like her corn.

Oh, give to us, in times like these,
    The vision of her eyes;
And make her fields and fruited trees
    Our golden prophecies.

Oh, give to us her finer ear,
    Above this stormy din.
We too would hear the bells of cheer
    Ring peace and freedom in.

JAMES RUSSELL LOWELL (1819–1891) ✍

Ode Recited at the Harvard Commemoration,
July 21, 1865

I   Weak-winged is song,
Nor aims at that clear-ethered height
Whither the brave deed climbs for light:
     We seem to do them wrong,
Bringing our robin's-leaf to deck their hearse
Who in warm life-blood wrote their nobler verse,
Our trivial song to honor those who come
With ears attuned to strenuous trump and drum,
And shaped in squadron-strophes their desire,
Live battle-odes whose lines were steel and fire:
     Yet sometimes feathered words are strong,
A gracious memory to buoy up and save
From Lethe's dreamless ooze, the common grave
     Of the unventurous throng.

II   To-day our Reverend Mother welcomes back
     Her wisest Scholars, those who understood
The deeper teaching of her mystic tome,
     And offered their fresh lives to make it good:

No lore of Greece or Rome,
No science peddling with the names of things,
Or reading stars to find inglorious fates,
Can lift our life with wings
Far from Death's idle gulf that for the many waits,
And lengthen out our dates
With that clear fame whose memory sings
In manly hearts to come, and nerves them and dilates:
Nor such thy teaching, Mother of us all!
Not such the trumpet-call
Of thy diviner mood,
That could thy sons entice
From happy homes and toils, the fruitful nest
Of those half-virtues which the world calls best,
Into War's tumult rude;
But rather far that stern device
The sponsors chose that round thy cradle stood
In the dim, unventured wood,
The VERITAS that lurks beneath
The letter's unprolific sheath,
Life of whate'er makes life worth living,
Seed-grain of high emprise, immortal food,
One heavenly thing whereof earth hath the giving.

III   Many loved Truth, and lavished life's best oil
Amid the dust of books to find her,
Content at last, for guerdon of their toil,
With the cast mantle she hath left behind her.
Many in sad faith sought for her,
Many with crossed hands sighed for her;
But these, our brothers, fought for her,

At life's dear peril wrought for her,

So loved her that they died for her,

Tasting the raptured fleetness

Of her divine completeness:

Their higher instinct knew

Those love her best who to themselves are true,

And what they dare to dream of, dare to do;

They followed her and found her

Where all may hope to find,

Not in the ashes of the burnt-out mind,

But beautiful, with danger's sweetness round her.

Where faith made whole with deed

Breathes its awakening breath

Into the lifeless creed,

They saw her plumed and mailed,

With sweet, stern face unveiled,

And all-repaying eyes, look proud on them in death.

IV   Our slender life runs rippling by, and glides

Into the silent hollow of the past;

What is there that abides

To make the next age better for the last?

Is earth too poor to give us

Something to live for here that shall outlive us?

Some more substantial boon

Than such as flows and ebbs with Fortune's fickle moon?

The little that we see

From doubt is never free;

The little that we do

Is but half-nobly true;

With our laborious hiving

What men call treasure, and the gods call dross,
  Life seems a jest of Fate's contriving,
  Only secure in every one's conniving,
A long account of nothings paid with loss,
Where we poor puppets, jerked by unseen wires,
  After our little hour of strut and rave,
With all our pasteboard passions and desires,
Loves, hates, ambitions, and immortal fires,
  Are tossed pell-mell together in the grave.
  But stay! no age was e'er degenerate,
  Unless men held it at too cheap a rate,
  For in our likeness still we shape our fate.
    Ah, there is something here
  Unfathomed by the cynic's sneer,
  Something that gives our feeble light
  A high immunity from Night,
  Something that leaps life's narrow bars
To claim its birthright with the hosts of heaven;
  A seed of sunshine that can leaven
  Our earthly dullness with the beams of stars,
      And glorify our clay
  With light from fountains elder than the Day;
    A conscience more divine than we,
    A gladness fed with secret tears,
    A vexing, forward-reaching sense
    Of some more noble permanence;
      A light across the sea,
  Which haunts the soul and will not let it be,
Still beaconing from the heights of undegenerate years.

V   Whither leads the path
        To ampler fates that leads?
        Not down through flowery meads,
        To reap an aftermath
      Of youth's vainglorious weeds,
      But up the steep, amid the wrath
    And shock of deadly-hostile creeds,
    Where the world's best hope and stay
By battle's flashes gropes a desperate way,
And every turf the fierce foot clings to bleeds.
    Peace hath her not ignoble wreath,
    Ere yet the sharp, decisive word
Light the black lips of cannon, and the sword
      Dreams in its easeful sheath;
But some day the live coal behind the thought,
      Whether from Baal's stone obscene,
      Or from the shrine serene
      Of God's pure altar brought,
Bursts up in flame; the war of tongue and pen
Learns with what deadly purpose it was fraught,
And, helpless in the fiery passion caught,
Shakes all the pillared state with shock of men:
Some day the soft Ideal that we wooed
Confronts us fiercely, foe-beset, pursued,
And cries reproachful: "Was it, then, my praise,
And not myself was loved? Prove now thy truth;
I claim of thee the promise of thy youth;
Give me thy life, or cower in empty phrase,
The victim of thy genius, not its mate!"
    Life may be given in many ways,
    And loyalty to Truth be sealed

As bravely in the closet as the field,
    So bountiful is Fate;
    But then to stand beside her,
    When craven churls deride her,
To front a lie in arms and not to yield,
    This shows, methinks, God's plan
    And measure of a stalwart man,
    Limbed like the old heroic breeds,
    Who stands self-poised on manhood's solid earth,
    Not forced to frame excuses for his birth,
Fed from within with all the strength he needs.

VI   Such was he, our Martyr-Chief,
    Whom late the Nation he had led,
    With ashes on her head,
Wept with the passion of an angry grief:
Forgive me, if from present things I turn
To speak what in my heart will beat and burn,
And hang my wreath on his world-honored urn.
    Nature, they say, doth dote,
    And cannot make a man
    Save on some worn-out plan,
    Repeating us by rote:
For him her Old-World moulds aside she threw,
    And, choosing sweet clay from the breast
    Of the unexhausted West,
With stuff untainted shaped a hero new,
Wise, steadfast in the strength of God, and true.
    How beautiful to see
Once more a shepherd of mankind indeed,
Who loved his charge, but never loved to lead;

One whose meek flock the people joyed to be,
    Not lured by any cheat of birth,
    But by his clear-grained human worth,
And brave old wisdom of sincerity!
    They knew that outward grace is dust;
    They could not choose but trust
In that sure-footed mind's unfaltering skill,
    And supple-tempered will
That bent like perfect steel to spring again and thrust.
    His was no lonely mountain-peak of mind,
    Thrusting to thin air o'er our cloudy bars,
    A sea-mark now, now lost in vapors blind;
    Broad prairie rather, genial, level-lined,
    Fruitful and friendly for all human kind,
Yet also nigh to heaven and loved of loftiest stars.
      Nothing of Europe here,
Or, then, of Europe fronting mornward still,
    Ere any names of Serf and Peer
    Could Nature's equal scheme deface
    And thwart her genial will;
    Here was a type of the true elder race,
And one of Plutarch's men talked with us face to face.
    I praise him not; it were too late;
And some innative weakness there must be
In him who condescends to victory
Such as the Present gives, and cannot wait,
    Safe in himself as in a fate.
      So always firmly he:
      He knew to bide his time,
      And can his fame abide,
Still patient in his simple faith sublime,

Till the wise years decide.
Great captains, with their guns and drums,
Disturb our judgment for the hour,
But at last silence comes;
These all are gone, and, standing like a tower,
Our children shall behold his fame.
The kindly-earnest, brave, foreseeing man,
Sagacious, patient, dreading praise, not blame,
New birth of our new soil, the first American.

VII   Long as man's hope insatiate can discern
Or only guess some more inspiring goal
Outside of Self, enduring as the pole,
Along whose course the flying axles burn
Of spirits bravely-pitched, earth's manlier brood;
Long as below we cannot find
The meed that stills the inexorable mind;
So long this faith to some ideal Good,
Under whatever mortal names it masks,
Freedom, Law, Country, this ethereal mood
That thanks the Fates for their severer tasks,
Feeling its challenged pulses leap,
While others skulk in subterfuges cheap,
And, set in Danger's van, has all the boon it asks,
Shall win man's praise and woman's love,
Shall be a wisdom that we set above
All other skills and gifts to culture dear,
A virtue round whose forehead we inwreathe
Laurels that with a living passion breathe
When other crowns grow, while we twine them, sear.
What brings us thronging these high rites to pay,

And seal these hours the noblest of our year,
　　Save that our brothers found this better way?

VIII　We sit here in the Promised Land
　　That flows with Freedom's honey and milk;
　　But 't was they won it, sword in hand,
Making the nettle danger soft for us as silk.
　　We welcome back our bravest and our best; —
　　Ah me! not all! some come not with the rest,
Who went forth brave and bright as any here!
I strive to mix some gladness with my strain,
　　　　But the sad strings complain,
　　　　And will not please the ear:
I sweep them for a pæan, but they wane
　　　　Again and yet again
Into a dirge, and die away, in pain.
In these brave ranks I only see the gaps,
Thinking of dear ones whom the dumb turf wraps,
Dark to the triumph which they died to gain:
　　Fitlier may others greet the living,
　　For me the past is unforgiving;
　　　　I with uncovered head
　　　　Salute the sacred dead,
Who went, and who return not. — Say not so!
'T is not the grapes of Canaan that repay,
But the high faith that failed not by the way;
Virtue treads paths that end not in the grave;
No ban of endless night exiles the brave;
　　　　And to the saner mind
We rather seem the dead that stayed behind
Blow, trumpets, all your exultations blow!

For never shall their aureoled presence lack:
I see them muster in a gleaming row,
With ever-youthful brows that nobler show;
We find in our dull road their shining track;
In every nobler mood
We feel the orient of their spirit glow,
Part of our life's unalterable good,
Of all our saintlier aspiration;
They come transfigured back,
Secure from change in their high-hearted ways,
Beautiful evermore, and with the rays
Of morn on their white Shields of Expectation!

IX   But is there hope to save
Even this ethereal essence from the grave?
What ever 'scaped Oblivion's subtle wrong
Save a few clarion names, or golden threads of song?
Before my musing eye
The mighty ones of old sweep by,
Disvoicèd now and insubstantial things,
As noisy once as we; poor ghosts of kings,
Shadows of empire wholly gone to dust,
And many races, nameless long ago,
To darkness driven by that imperious gust
Of ever-rushing Time that here doth blow:
O visionary world, condition strange,
Where naught abiding is but only Change,
Where the deep-bolted stars themselves still shift and range!
Shall we to more continuance make pretence?
Renown builds tombs; a life-estate is Wit;
And, bit by bit,

The cunning years steal all from us but woe;

    Leaves are we, whose decays no harvest sow.

        But, when we vanish hence,

Shall they lie forceless in the dark below,

Save to make green their little length of sods,

Or deepen pansies for a year or two,

Who now to us are shining-sweet as gods;

Was dying all they had the skill to do?

That were not fruitless: but the Soul resents

Such short-lived service, as if blind events

Ruled without her, or earth could so endure;

She claims a more divine investiture

Of longer tenure than Fame's airy rents;

Whate'er she touches doth her nature share;

Her inspiration haunts the ennobled air,

      Gives eyes to mountains blind,

Ears to the deaf earth, voices to the wind,

And her clear trump sings succor everywhere

By lonely bivouacs to the wakeful mind;

For soul inherits all that soul could dare:

      Yea, Manhood hath a wider span

And larger privilege of life than man.

The single deed, the private sacrifice,

So radiant now through proudly-hidden tears,

Is covered up erelong from mortal eyes

With thoughtless drift of the deciduous years;

But that high privilege that makes all men peers,

The leap of heart whereby a people rise

     Up to a noble anger's height,

And, flamed on by the Fates, not shrink, but grow more bright,

    That swift validity in noble veins,

Of choosing danger and disdaining shame,
Of being set on flame
By the pure fire that flies all contact base
But wraps its chosen with angelic might,
These are imperishable gains,
Sure as the sun, medicinal as light,
These hold great futures in their lusty reins
And certify to earth a new imperial race

X   Who now shall sneer?
Who dare again to say we trace
Our lines to a plebeian race?
Roundhead and Cavalier!
Dumb are those names erewhile in battle loud;
Dream-footed as the shadow of a cloud,
They flit across the ear:
That is best blood that hath most iron in 't.
To edge resolve with, pouring without stint
For what makes manhood dear.
Tell us not of Plantagenets,
Hapsburgs, and Guelfs, whose thin bloods crawl
Down from some victor in a border-brawl!
How poor their outworn coronets,
Matched with one leaf of that plain civic wreath
Our brave for honor's blazon shall bequeath,
Through whose desert a rescued Nation sets
Her heel on treason, and the trumpet hears
Shout victory, tingling Europe's sullen ears
With vain resentments and more vain regrets!

XI   Not in anger, not in pride,

Pure from passion's mixture rude

Ever to base earth allied,

But with far-heard gratitude,

Still with heart and voice renewed,

To heroes living and dear martyrs dead,

The strain should close that consecrates our brave.

Lift the heart and lift the head!

Lofty be its mood and grave,

Not without a martial ring,

Not without a prouder trend

And a peal of exultation:

Little right has he to sing

Through whose heart in such an hour

Beats no march of conscious power,

Sweeps no tumult of elation!

'T is no Man we celebrate,

By his country's victories great,

A hero half, and half the whim of Fate,

But the pith and marrow of a Nation

Drawing force from all her men,

Highest, humblest, weakest, all,

For her time of need, and then

Pulsing it again through them,

Till the basest can no longer cower,

Feeling his soul spring up divinely tall,

Touched but in passing by her mantle-hem.

Come back, then, noble pride, for ' tis her dower!

How could poet ever tower,

If his passions, hopes, and fears,

If his triumphs and his tears,

Kept not measure with his people?
Boom, cannon, boom to all the winds and waves!
Clash out, glad bells, from every rocking steeple!
Banners, adance with triumph, bend your staves!
        And from every mountain-peak
        Let beacon-fire to answering beacon speak,
        Katahdin tell Monadnock, Whiteface he,
And so leap on in light from sea to sea,
            Till the glad news be sent
            Across a kindling continent,
Making earth feel more firm and air breathe braver:
"Be proud! for she is saved, and all have helped to save her!
        She that lifts up the manhood of the poor,
        She of the open soul and open door,
        With room about her hearth for all mankind!
        The fire is dreadful in her eyes no more;
        From her bold front the helm she doth unbind,
        Sends all her handmaid armies back to spin,
        And bids her navies, that so lately hurled
        Their crashing battle, hold their thunders in,
        Swimming like birds of calm along the unharmful shore.
        No challenge sends she to the elder world,
        That looked askance and hated; a light scorn
        Plays o'er her mouth, as round her mighty knees
        She calls her children back, and waits the morn
Of nobler day, enthroned between her subject seas."

XII   Bow down, dear Land, for thou hast found release!
        Thy God, in these distempered days,
        Hath taught thee the sure wisdom of
            His ways,

And through thine enemies hath wrought thy peace!

    Bow down in prayer and praise!

No poorest in thy borders but may now

Lift to the juster skies a man's enfranchised brow.

O Beautiful! my Country! ours once more!

Something thy gold of war-dishevelled hair

O'er such sweet brows as never other wore,

    And letting thy set lips,

    Freed from wrath's pale eclipse,

The rosy edges of their smile lay bare,

What words divine of lover or of poet

Could tell our love and make thee know it,

Among the Nations bright beyond compare?

    What were our lives without thee?

    What all our lives to save thee?

    We reck not what we gave thee;

    We will not dare to doubt thee,

But ask whatever else, and we will dare!

A poem published after the war and recalling Lee's first great battle after he took command of the Army of Northern Virginia. Lee sent infantry charging Federal artillery emplaced in great strength atop Malvern Hill near the James River. The Confederates were slaughtered by canister. Melville writes of the bucolic place that knew such terror.

HERMAN MELVILLE (1819–1891) ❧

Malvern Hill
(July 1862)

Ye elms that wave on Malvern Hill
   In prime of morn and May,
Recall ye how McClellan's men
    Here stood at bay?
While deep within yon forest dim
   Our rigid comrades lay—
Some with the cartridge in their mouth,
Others with fixed arms lifted South—
    Invoking so
The cypress glades? Ah wilds of woe!

The spires of Richmond, late beheld
   Through rifts in musket-haze,
Were closed from view in clouds of dust
    On leaf-walled ways,
Where streamed our wagons in caravan;
   And the Seven Nights and Days
Of march and fast, retreat and fight,
Pinched our grimed faces to ghastly plight—

Union General George B. McClellan

Does the elm wood
Recall the haggard beards of blood?

The battle-smoked flag, with stars eclipsed,
    We followed (it never fell!)—
In silence husbanded our strength—
    Received their yell;
Till on this slope we patient turned
    With cannon ordered well;
Reverse we proved was not defeat;
But ah, the sod what thousands meet!—
    Does Malvern Wood
Bethink itself, and muse and brood?

We elms of Malvern Hill
    Remember every thing;
But sap the twig will fill:
Wag the world how it will,
    Leaves must be green in Spring.

Part of the Chickamauga battlefield

At Chickamauga Creek in September 1863, just South of Chattanooga, a Confederate force under Braxton Bragg defeated the Federals under General William Rosecrans in one of the hottest battles of the war. Killed and wounded on both sides totaled about 35,000. The Federals withdrew into Chattanooga, but the Confederates were in no position to exploit their "victory." Melville's point, frequently made in his poetry, is that the dead in battle have no idea how it all came out.

HERMAN MELVILLE (1819–1891) ⬿

Memorial on the Slain at Chickamauga

Happy are they and charmed in life
   Who through long wars arrive unscarred
At peace. To such the wreath be given,
If they unfalteringly have striven—
   In honor, as in limb, unmarred.
Let cheerful praise be rife,
   And let them live their years at ease,
Musing on brothers who victorious died—
   Loved mates whose memory shall ever please.

And yet mischance is honorable too—
   Seeming defeat in conflict justified
Whose end to closing eyes is hid from view.
The will, that never can relent—
The aim, survivor of the bafflement,
   Make this memorial due.

WALT WHITMAN (1819–1892) ❧

To a Certain Civilian

Did you ask dulcet rhymes from me?
Did you seek the civilian's peaceful and languishing rhymes?
Did you find what I sang erewhile so hard to follow?
Why I was not singing erewhile for you to follow, to understand—nor am I now;
(I have been born of the same as the war was born,
The drum-corps' rattle is ever to me sweet music, I love well the martial dirge,
With slow wail and convulsive throb leading the officer's funeral;)
What to such as you anyhow such a poet as I? therefore leave my works,
And go lull yourself with what you can understand, and with piano-tunes,
For I lull nobody, and you will never understand me.

When the war ended, many who had endured it realized that it had been an experience whose drama would never be repeated in their lives. Whitman's poem reflects a common nostalgia for the terrifying years of conflict.

WALT WHITMAN (1819–1892)

Spirit Whose Work Is Done

(Washington City, 1865)

Spirit whose work is done—spirit of dreadful hours!
Ere departing fade from my eyes your forests of bayonets;
Spirit of gloomiest fears and doubts, (yet onward ever unfaltering pressing,)
Spirit of many a solemn day and many a savage scene—electric spirit,
That with muttering voice through the war now closed, like a tireless phantom flitted,
Rousing the land with breath of flame, while you beat and beat the drum,
Now as the sound of the drum, hollow and harsh to the last, reverberates round me,
As your ranks, your immortal ranks, return, return from the battles,
As the muskets of the young men yet lean over their shoulders,
As I look on the bayonets bristling over their shoulders,
As those slanted bayonets, whole forests of them appearing in the distance, approach and
 pass on, returning homeward,
Moving with steady motion, swaying to and fro to the right and left,
Evenly lightly rising and falling while the steps keep time;
Spirit of hours I knew, all hectic red one day, but pale as death next day,
Touch my mouth ere you depart, press my lips close,
Leave me your pulses of rage—beneath them to me—fill me with currents convulsive,
Let them scorch and blister out of my chants when you are gone,
Let them identify you to the future in these songs.

JOHN REUBEN THOMPSON (1823–1873)

Music in Camp

It is hard to say whether Thompson's poem is about a real event. At Christmas in 1914 German and English troops joined in singing Christmas carols across the trenches, and music has always been a great connector. "Home Sweet Home" was one of the most popular songs in the war. In the dark winter of 1862–1863, after Federal forces were slaughtered at Fredericksburg, the song was forbidden in the Army of the Potomac lest it lower morale.

Two armies covered hill and plain,
   Where Rappahannock's waters
Ran deeply crimsoned with the stain
   Of battle's recent slaughters.

The summer clouds lay pitched like tents
   In meads of heavenly azure;
And each dread gun of the elements
   Slept in its high embrasure.

The breeze so softly blew, it made
   No forest leaf to quiver;
And the smoke of the random cannonade
   Rolled slowly from the river.

And now, where circling hills looked down
   With cannon grimly planted,
O'er listless camp and silent town
   The golden sunset slanted.

Band, 4th Michigan Infantry

When on the fervid air there came
    A strain, now rich, now tender,
The music seemed itself aflame
    With day's departing splendor.

A Federal band, which eve and morn
    Played measures brave and nimble,
Had just struck up, with flute and horn
    And lively clash of cymbal.

Down flocked the soldiers to the banks;
    Till, margined by its pebbles,
One wooded shore was blue with "Yanks,"
    And one was gray with "Rebels."

Then all was still; and then the band,
    With movement light and tricksy,
Made stream and forest, hill and strand,
    Reverberate with "Dixie."

The conscious stream, with burnished glow,
    Went proudly o'er its pebbles,
But thrilled throughout its deepest flow
    With yelling of the Rebels.

Again a pause; and then again
    The trumpet pealed, sonorous,
And "Yankee Doodle" was the strain
    To which the shore gave chorus.

The laughing ripple shoreward flew
    To kiss the shining pebbles;
Loud shrieked the swarming Boys in Blue
    Defiance to the Rebels.

And yet once more the bugle sang
    Above the stormy riot;
No shout upon the evening rang,—
    There reigned a holy quiet.

The sad, slow stream its noiseless flood
    Poured o'er the glistening pebbles;
All silent now the Yankees stood,
    All silent stood the Rebels.

No unresponsive soul had heard
    That plaintive note's appealing,
So deeply "Home, Sweet Home" had stirred
    The hidden founts of feeling.

Or Blue, or Gray, the soldier sees,
    As by the wand of fairy,
The cottage 'neath the live oak trees,
    The cabin by the prairie.

Or cold, or warm, his native skies
    Bend in their beauty o'er him;
Seen through the tear-mist in his eyes,
    His loved ones stand before him.

As fades the iris after rain
In April's tearful weather,
The vision vanished as the strain
And daylight died together.

But Memory, waked by Music's art,
Expressed in simple numbers,
Subdued the sternest Yankee's heart,
Made light the Rebel's slumbers.

And fair the form of Music shines, —
That bright celestial creature, —
Who still 'mid War's embattled lines
Gave this one touch of Nature.

CAROLINE AUGUSTA BALL (b. 1825)

The Jacket of Gray

Fold it up carefully, lay it aside;
Tenderly touch it, look on it with pride;
For dear to our hearts must it be evermore,
The jacket of gray our loved soldier-boy wore.

Can we ever forget when he joined the brave band
That rose in defense of our dear Southern land,
And in his bright youth hurried on to the fray,
How proudly he donned it—the jacket of gray?

His fond mother blessed him and looked up above,
Commending to Heaven the child of her love;
What anguish was her's mortal tongue cannot say,
When he passed from her sight in the jacket of gray.

But her country had called and she would not repine,
Though costly the sacrifice placed on its shrine;
Her heart's dearest hopes on its altar she lay,
When she sent out her boy in the jacket of gray.

Dead Confederate soldier in the trenches, April 3, 1865, Petersburg, Virginia

Months passed, and war's thunders rolled over the land,
Unsheathed was the sword, and lighted the brand;
We heard in the distance the sounds of the fray,
And prayed for our boy in the jacket of gray.

Ah vain, all in vain, were our prayers and our tears,
The glad shout of victory rang in our ears;
But our treasured one on the red battle-field lay,
While the life-blood oozed out of the jacket of gray.

His young comrades found him, and tenderly bore
The cold lifeless form to his home by the shore;
Oh, dark were our hearts on that terrible day,
When we saw our dead boy in the jacket of gray.

Ah! spotted and tattered, and stained now with gore,
Was the garment which once he so proudly wore;
We bitterly wept as we took it away,
And replaced with death's white robes the jacket of gray.

We laid him to rest in his cold narrow bed,
And graved on the marble we placed o'er his head
As the proudest tribute our sad hearts could pay—
"He never disgraced it, the jacket of gray."

Then fold it up carefully, lay it aside,
Tenderly touch it, look on it with pride;
For dear must it be to our hearts evermore,
The jacket of gray our loved soldier-boy wore!

BAYARD TAYLOR (1825–1878) 🖎

Gettysburg Ode

(Dedication of the National Monument, July 1, 1869)

Taylor sets Lincoln's "Gettysburg
Address" to rhyme, an act
approximate to setting Beethoven's
Ninth to music. Yet this
sentimental poem has a strange
power. Everything is here—the
loss of young men in their prime,
the faith that their sacrifice could
not have been in vain, the gratitude
for the nation that is a communion,
a breaking of bread with the dead.
There is also the nineteenth-century
conviction that progress comes by a
dialectic, faith against doubt,
freedom against oppression, law
from discord. The poem is a
determined resolve to make
meaning out of the most chaotic
experience in our history.

I   After the eyes that looked, the lips that spake

Here, from the shadows of impending death,

    Those words of solemn breath,

    What voice may fitly break

The silence, doubly hallowed, left by him?

We can but bow the head, with eyes grown dim,

    And, as a Nation's litany, repeat

The phrase his martyrdom hath made complete,

Noble as then, but now more sadly-sweet:

"Let us, the Living, rather dedicate

Ourselves to the unfinished work, which they

Thus far advanced so nobly on its way,

    And save the perilled State!

Let us, upon this field where they, the brave,

Their last full measure of devotion gave,

Highly resolve they have not died in vain! —

That, under God, the Nation's later birth

    Of freedom, and the people's gain

Of their own Sovereignty, shall never wane

And perish from the circle of the earth!"
From such a perfect text, shall Song aspire
    To light her faded fire,
    And into wandering music turn
Its virtue, simple, sorrowful, and stern?
His voice all elegies anticipated;
      For, whatsoe'er the strain,
      We hear that one refrain:
"We consecrate ourselves to them, the Consecrated!"

II   After the thunder-storm our heaven is blue:
    Far-off, along the borders of the sky,
    In silver folds the clouds of battle lie,
With soft, consoling sunlight shining through;
And round the sweeping circle of your hills
      The crashing cannon-thrills
Have faded from the memory of the air;
And Summer pours from unexhausted fountains
      Her bliss on yonder mountains:
The camps are tenantless, the breastworks bare:
Earth keeps no stain where hero-blood was poured:
    The hornets, humming on their wings of lead,
    Have ceased to sting, their angry swarms are dead,
And, harmless in its scabbard, rusts the sword!

III   O, not till now,—O, now we dare, at last,
    To give our heroes fitting consecration!
Not till the soreness of the strife is past,
    And Peace hath comforted the weary Nation!
So long her sad, indignant spirit held
One keen regret, one throb of pain, unquelled;

So long the land about her feet was waste,

    The ashes of the burning lay upon her,

We stood beside their graves with brows abased,

    Waiting the purer mood to do them honor!

They, through the flames of this dread holocaust,

The patriot's wrath, the soldier's ardor, lost:

They sit above us and above our passion,

    Disparaged even by our human tears, —

Beholding truth our race, perchance, may fashion

    In the slow process of the creeping years.

We saw the still reproof upon their faces;

We heard them whisper from the shining spaces:

"To-day ye grieve: come not to us with sorrow!

    Wait for the glad, the reconciled To-morrow!

Your grief but clouds the ether where we dwell;

    Your anger keeps your souls and ours apart:

But come with peace and pardon, all is well!

    And come with love, we touch you, heart to heart!"

IV   Immortal Brothers, we have heard!

Our lips declare the reconciling word:

For Battle taught, that set us face to face,

    The stubborn temper of the race,

And both, from fields no longer alien, come,

    To grander action equally invited, —

Marshalled by Learning's trump, by Labor's drum,

    In strife that purifies and makes united!

We force to build, the powers that would destroy;

The muscles, hardened by the sabre's grasp,

    Now give our hands a firmer clasp:

We bring not grief to you, but solemn joy!

And, feeling you so near;
Look forward with your eyes, divinely clear,
To some sublimely-perfect, sacred year,
When sons of fathers whom ye overcame
Forget in mutual pride the partial blame,
And join with us, to set the final crown
Upon your dear renown,—
The People's Union in heart and name!

V   And yet, ye Dead!—and yet
Our clouded natures cling to our regret:
We are not all resigned
To yield, with even mind,
Our scarcely-risen stars, that here untimely set.
We needs must think of History that waits
For lines that live but in their proud beginning,—
Arrested promises and cheated fates,—
Youth's boundless venture and its single winning!
We see the ghosts of deeds they might have done,
The phantom homes that beaconed their endeavor;
The seeds of countless lives, in them begun,
That might have multiplied for us forever!
We grudge the better strain of men
That proved itself, and was extinguished then—
The field, with strength and hope so thickly sown,
Wherefrom no other harvest shall be mown:
For all the land, within its clasping seas,
Is poorer now in bravery and beauty,
Such wealth of manly loves and energies
Was given to teach us all the freeman's sacred duty!

VI   Again 't is they, the Dead,
     By whom our hearts are comforted.
Deep as the land-blown murmurs of the waves
The answer cometh from a thousand graves:
    "Not so! we are not orphaned of our fate!
Though life were warmest, and though love were sweetest,
We still have portion in their best estate:
    Our fortune is the fairest and completest!
Our homes are everywhere: our loves are set
    In hearts of man and woman, sweet and vernal:
Courage and Truth, the children we beget,
    Unmixed of baser earth, shall be eternal.
A finer spirit in the blood shall give
The token of the lines wherein we live, —
Unselfish force, unconscious nobleness
    That in the shocks of fortune stands unshaken, —
The hopes that in their very being bless,
    The aspirations that to deeds awaken!
If aught of finer virtue ye allow
    To us, that faith alone its like shall win you;
So, trust like ours shall ever lift the brow;
    And strength like ours shall ever steel the sinew!
We are the blossoms which the storm has cast
    From the Spring promise of our Freedom's tree,
Pruning its overgrowths, that so, at last,
    Its later fruit more bountiful shall be! —
Content, if, when the balm of Time assuages
The branch's hurt, some fragrance of our lives
      In all the land survives,
And makes their memory sweet through still expanding ages!"

VII   Thus grandly, they we mourn, themselves console us;
And, as their spirits conquer and control us,
We hear, from some high realm that lies beyond,
The hero-voices of the Past respond.
From every State that reached a broader right
Through fiery gates of battle; from the shock
Of old invasions on the People's rock;
From tribes that stood, in Kings' and Priests' despite;
From graves, forgotten in the Syrian sand,
Or nameless barrows of the Northern strand,
Or gorges of the Alps and Pyrenees,
Or the dark bowels of devouring seas, —
Wherever Man for Man's sake died, — wherever
Death stayed the march of upward-climbing feet,
   Leaving their Present incomplete,
But through far Futures crowning their endeavor, —
Their ghostly voices to our ears are sent,
As when the high note of a trumpet wrings
   Æolian answers from the strings
Of many a mute, unfingered instrument!
Platæan cymbals thrill for us to-day;
The horns of Sempach in our echoes play,
And nearer yet, and sharper, and more stern,
The slogan rings that startled Bannockburn;
Till from the field, made green with kindred deed,
   The shields are clashed in exultation
     Above the dauntless Nation,
That for a Continent has fought its Runnymede!

VIII   Aye, for a Continent! The heart that beats
>With such rich blood of sacrifice
Shall, from the Tropics, drowsed with languid heats,
>To the blue ramparts of the Northern ice,
Make felt its pulses, all this young world over! —
>Shall thrill, and shake, and sway
Each land that bourgeons in the Western day,
Whatever flag may float, whatever shield may cover!
With fuller manhood every wind is rife,
>In every soil are sown the seeds of valor,
Since out of death came forth such boundless life,
>Such ruddy beauty out of anguished pallor!
>And that first deed, along the Southern wave,
>Spoiled not the sister-land, but lent an arm to save!

IX   Now, in her seat secure,
Where distant menaces no more can reach her,
>Our land, in undivided freedom pure,
Becomes the unwilling world's unconscious teacher;
And, day by day, beneath serener skies,
The unshaken pillars of her palace rise, —
The Doric shafts, that lightly upward press,
And hide in grace their giant massiveness.
What though the sword has hewn each corner-stone,
>And precious blood cements the deep foundation!
Never by other force have empires grown;
>From other basis never rose a nation!
For strength is born of struggle, faith of doubt,
>Of discord law, and freedom of oppression:
We hail from Pisgah, with exulting shout,

The Promised Land below us, bright with sun,
        And deem its pastures won,
Ere toil and blood have earned us their possession!
Each aspiration of our human earth
Becomes an act through keenest pangs of birth;
Each force, to bless, must cease to be a dream
And conquer life through agony supreme;
Each inborn right must outwardly be tested
        By stern material weapons, ere it stand
        In the enduring fabric of the land,
Secured for these who yielded it, and those who wrested!

X   This they have done for us who slumber here, —
        Awake, alive, though now so dumbly sleeping;
Spreading the board, but tasting not its cheer,
        Sowing, but never reaping; —
Building, but never sitting in the shade
Of the strong mansion they have made; —
Speaking their word of life with mighty tongue,
But hearing not the echo, million-voiced,
        Of brothers who rejoiced,
From all our river vales and mountains flung!
So take them, Heroes of the songful Past!
Open your ranks, let every shining troop
        Its phantom banners droop,
To hail Earth's noblest martyrs, and her last!
        Take them, O Fatherland!
    Who, dying, conquered in thy name;
        And, with a grateful hand,
Inscribe their deed who took away thy blame, —

Give, for their grandest all, thine insufficient fame!
        Take them, O God! our Brave,
    The glad fulfillers of Thy dread decree;
    Who grasped the sword for Peace, and smote to save,
And, dying here for Freedom, also died for Thee!

One of the most famous poems to come after the war, published about 1867. The nation quickly re-establishes itself.

FRANCIS MILES FINCH (1827–1907) ❦

The Blue and the Gray
(1867)

By the flow of the inland river,
　Whence the fleets of iron have fled,
Where the blades of the grave-grass quiver,
　Asleep are the ranks of the dead:
　　Under the sod and the dew,
　　　Waiting the Judgment Day:
　　Under the one, the Blue,
　　　Under the other, the Gray.

These in the robings of glory,
　Those in the gloom of defeat,
All with the battle-blood gory,
　In the dusk of eternity meet:
　　Under the sod and the dew,
　　　Waiting the Judgment Day:
　　Under the laurel, the Blue,
　　　Under the willow, the Gray.

From the silence of sorrowful hours
   The desolate mourners go,
Lovingly laden with flowers
   Alike for the friend and the foe:
      Under the sod and the dew,
         Waiting the Judgment Day:
      Under the roses, the Blue,
         Under the lilies, the Gray.

So with an equal splendor,
   The morning sunrays fall,
With a touch impartially tender,
   On the blossoms blooming for all:
      Under the sod and the dew,
         Waiting the Judgment Day:
      Broidered with gold, the Blue,
         Mellowed with gold, the Gray.

So, when the summer calleth,
   On forest and field of grain,
With an equal murmur falleth
   The cooling drip of the rain:
      Under the sod and the dew,
         Waiting the Judgment Day:
      Wet with the rain, the Blue,
         Wet with the rain, the Gray.

Sadly, but not with upbraiding,
   The generous deed was done,
In the storm of the years that are fading
   No braver battle was won:

Under the sod and the dew,
   Waiting the Judgment Day:
Under the blossoms, the Blue,
   Under the garlands, the Gray.

No more shall the war-cry sever,
   Or the winding rivers be red;
They banish our anger forever
   When they laurel the graves of our dead!
Under the sod and the dew,
   Waiting the Judgment Day:
Love and tears for the Blue,
   Tears and love for the Gray.

PATRICK SARSFIELD GILMORE (1829–1892) ❧

When Johnny Comes Marching Home

A popular poem set to rousing music and enduring as a camp song into the twentieth century. The poem/song takes no sides. Johnny is probably a Union soldier since he is marching home in triumph, but he could easily be a Confederate.

When Johnny comes marching home again,
  Hurrah! hurrah!
We'll give him a hearty welcome then,
  Hurrah! hurrah!
The men will cheer, the boys will shout,
The ladies, they will all turn out,
  And we'll all feel gay,
When Johnny comes marching home.

The old church-bell will peal with joy,
  Hurrah! hurrah!
To welcome home our darling boy,
  Hurrah! hurrah!
The village lads and lasses say,
With roses they will strew the way;
  And we'll all feel gay,
When Johnny comes marching home.

Union infantry private on post

Get ready for the jubilee,
   Hurrah! hurrah!
We'll give the hero three times three,
   Hurrah! hurrah!
The laurel-wreath is ready now
To place upon his loyal brow,
   And we'll all feel gay,
When Johnny comes marching home.

Let love and friendship on that day,
   Hurrah! hurrah!
Their choicest treasures then display,
   Hurrah! hurrah!
And let each one perform some part,
To fill with joy the warrior's heart;
   And we'll all feel gay,
When Johnny comes marching home.

HENRY TIMROD (1829–1867)

Ode

(Sung on the occasion of decorating the graves of the Confederate dead, at Magnolia Cemetery, Charleston, South Carolina, 1867)

Sleep sweetly in your humble graves,
　　Sleep, martyrs of a fallen cause;
Though yet no marble column craves
　　The pilgrim here to pause.

In seeds of laurel in the earth
　　The blossom of your fame is blown,
And somewhere, waiting for its birth,
　　The shaft is in the stone!

Meanwhile, behalf the tardy years
　　Which keep in trust your storied tombs,
Behold! your sisters bring their tears,
　　And these memorial blooms.

Small tributes! but your shades will smile
　　More proudly on these wreaths to-day,
Than when some cannon-moulded pile
　　Shall overlook this bay.

Stoop, angels, hither from the skies,
There is no holier spot of ground
Than where defeated valor lies,
By mourning beauty crowned.

The unreconstructed Rebel,
defiant to the end. He hates the
Declaration of Independence
because it asserts the equality of all
men. The use of dialect allows us
to think that part of the spirit of this
poem is boffo humor rather than
serious hatred, but it is hard to tell.

INNES RANDOLPH (1837–1887)

The Rebel

Oh, I'm a good old Rebel,
   Now that's just what I am;
For this "fair Land of Freedom"
I do not care a dam.
I'm glad I fit against it —
   I only wish we'd won,
And I don't want no pardon
   For anything I've done.

I hates the Constitution,
   This great Republic, too;
I hates the Freedmen's Buro,
   In uniforms of blue.
I hates the nasty eagle,
   With all his brag and fuss;
The lyin', thievin' Yankees,
   I hates 'em wuss and wuss.

Edmund Ruffin, private in the Confederate Army, fired the first shot at Fort Sumter

I hate the Yankee Nation
  And everything they do;
I hate the Declaration
  Of Independence, too.
I hates the glorious Union,
  'Tis dripping with our blood;
I hates the striped banner—
  I fit it all I could.

I followed old Mars' Robert
  For four year, near about,
Got wounded in three places,
  And starved at Pint Lookout.
I cotch the roomatism
  A-campin' in the snow,
But I killed a chance of Yankees—
  I'd like to kill some mo'.

Three hundred thousand Yankees
  Is stiff in Southern dust;
We got three hundred thousand
  Before they conquered us.
They died of Southern fever
  And Southern steel and shot;
I wish it was three millions
  Instead of what we got.

I can't take up my musket
  And fight 'em now no more,
But I ain't agoin' to love 'em,
  Now that is sartin sure.

And I don't want no pardon
For what I was and am;
I won't be reconstructed,
And I don't care a dam.

KATE PUTNAM OSGOOD (1841–1910) ❦

Driving Home the Cows

Out of the clover and blue-eyed grass,
 He turned them into the river-lane;
One after another he let them pass,
 Then fastened the meadow bars again.

Under the willows, and over the hill,
 He patiently followed their sober pace;
The merry whistle for once was still,
 And something shadowed the sunny face.

Only a boy! and his father had said
 He never could let his youngest go;
Two already were lying dead
 Under the feet of the trampling foe.

But after the evening work was done,
 And the frogs were loud in the meadow swamp,
Over his shoulder he slung his gun,
 And stealthily followed the footpath damp.

Across the clover and through the wheat,
  With resolute heart and purpose grim,
Though cold was the dew on his hurrying feet,
  And the blind bat's flitting startled him.

Thrice since then had the lanes been white,
  And the orchards sweet with apple-bloom;
And now when the cows came back at night,
  The feeble father drove them home.

For news had come to the lonely farm
  That three were lying where two had lain;
And the old man's tremulous, palsied arm
  Could never lean on a son's again.

The summer day grew cold and late,
  He went for the cows when the work was done;
But down the lane, as he opened the gate,
  He saw them coming, one by one, —

Brindle, Ebony, Speckle, and Bess,
  Shaking their horns in the evening wind;
Cropping the buttercups out of the grass, —
  But who was it following close behind?

Loosely swung in the idle air
  The empty sleeve of army blue;
And worn and pale from the crisping hair
  Looked out a face that the father knew.

For the Southern prisons will sometimes yawn,
    And yield their dead unto life again;
And the day that comes with a cloudy dawn
    In golden glory at last may wane.

The great tears sprang to their meeting eyes;
    For the heart must speak when the lips are dumb;
And under the silent evening skies,
    Together they followed the cattle home.

AMBROSE BIERCE (1842–1914?) 🖋

To E. S. Salomon

Who in a Memorial Day oration protested bitterly
against decorating the graves of Confederate dead

Ambrose Bierce enlisted in the
Union Army when he was 18. He
was a talented field mapmaker,
performing under fire an invaluable
service for officers charged with
moving troops in territory they did
not know. He was severely
wounded in the fighting for
Atlanta. Few writers saw better
the ironies and stupidities of the
war, and few had his devastating
wit. This poem illustrates the
kinship soldiers on both sides had
for each other against civilians who
wanted to continue hatreds when
the war was over.

What! Salomon! such words from you,
   Who call yourself a soldier? Well,
   The Southern brother where he fell
Slept all your base oration through.

Alike to him—he cannot know
   Your praise or blame: as little harm
   Your tongue can do him as your arm
A quarter-century ago.

The brave respect the brave. The brave
   Respect the dead; but *you*—you draw
   That ancient blade, the ass's jaw,
And shake it o'er a hero's grave.

Are you not he who makes to-day
   A merchandise of old renown
   Which he persuades this easy town
He won in battle far away?

Nay, those the fallen who revile
   Have ne'er before the living stood
   And stoutly made their battle good
And greeted danger with a smile.

What if the dead whom still you hate
   Were wrong? Are you so surely right?
   We know the issues of the fight—
The sword is but an advocate.

Men live and die, and other men
   Arise with knowledges diverse:
   What seemed a blessing seems a curse,
And Now is still at odds with Then.

The years go on, the old comes back
   To mock the new—beneath the sun
   Is *nothing* new; ideas run
Recurrent in an endless track.

What most we censure, men as wise
   Have reverently practised; nor
   Will future wisdom fail to war
On principles we dearly prize.

We do not know—we can but deem,
   And he is loyalest and best
   Who takes the light full on his breast
And follows it throughout the dream.

The broken light, the shadows wide—
   Behold the battle-field displayed!
   God save the vanquished from the blade,
The victor from the victor's pride!

If, Salomon, the blessed dew
   That falls upon the Blue and Gray
   Is powerless to wash away
The sin of differing from you,

Remember how the flood of years
   Has rolled across the erring slain;
   Remember, too, the cleansing rain
Of widows' and of orphans' tears.

The dead are dead—let that atone:
   And though with equal hand we strew
   The blooms on saint and sinner too,
Yet God will know to choose his own.

The wretch, whate'er his life and lot,
   Who does not love the harmless dead
   With all his heart and all his head—
May God forgive him, *I* shall not.

When, Salomon, you come to quaff
   The Darker Cup with meeker face,
   I, loving you at last, shall trace
Upon your tomb this epitaph:

"Draw near, ye generous and brave—
    Kneel round this monument and weep
    For one who tried in vain to keep
A flower from a soldier's grave."

AMBROSE BIERCE (1842–1914?)

The Confederate Flags

The poet somewhat humorously pleads for the return of Confederate battle flags taken by Northern armies. Flags marked the location of units on battlefields amid the smoke and noise, and to capture one was considered a great feat, to lose one a great shame.

Tut-tut! give back the flags—how can you care,
    You veterans and heroes?
Why should you at a kind intention swear
    Like twenty Neros?

Suppose the act was not so overwise—
    Suppose it was illegal;
Is't well on such a question to arise
    And pinch the Eagle?

Nay, let's economize his breath to scold
    And terrify the alien
Who tackles him, as Hercules of old
    The bird Stymphalian.

Among the rebels when we made a breach
    Was it to get their banners?
That was but incidental—'twas to teach
    Them better manners.

They know the lesson well enough to-day;
    Now, let us try to show them
That we're not only stronger far than they,
    (How we did mow them!)

But more magnanimous. My lads, 'tis plain
    'Twas an uncommon riot;
The warlike tribes of Europe fight for gain;
    We fought for quiet.

If we were victors, then we all must live
    With the same flag above us;
'Twas all in vain unless we now forgive
    And make them love us.

Let kings keep trophies to display above
    Their doors like any savage;
The freeman's trophy is the foeman's love,
    Despite war's ravage.

"Make treason odious?" My friends, you'll find
    You can't, in right and reason,
While "Washington" and "treason" are combined—
    "Hugo" and "treason."

All human governments must take the chance
    And hazard of sedition.
O wretch! to pledge your manhood in advance
    To blind submission.

It may be wrong, it may be right, to rise
    In warlike insurrection:
The loyalty that fools so dearly prize
    May mean subjection.

Be loyal to your country, yes—but how
    If tyrants hold dominion?
The South believed they did; can't you allow
    For that opinion?

He who will never rise though rulers plot,
    His liberties despising—
How is he manlier than the *sans-culottes*
    Who's always rising?

Give back the foolish flags whose bearers fell,
    Too valiant to forsake them.
Is it presumptuous, this counsel? Well,
    I helped to take them.

Bierce recognizes the irony of a
war fought to free the slaves that
results in efforts to prevent the freed
men from gaining political rights.
A sadness lurks beneath these
lines. What was the war about?

AMBROSE BIERCE (1842–1914?) ❧

The Hesitating Veteran

When I was young and full of faith
    And other fads that youngsters cherish
A cry rose as of one that saith
    With emphasis: "Help or I perish!"
'Twas heard in all the land, and men
    The sound were each to each repeating.
It made my heart beat faster then
    Than any heart can now be beating.

For the world is old and world is gray—
    Grown prudent and, I think, more witty.
She's cut her wisdom teeth, they say,
    And doesn't now go in for Pity.
Besides, the melancholy cry
    Was that of one, 'tis now conceded,
Whose plight no one beneath the sky
    Felt half so poignantly as he did.

Moreover, he was black. And yet
    That sentimental generation
With an austere compassion set
    Its face and faith to the occasion.
Then there were hate and strife to spare,
    And various hard knocks a-plenty;
And I ('twas more than my true share,
    I must confess) took five-and-twenty.

That all is over now—the reign
    Of love and trade stills all dissensions,
And the clear heavens arch again
    Above a land of peace and pensions.
The black chap—at the last we gave
    Him everything that he had cried for,
Though many white chaps in the grave
    'Twould puzzle to say what they died for.

I hope he's better off—I trust
    That his society and his master's
Are worth the price we paid, and must
    Continue paying, in disasters;
But sometimes doubts press thronging round
    ('Tis mostly when my hurts are aching)
If war for Union was a sound
    And profitable undertaking.

'Tis said they mean to take away
    The Negro's vote for he's unlettered.
'Tis true he sits in darkness day
    And night, as formerly, when fettered;

But pray observe—howe'er he vote
    To whatsoever party turning,
He'll be with gentlemen of note
    And wealth and consequence and learning.

With saints and sages on each side,
    How could a fool through lack of knowledge,
Vote wrong? If learning is no guide
    Why ought one to have been in college?
O Son of Day, O Son of Night!
    What are your preferences made of?
I know not which of you is right,
    Nor which to be the more afraid of.

The world is old and the world is bad,
    And creaks and grinds upon its axis;
And man's an ape and the gods are mad!—
    There's nothing sure, not even our taxes.
No mortal man can Truth restore,
    Or say where she is to be sought for.
I know what uniform I wore—
    O, that I knew which side I fought for!

AMBROSE BIERCE (1842–1914?) 🪶

The Death of Grant

Grant died painfully of throat cancer in the summer of 1885, having just finished his memoirs in an effort to leave his family enough money to live on. Bierce praises Grant for his magnanimity but expresses doubt in the ultimate purpose of the war that Grant led.

Father! whose hard and cruel law
   Is part of thy compassion's plan,
   Thy works presumptuously we scan
For what the prophets say they saw.

Unbidden still the awful slope
   Walling us in we climb to gain
   Assurance of the shining plain
That faith has certified to hope.

In vain! — beyond the circling hill
   The shadow and the cloud abide.
   Subdue the doubt, our spirits guide
To trust the record and be still.

To trust it loyally as he
   Who, heedful of his high design,
   Ne'er raised a seeking eye to thine,
But wrought thy will unconsciously,

Disputing not of chance or fate,
    Nor questioning of cause or creed;
    For anything but duty's deed
Too simply wise, too humbly great.

The cannon syllabled his name;
    His shadow shifted o'er the land,
    Portentous, as at his demand
Successive bastions sprang to flame!

He flared the continent with fire,
    The rivers ran in lines of light!
    Thy will be done on earth—if right
Or wrong he cared not to inquire.

His was the heavy hand, and his
    The service of the despot blade;
    His the soft answer that allayed
War's giant animosities.

Let us have peace: our clouded eyes,
    Fill, Father, with another light,
    That we may see with clearer sight
Thy servant's soul in Paradise.

AMBROSE BIERCE (1842–1914?) 🖋

General B. F. Butler

Butler was an unsuccessful political general, often ridiculed, but a man of some shrewd perceptions. He commanded Federal troops in New Orleans with an iron rule that made citizens confer on him the name "Beast Butler." After the war he became a radical Republican. Many people hated him. He died in 1891.

Thy flesh to earth, thy soul to God,
    We gave, O gallant brother;
And o'er thy grave the awkward squad
    Fired into one another!

*A poem of reconciliation, showing
again the kinship felt by men on
both sides who had fought in the
war and their common scorn for
civilians who tried to carry on
hatreds the soldiers thought the war
should have buried. Note, too, the
somewhat vague sense of divine
Providence here, that the war
turned out for the best.*

MAURICE THOMPSON (1844–1901) ❧

An Address by an Ex-Confederate Soldier to the Grand Army of the Republic

I   I was a rebel, if you please,
      A reckless fighter to the last,
    Nor do I fall upon my knees
      And ask forgiveness for the past.

A traitor? *I* a traitor? No!
      I was a patriot to the core;
The South was mine, I loved her so,
      I gave her all, — I could no more.

You scowl at me. And was it wrong
      To wear the gray my father wore?
Could I slink back, though young and strong,
      From foes before my mother's door?

My mother's kiss was hot with fight,
      My father's frenzy filled his son,
Through reeking day and sodden night
      My sister's courage urged me on.

And I, a missile steeped in hate,
   Hurled forward like a cannon-ball
By the resistless hand of fate,
   Rushed wildly, madly through it all.

I stemmed the level flames of hell,
   O'er bayonet bars of death I broke,
I was so near when Cleburne fell,
   I heard the muffled bullet stroke!

But all in vain. In dull despair
   I saw the storm of conflict die;
Low lay the Southern banner fair,
   And yonder flag was waving high.

God, what a triumph had the foe!
   Laurels, arches, trumpet-blare;
All around the earth their songs did go,
   Thundering through heaven their shouts did tear.

My mother, gray and bent with years,
   Hoarding love's withered aftermath,
Her sweet eyes burnt too dry for tears,
   Sat in the dust of Sherman's path.

My father, broken, helpless, poor,
   A gloomy, nerveless giant stood,
Too strong to cower and endure,
   Too weak to fight for masterhood.

My boyhood's home, a blackened heap
    Where lizards crawled and briers grew,
Had felt the fire of vengeance creep,
    The crashing round-shot hurtle through.

I had no country, all was lost,
    I closed my eyes and longed to die,
While past me stalked the awful ghost
    Of mangled, murdered Liberty.

The scars upon my body burned,
    I felt a heel upon my throat,
A heel that ground and grinding turned
    With each triumphal trumpet note.

"Grind on!" I cried, "nor doubt that I,
    (If all your necks were one and low
As mine is now) delightedly
    Would cut it by a single blow!"

II   That was dark night; but day is here,
    The crowning victory is won;
Hark, how the sixty millions cheer,
    With Freedom's flag across the sun!

I a traitor! Who are *you*
    That dare to breathe that word to me?
You never wore the Union blue,
    No wounds attest *your* loyalty!

I do detest the sutler's clerk,
  Who skulked and dodged till peace had come,
Then found it most congenial work
  To beat the politician's drum.

I clasp the hand that made my scars,
  I cheer the flag my foemen bore,
I shout for joy to see the stars
  All on our common shield once more.

I do not cringe before you now,
  Or lay my face upon the ground;
I am a man, of men a peer,
  And not a cowering, cudgeled hound!

I stand and say that you were right,
  I greet you with uncovered head,
Remembering many a thundering fight,
  Where whistling death between us sped.

Remembering the boys in gray,
  With thoughts too deep and fine for words,
I lift this cup of love to-day
  To drink what only love affords.

Soldiers in blue, a health to you!
  Long life and vigor oft renewed,
While on your hearts, like honey-dew,
  Falls our great country's gratitude.

MAURICE THOMPSON (1844–1901) ✌

To the South

O subtle, musky, slumbrous clime!
  O swart, hot land of pine and palm,
Of fig, peach, guava, orange, lime,
  And terebinth and tropic balm!
Land where our Washington was born,
When truth in hearts of gold was worn;
Mother of Marion, Moultrie, Lee,
Widow of fallen chivalry!
No longer sadly look behind,
But turn and face the morning wind,
And feel sweet comfort in the thought:
  *"With each fierce battle's sacrifice
  I sold the wrong at awful price,
And bought the good; but knew it not."*

Cheer up! Reach out! Breathe in new life!
Brood not on unsuccessful strife
Against the current of the age;
The Highest is thy heritage!

Leave off this death's-head scowl at Fate,
And into thy true heart sink this:
"God loves to walk where Freedom is!"

There is no sweet in dregs and lees;
There is no fruit on girdled trees.
Plant new vineyards, sow new fields,
For bread and wine the Future yields;
Out of free soil fresh spathes shall start;
Now is the budding-time of Art!

But hark! O hear! My senses reel!
Some grand presentiment I feel!
A voice of love, bouquet of truth,
The quick sound of the feet of youth!

Lo! from the war-cloud, dull and dense,
  Loyal and chaste and brave and strong,
Comes forth the South with frankincense,
  And vital freshness in her song.
The weight is fallen from her wings;
To find a purer air she springs
Out of the Night into the Morn,
Fair as cotton, sound as corn.

Hold! Shall a Northman, fierce and grim,
With hoary beard and boreal vim,
Thus fling, from some bleak waste of ice,
Frost-crystals of unsought advice
  To those who dwell by Coosa's stream,
Or on dark hummocks plant the cane

Beside the lovely Pontchartrain,
    Or in gay sail-boats drift and dream
Where Caribbean breezes stray
On Pensacola's drowsy bay?

Not so! I am a Southerner;
I love the South; I dared for her
To fight from Lookout to the sea,
With her proud banner over me:
But from my lips thanksgiving broke,
As God in battle thunder spoke,
And that Black Idol, breeding drouth
And dearth of human sympathy
Throughout the sweet and sensuous South,
    Was, with its chains and human yoke,
Blown hellward from the cannon's mouth,
    While Freedom cheered behind the smoke!

EDGAR LEE MASTERS (1869–1950)

Veterans of the Wars

A somewhat contradictory anti-war poem in which the adage "A rich man's war, a poor man's fight" finds expression in the words of the widow of a veteran. She sees war driven by "usurers," the profiteers. The good men went to war, the widow says; the bad men stayed behind and did not profit but rather became the refuse of humanity.

Edwin, your father has never ceased to be
My admiration, and I can close my eyes
And see his soldier shape arise
In vivid memory.

And I recall him as he used to stride
So straight, and how he never stayed or shirked
Through the long years, and how he worked
For wages to provide

For you and for his brood; and by great care
Saved from small earnings enough to buy a house,
A garden and some apple boughs
For his Sunday and evening chair,

When with his duties ended he would read
Of Antietam, Shiloh, the Wilderness,
Of battles he had fought, of stress,
Of victory and stampede.

And when old age and agonized disease
Racked him he bore them with heroic will,
As one who knew the battle's drill,
And prized the good of peace.

What training like the soldier's life commands
For all men's days such strength and discipline,
For all the labors, trials wherein
The soul deserts or stands?

Were soldiers not of money plots the pawn;
Or did not after wars vote as they fought,
Who would not have the youthful wrought
Into such will and brawn?

Were there some way to keep the usurers chained
Against the use of souls by Mars refined
Above the mass of humankind,
Who would not have them trained?

For those who were in mind your father's peers,
But dodged the battle, were about our town
The drunkards, failures, drooped and down,
Who crawled the idiot years.

MINNA IRVING (b. 1872)

Marching Still

She is old, and bent, and wrinkled,
   In her rocker in the sun,
And the thick, gray, woollen stocking
   That she knits is never done.
She will ask the news of battle
   If you pass her when you will,
For to her the troops are marching,
     Marching still.

Seven tall sons about her growing
   Cheered the widowed mother's soul;
One by one they kissed and left her
   When the drums began to roll.
They are buried in the trenches,
   They are bleaching on the hill;
But to her the boys are marching,
     Marching still.

She was knitting in the corner
    When the fatal news was read,
How the last and youngest perished, —
    And the letter, ending, said:
"I am writing on my knapsack
    By the road, with borrowed quill,
For the Union army's marching,
        Marching still."

Reason sank and died within her
    Like a flame for want of air;
So she knits the woollen stockings
    For the soldier lads to wear,
Waiting till the war is ended
    For her sons to cross the sill;
For she thinks they all are marching,
        Marching still.

A meditation on idealism, on belief, on time that takes all things away, even something so grand as the Civil War.

ROBERT FROST (1874–1963)

The Black Cottage

We chanced in passing by that afternoon
To catch it in a sort of special picture
Among tar-banded ancient cherry trees,
Set well back from the road in rank lodged grass,
The little cottage we were speaking of,
A front with just a door between two windows,
Fresh painted by the shower a velvet black.
We paused, the minister and I, to look.
He made as if to hold it at arm's length
Or put the leaves aside that framed it in.
"Pretty," he said. "Come in. No one will care."
The path was a vague parting in the grass
That led us to a weathered windowsill.
We pressed our faces to the pane. "You see," he said,
"Everything's as she left it when she died.
Her sons won't sell the house or the things in it.
They say they mean to come and summer here
Where they were boys. They haven't come this year.
They live so far away—one is out West—

It will be hard for them to keep their word.
Anyway they won't have the place disturbed."
A buttoned haircloth lounge spread scrolling arms
Under a crayon portrait on the wall,
Done sadly from an old daguerreotype.
"That was the father as he went to war.
She always, when she talked about the war,
Sooner or later came and leaned, half knelt,
Against the lounge beside it, though I doubt
If such unlifelike lines kept power to stir
Anything in her after all the years.
He fell at Gettysburg or Fredericksburg,
I ought to know—it makes a difference which:
Fredericksburg wasn't Gettysburg, of course.
But what I'm getting to is how forsaken
A little cottage this has always seemed;
Since she went, more than ever, but before—
I don't mean altogether by the lives
That had gone out of it, the father first,
Then the two sons, till she was left alone.
(Nothing could draw her after those two sons.
She valued the considerate neglect
She had at some cost taught them after years.)
I mean by the world's having passed it by—
As we almost got by this afternoon.
It always seems to me a sort of mark
To measure how far fifty years have brought us.
Why not sit down if you are in no haste?
These doorsteps seldom have a visitor.
The warping boards pull out their own old nails
With none to tread and put them in their place.

She had her own idea of things, the old lady.
And she liked talk. She had seen Garrison
And Whittier, and had her story of them.
One wasn't long in learning that she thought,
Whatever else the Civil War was for,
It wasn't just to keep the States together,
Nor just to free the slaves, though it did both.
She wouldn't have believed those ends enough
To have given outright for them all she gave.
Her giving somehow touched the principle
That all men are created free and equal.
And to hear her quaint phrases—so removed
From the world's view today of all those things.
That's a hard mystery of Jefferson's.
What did he mean? Of course the easy way
Is to decide it simply isn't true.
It may not be. I heard a fellow say so.
But never mind, the Welshman got it planted
Where it will trouble us a thousand years.
Each age will have to reconsider it.
You couldn't tell her what the West was saying,
And what the South, to her serene belief.
She had some art of hearing and yet not
Hearing the latter wisdom of the world.
White was the only race she ever knew.
Black she had scarcely seen, and yellow never.
But how could they be made so very unlike
By the same hand working in the same stuff?
She had supposed the war decided that.
What are you going to do with such a person?
Strange how such innocence gets its own way.

I shouldn't be surprised if in this world
It were the force that would at last prevail.
Do you know but for her there was a time
When, to please younger members of the church,
Or rather say non-members in the church,
Whom we all have to think of nowadays,
I would have changed the Creed a very little?
Not that she ever had to ask me not to;
It never got so far as that; but the bare thought
Of her old tremulous bonnet in the pew,
And of her half asleep, was too much for me.
Why, I might wake her up and startle her.
It was the words 'descended into Hades'
That seemed too pagan to our liberal youth.
You know they suffered from a general onslaught.
And well, if they weren't true why keep right on
Saying them like the heathen? We could drop them.
Only—there was the bonnet in the pew.
Such a phrase couldn't have meant much to her.
But suppose she had missed it from the Creed,
As a child misses the unsaid Good-night
And falls asleep with heartache—how should *I* feel?
I'm just as glad she made me keep hands off,
For, dear me, why abandon a belief
Merely because it ceases to be true.
Cling to it long enough, and not a doubt
It will turn true again, for so it goes.
Most of the change we think we see in life
Is due to truths being in and out of favor.
As I sit here, and oftentimes, I wish
I could be monarch of a desert land

I could devote and dedicate forever
To the truths we keep coming back and back to.
So desert it would have to be, so walled
By mountain ranges half in summer snow,
No one would covet it or think it worth
The pains of conquering to force change on.
Scattered oases where men dwelt, but mostly
Sand dunes held loosely in tamarisk
Blown over and over themselves in idleness.
Sand grains should sugar in the natal dew
The babe born to the desert, the sandstorm
Retard mid-waste my cowering caravans—

"There are bees in this wall." He struck the clapboards,
Fierce heads looked out; small bodies pivoted.
We rose to go. Sunset blazed on the windows.

One of the most famous modern poems and one of the best about the Civil War. Tate was much influenced by T. S. Eliot, and this poem reflects Eliot's sense of how time buries all things. This is a meditation on how all the fury of war comes down to the silence of autumn, the oblivion of the turning seasons.

ALLEN TATE (1899–1979)

Ode to the Confederate Dead

Row after row with strict impunity
The headstones yield their names to the element,
The wind whirrs without recollection;
In the riven troughs the splayed leaves
Pile up, of nature the casual sacrament
To the seasonal eternity of death;
Then driven by the fierce scrutiny
Of heaven to their election in the vast breath,
They sough the rumour of mortality.

Autumn is desolation in the plot
Of a thousand acres where these memories grow
From the inexhaustible bodies that are not
Dead, but feed the grass row after rich row.
Think of the autumns that have come and gone! —
Ambitious November with the humors of the year,
With a particular zeal for every slab,
Staining the uncomfortable angels that rot
On the slabs, a wing chipped here, an arm there:

National Cemetery, Andersonville, Georgia

The brute curiosity of an angel's stare
Turns you, like them, to stone,
Transforms the heaving air
Till plunged to a heavier world below
You shift your sea-space blindly
Heaving, turning like the blind crab.

Dazed by the wind, only the wind
The leaves flying, plunge

You know who have waited by the wall
The twilight certainty of an animal,
Those midnight restitutions of the blood
You know—the immitigable pines, the smoky frieze
Of the sky, the sudden call: you know the rage,
The cold pool left by the mounting flood,
Of muted Zeno and Parmenides.
You who have waited for the angry resolution
Of those desires that should be yours tomorrow,
You know the unimportant shrift of death
And praise the vision
And praise the arrogant circumstance
Of those who fall
Rank upon rank, hurried beyond decision—
Here by the sagging gate, stopped by the wall.

Seeing, seeing only the leaves
Flying, plunge and expire

Turn your eyes to the immoderate past,
Turn to the inscrutable infantry rising

Demons out of the earth—they will not last.
Stonewall, Stonewall, and the sunken fields of hemp.
Shiloh, Antietam, Malvern Hill, Bull Run.
Lost in that orient of the thick-and-fast
You will curse the setting sun.

   Cursing only the leaves crying
   Like an old man in a storm

You hear the shout, the crazy hemlocks point
With troubled fingers to the silence which
Smothers you, a mummy, in time.

             The hound bitch
Toothless and dying, in a musty cellar
Hears the wind only.

          Now that the salt of their blood
Stiffens the saltier oblivion of the sea,
Seals the malignant purity of the flood,
What shall we who count our days and bow
Our heads with a commemorial woe
In the ribboned coats of grim felicity,
What shall we say of the bones, unclean,
Whose verdurous anonymity will grow?
The ragged arms, the ragged heads and eyes
Lost in these acres of the insane green?
The gray lean spiders come, they come and go;
In a tangle of willows without light
The singular screech-owl's tight
Invisible lyric seeds the mind

With the furious murmur of their chivalry.

We shall say only the leaves
Flying, plunge and expire

We shall say only the leaves whispering
In the improbable mist of nightfall
That flies on multiple wing;
Night is the beginning and the end

And in between the ends of distraction
Waits mute speculation, the patient curse
That stones the eyes, or like the jaguar leaps
For his own image in a jungle pool, his victim.

What shall we say who have knowledge
Carried to the heart? Shall we take the act
To the grave? Shall we, more hopeful, set up the grave
In the house? The ravenous grave?

Leave now
The shut gate and the decomposing wall:
The gentle serpent, green in the mulberry bush,
Riots with his tongue through the hush—
Sentinel of the grave who counts us all!

JOHN BERRYMAN (1914–1972)

Boston Common

A Meditation upon the Hero

A modernist poem, difficult to interpret. The narrator comes upon a homeless man, asleep on a February night under the Saint-Gaudens statue of Robert Gould Shaw on the Boston Common. The great movements of history pass some individuals by. What does past honor mean on a cold night in the present when human beings are reduced to their elements?

I   Slumped under the impressive genitals
        Of the bronze charger, protected by bronze,
        By darkness from patrols, by sleep from what
        Assailed him earlier and left him here,
        The man lies. Clothing and organs. These were once
        Shoes. Faint in the orange light
        Flooding the portico above: the whole
        Front of the State House. On a February night.

II   Dramatic bivouac for the casual man!
        Beyond the exedra the Common falls,
        Famous and dark, away; a lashing wind;
        Immortal heroes in a marble frame
        Who broke their bodies on Fort Wagner's walls,
        Robert Gould Shaw astride, and his
        Negroes without name, who followed, who fell
        Screaming or calm, wet cold, sick or oblivious.

III   Who now cares how? here they are in their prime,—
Paradigm, pitching imagination where
The crucible night all singularity,
Idiosyncrasy and creed, burnt out
And brought them, here, a common character.
Imperishable march below
The mounted man below the Angel, and
Under, the casual man, the possible hero.

IV   Hero for whom under a sky of bronze,
Saint-Gaudens' sky? Passive he seems to lie,
The last straw of contemporary thought,
In shapeless failure; but may be this man
Before he came here, or he comes to die,
Blazing with force or fortitude
Superb of civil soul may stand or may
After young Shaw within that crucible have stood.

V   For past her assignation when night fell
And the men forward,—poise and shock of dusk
As daylight rocking passes the horizon,—
The Angel spread her wings still. War is the
Congress of adolescents, love in a mask,
Bestial and easy, issueless,
Or gets a man of bronze. No beating heart
Until the casual man can see the Angel's face.

VI   Where shall they meet? what ceremony find,
Loose in the brothel of another war
This winter night? Can citizen enact
His timid will and expectation where,

Exact a wedding or her face O where
Tanks and guns, tanks and guns,
Move and must move to their conclusions, where
The will is mounted and gregarious and bronze?

VII For ceremony, in the West, in the East,
The pierced sky, iced air, and the rent of cloud
As, moving to his task at dawn, who'd been
Hobbledehoy of the cafeteria life
Swung like a hobby in the blue and rode
The shining body of his choice
To the eye and time of his bombardier;—
Stiffened in the racket, and relaxed beyond noise.

VIII "Who now cares how?"—the quick, the index! Question
Your official heroes in a magazine,
Wry voices past the river. Dereliction,
Lust and bloodlust, error and goodwill, this one
Died howling, craven, this one was a swine
From childhood. Man and animal
Sit for their photographs to Fame, and dream
Barbershop hours . . vain, compassionate parable.

IX "Accidents of history, memorials"—
A considering and quiet voice. "I see
Photograph and bronze upon another shore
Do not arrive; the light is where it is,
Indifferent to honour. Let honour be
Consolation to those who give,
None to the Hero, and no sign of him:
All unrecorded, flame-like, perish and live."

X Diminishing beyond the elms. Rise now
  The chivalry and defenders of our time,
  From Spain and China, the tortured continents,
  Leningrad, Syria, Corregidor,—
  Upon a primitive theme high variations
  Like soaring Beethoven's.—Lost, lost
  Whose eyes flung faultless to one horizon
  Their fan look. Fiery night consumes a summoned ghost.

XI Images of the Possible, the top,
  Their time they taxed,—after the tanks came through,
  When orderless and by their burning homes'
  Indelible light, with knee and nail they struck
  (The improvised the real) man's common foe,
  Misled blood-red statistical men.
  Images of conduct in a crucible,
  Their eyes, and nameless eyes, which will not come again.

XII *We hope will not again.* Therefore those eyes
  Fix me again upon the terrible shape,
  Defeated and marvellous, of the man I know,
  Jack under the stallion. We have passed him by,
  Wandering, prone, and he is our whole hope,
  Our fork's one tine and our despair,
  The heart of the Future beating. How far far
  We sent our subtle messengers! when he is here.

XIII Who chides our clamour and who would forget
  The death of heroes: never know the shore
  Where, hair to the West, Starkatterus was burnt;
  And undergo no more that spectacle—

Perpetually verdant the last pyre,
Fir, cypress, yew, the phoenix bay
And voluntary music—which to him
Threw never meat or truth. He looks another way.

XIV   Watching who labour O that all may see
And savour the blooming world, flower and sound,
Tending and tending to peace,—be what their blood,
Prayer, occupation may,—so tend for all:
A common garden in a private ground.
Who labour in the private dark
And silent dark for birthday music and light,
Fishermen, gardeners, about their violent work.

XV   Lincoln, the lanky lonely and sad man
Who suffered in Washington his own, his soul;
Mao Tse-tung, Teng Fa, fabulous men,
Laughing and serious men; or Tracy Doll
Tracing the future on the wall of a cell—
There, there, on the wall of a cell
The face towards which we hope all history,
Institutions, tears move, there the Individual.

XVI   Ah, it may not be so. Still the crucial night
Fastens you all upon this frame of hope:
Each in his limited sick world with them,
The figures of his reverence, his awe,
His shivering devotion,—that they shape
Shelter, action, salvation.
. . Legends and lies. Kneel if you will, but rise
Homeless, alone, and be the kicking working one.

XVII   None anywhere alone! The turning world
           Brings unaware us to our enemies,
           Artist to assassin, Saint-Gaudens' bronze
           To a free shelter, images to end.
           The cold and hard wind has tears in my eyes,
           Long since, long since, I heard the last
           Traffic unmeshing upon Boylston Street,
           I halted here in the orange light of the Past,

XVIII   Helpless under the great crotch lay this man
           Huddled against woe, I had heard defeat
           All day, I saw upon the sands assault,
           I heard the voice of William James, the wind,
           And poured in darkness or in my heartbeat
           Across my hearing and my sight
           Worship and love irreconcilable
           Here to be reconciled. On a February night.

DUDLEY RANDALL (1914–) ❧

Memorial Wreath

*(For the more than 200,000 Negroes who served
in the Union Army during the Civil War)*

*An expression of pride and
gratitude to the black soldiers who
fought to end slavery. Toussaint
L'Ouverture (1744–1803) led
blacks in Haiti against British,
Spanish, and French domination.*

In this green month when resurrected flowers,
Like laughing children ignorant of death,
Brighten the couch of those who wake no more,
Love and remembrance blossom in our hearts
For you who bore the extreme sharp pang for us,
And bought our freedom with your lives.

                                    And now,
Honoring your memory, with love we bring
These fiery roses, white-hot cotton flowers
And violets bluer than cool northern skies
You dreamed of in the burning prison fields
When liberty was only a faint north star,
Not a bright flower planted by your hands
Reaching up hardy nourished with your blood.

Group of black workers

Fit gravefellows you are for Lincoln, Brown
And Douglass and Toussaint . . . all whose rapt eyes
Fashioned a new world in this wilderness.

American earth is richer for your bones;
Our hearts beat prouder for the blood we inherit.

A humorous poem, mocking the glorification of war and the heroic legends people create about it.

ALAN DUGAN (1923–) ❦

Fabrication of Ancestors

*(For Old Billy Dugan, Shot in the Ass in
the Civil War, My Father Said)*

The old wound in my ass
has opened up again, but I
am past the prodigies
of youth's campaigns, and weep
where I used to laugh
in war's red humors, half
in love with silly-assed pains
and half not feeling them.
I have to sit up with
an indoor unsittable itch
before I go down late
and weeping to the storm-
cellar on a dirty night
and go to bed with the worms.
So pull the dirt up over me
and make a family joke
for Old Billy Blue Balls,
the oldest private in the world
with two ass-holes and no

place more to go to for a laugh
except the last one. Say:
The North won the Civil War
without much help from me
although I wear a proof
of the war's obscenity.

ROBERT LOWELL (1917–1977) ✍

For the Union Dead

"Relinquunt Omnia Servare Rem Publicam."

The old South Boston Aquarium stands
in a Sahara of snow now. Its broken windows are boarded:
The bronze weathervane cod has lost half its scales.
The airy tanks are dry.

Once my nose crawled like a snail on the glass;
my hand tingled
to burst the bubbles
drifting from the noses of the cowed, compliant fish.

My hand draws back. I often sigh still
for the dark downward and vegetating kingdom
of the fish and reptile. On a morning last March,
I pressed against the new barbed and galvanized

fence on the Boston Common. Behind their cage,
yellow dinosaur steamshovels were grunting
as they cropped up tons of mush and grass
to gouge their underworld garage.

Inside the trenches before Petersburg, Virginia

Parking spaces luxuriate like civic
sandpiles in the heart of Boston.
A girdle of orange, Puritan-pumpkin colored girders
braces the tingling Statehouse,

shaking over the excavations, as it faces Colonel Shaw
and his bell-cheeked Negro infantry
on St. Gaudens shaking Civil War relief,
propped by a plank splint against the garage's earthquake.

Two months after marching through Boston,
half the regiment was dead;
at the dedication,
William James could almost hear the bronze Negroes breathe.

Their monument sticks like a fishbone
in the city's throat.
Its Colonel is as lean
as a compass-needle.

He has an angry wrenlike vigilance,
a greyhound's gentle tautness;
he seems to wince at pleasure,
and suffocate for privacy.

He is out of bounds now. He rejoices in man's lovely,
peculiar power to choose life and die—
when he leads his black soldiers to death,
he cannot bend his back.

On a thousand small town New England greens,
the old white churches hold their air
of sparse, sincere rebellion; frayed flags
quilt the graveyards of the Grand Army of the Republic.

The stone statues of the abstract Union Soldier
grow slimmer and younger each year—
wasp-waisted, they doze over muskets
and muse through their sideburns . . .

Shaw's father wanted no monument
except the ditch,
where his son's body was thrown
and lost with his "niggers."

The ditch is nearer.
There are no statues for the last war here;
on Boylston Street, a commercial photograph
shows Hiroshima boiling

over a Mosler Safe, the "Rock of Ages"
that survived the blast. Space is nearer.
When I crouch to my television set,
the drained faces of Negro school-children rise like balloons.

Colonel Shaw
is riding on his bubble,
he waits
for the blessèd break.

The Aquarium is gone. Everywhere,
giant finned cars nose forward like fish;
a savage servility
slides by on grease.

A poem about mortality, joining
the narrator to the mortality of the
past and making her contemplate
time's burial of all the living. It is
a poem both private and public.

ELEANOR ROSS TAYLOR (1920–)

This Year's Drive to Appomattox

March comes,
and Eastern bluebird shows himself,
a long-awaited call, on the telephone wire,
   Confederate blue and old blood.

Make a fist. Okay, hold up your arm
like that a minute or two.
You'll have the lab report next week.
   If you still like mortality.

We go past church and stones, genesis, exodus.
That house played house to many bones;
these fields, to hoof and brogan,
   that hilltop woods to wind.

Wind whips her dress against her legs,
under the clothesline, taking down the ghosts.
It's cold. They aren't whipped out by wind,
   our ghosts—they drive the wind.

A future's hatching out of firmament,
an Oberland, and 1865 is drying mist—
and last year,
what recollection has last year—
two, not one, here?

DEREK WALCOTT (1930–) 🕊

The Arkansas Testament

(For Michael Harper)

Walcott is a West Indian black poet, winner of the Nobel Prize in Literature in 1992. Here he ponders with great ambivalence and many images not only the old Confederacy but the modern South, with its tradition of hostility to blacks, a tradition passed down from the slave times. Fayetteville is the location of the University of Arkansas whose teams are called the "Razorbacks."

I   Over Fayetteville, Arkansas,
a slope of memorial pines
guards the stone slabs of forces
fallen for the Confederacy
at some point in the Civil War.
The young stones, flat on their backs,
their beards curling like mosses,
have no names; an occasional surge
in the pines mutters their roster
while their centennial siege,
their entrenched metamorphosis
into cones and needles, goes on.
Over Arkansas, they can see
between the swaying cracks
in the pines the blue of the Union,
as the trunks get rustier.

II   It was midwinter. The dusk was
yielding in flashes of metal
from a slowly surrendering sun
on the billboards, storefronts, and signs
along Highway 71,
then on the brass-numbered doors
of my $17.50 motel,
and the slab of my cold key.
Jet-lagged and travel-gritty,
I fell back on the double bed
like Saul under neighing horses
on the highway to Damascus,
and lay still, as Saul does,
till my name re-entered me,
and felt, through the chained door,
dark entering Arkansas.

III   I stared back at the Celotex
ceiling of room 16,
my coat still on, for minutes
as the key warmed my palm—
TV, telephone, maid service,
and a sense of the parking lot
through cinder blocks—homesick
for islands with fringed shores
like the mustard-gold coverlet.
A roach crossed its oceanic
carpet with scurrying oars
to a South that it knew, calm
shallows of crystalline green.
I studied again how glare

dies on a wall, till a complex
neon scribbled its signature.

IV   At the desk, crouched over Mr._____
I had felt like changing my name
for one beat at the register.
Instead, I'd kept up the game
of pretending whoever I was,
or am, or will be, are the same:
"How'll you pay for this, sir?
Cash or charge?" I missed the
chance of answering, "In kind,
like my colour." But her gaze
was corn-country, her eyes frayed
denim. "American Express."
On a pennant, with snarling tusk,
a razorback charged. A tress
of loose hair lifted like maize
in the lounge's indigo dusk.

V   I dozed off in the early dark
to a smell of detergent pine
and they faded with me: the rug
with its shag, pine-needled floor,
the without-a-calendar wall
now hung with the neon's sign,
no thin-lipped Gideon Bible,
no bed lamp, no magazine,
no bristle-faced fiddler
sawing at "Little Brown Jug,"
or some brochure with a landmark

by which you know Arkansas,
or a mountain spring's white babble,
nothing on a shelf, no shelves;
just a smudge on a wall, the mark
left by two uncoiling selves.

VI I crucified my coat on one wire
hanger, undressed for bathing,
then saw that other, full-length,
alarmed in the glass coffin
of the bathroom door. Right there,
I decided to stay unshaven,
unsaved, if I found the strength.
Oh, for a day's dirt unshowered,
no plug for my grovelling razor,
to reek of the natural coward
I am, to make this a place for
disposable shavers as well
as my own disposable people!
On a ridge over Fayetteville,
higher than any steeple,
is a white-hot electric cross.

VII It burns the back of my mind.
It scorches the skin of night;
as a candle repeats the moment
of being blown out, it remained
when I switched off the ceiling light.
That night I slept like the dead,
or a drunk in the tank, like moss
on a wall, like a lover happier

in the loss of love, like soldiers
under the pines, but, as I dreaded,
rose too early. It was four.
Maybe five. I only guessed
by the watch I always keep
when my own house is at rest.
I opened the motel door.
The hills never turned in their sleep.

VIII Pyjamas crammed in my jacket,
the bottoms stuffed into trousers
that sagged, I needed my fix—
my 5 a.m. caffeine addiction.
No rooster crew brassily back at
the white-neon crucifix,
and Arkansas smelt as sweet
as a barn door opening. Like horses
in their starlit, metallic sweat,
parked cars grazed in their stalls.
Dawn was fading the houses
to an even Confederate grey.
On the far side of the highway,
a breeze turned the leaves of an aspen
to the First Epistle of Paul's
to the Corinthians.

IX The asphalt, quiet as a Sabbath,
by municipal sprinklers anointed,
shot its straight and narrow path
in the white, converging arrows
of Highway 71. They pointed

to Florida, as if tired warriors
dropped them on the Trail of Tears,
but nothing stirred in response
except two rabbinical willows
with nicotine beards, and a plaid
jacket Frisbeeing papers
from a bike to silvery lawns,
tires hissing the peace that passeth
understanding under the black elms,
and morning in Nazareth
was Fayetteville's and Jerusalem's.

X   Hugging walls in my tippler's hop—
the jive of shuffling bums,
a beat that comes from the chain—
I waited for a while by the grass
of a urinous wall to let
the revolving red eye on top
of a cruising police car pass.
In an all-night garage I saw
the gums of a toothless sybil
in garage tires, and she said:
STAY BLACK AND INVISIBLE
TO THE SIRENS OF ARKANSAS.
The snakes coiled on the pumps
hissed with their metal mouth:
Your shadow still hurts the South,
like Lee's slowly reversing sword.

XI   There's nothing to understand
in hunger. I watched the shell
of a white sun tapping its yolk
on the dark crust of Fayetteville,
and hurried up in my walk
past warming brick to the smell
of hash browns. Abounding light
raced towards me like a mongrel
hoping that it would be caressed
by my cold, roughening hand,
and I prayed that all could be blest
down Highway 71, the grey calm
of the lanes where a lion
lies down on its traffic island,
a post chevroning into a palm.
The world warmed to its work.

XII   But two doors down, a cafeteria
reminded me of my race.
A soak cursed his vinyl table
steadily, not looking up.
A tall black cook setting glazed
pies, a beehive-blond waitress,
lips like a burst strawberry,
and her "Mornin' " like maple syrup.
Four DEERE caps talking deer hunting.
I looked for my own area.
The muttering black decanter
had all I needed; it could sigh for
Sherman's smoking march to Atlanta
or the march to Montgomery.

I was still nothing. A cipher
in its bubbling black zeros, here.

XIII The self-contempt that it takes
to find my place card among any
of the faces reflected in lakes
of lacquered mahogany
comes easily now. I have laughed
loudest until silence kills
the shoptalk. A fork clicks
on its plate; a cough's rifle shot
shivers the chandeliered room.
A bright arm shakes its manacles.
Every candle-struck face stares into
the ethnic abyss. In the oval
of a silver spoon, the window
bent in a wineglass, the offal
of flattery fed to my craft,
I watch the bright clatter resume.

XIV I bagged the hot Styrofoam coffee
to the recently repealed law
that any black out after curfew
could be shot dead in Arkansas.
Liberty turns its face; the doctrine
of Aryan light is upheld
as sunrise stirs the lion-
coloured grasses of the veld.
Its seam glints in the mind
of the golden Witwatersrand,
whose clouds froth like a beer stein

in the Boer's sunburnt hand;
the world is flushed with fever.
In some plaid-flannel wood
a buck is roped to a fender—
it is something in their blood.

XV In a world I saw without end as
one highway with signs, low brown
motels, burger haciendas,
a neat, evangelical town
now pointed through decorous oaks
its calendar comfort—scary
with its simple, God-fearing folks.
Evil was as ordinary
here as good. I kept my word.
This, after all, was the South,
whose plough was still the sword,
its red earth dust in the mouth,
whose grey division and dates
swirl in the pine-scented air—
wherever the heart hesitates
that is its true frontier.

XVI On front porches every weak lamp
went out; on the frame windows
day broadened into the prose
of an average mid-American town.
My metre dropped its limp.
Sunlight flooded Arkansas.
Cold sunshine. I had to draw
my coat tight from the cold, or

suffer the nips of arthritis,
the small arrows that come with age;
the sun began to massage
the needles in the hill's shoulder
with its balsam, but hairs
fall on my collar as I write this
in shorter days, darker years,
more hatred, more racial rage.

XVII The light, being amber, ignored
the red and green traffic stops,
and, since it had never met me,
went past me without a nod.
It sauntered past the shops,
peered into AUTOMOBILE SALES,
where a serenely revolving Saab
sneered at it. At INDIAN CRAFTS
it regilded the Southern Gothic
sign, climbed one of the trails,
touching leaves as it sent
shadows squirrelling. Its shafts,
like the lasers of angels, went
through the pines guarding each slab
of the Confederate Cemetery,
piercing the dead with the quick.

XVIII Perhaps in these same pines runs,
with cross ties of bleeding thorns,
the track of the Underground Rail-
road way up into Canada,
and what links the Appalachians

is the tinkle of ankle chains
running north, where history is harder
to bear: the hypocrisy
of clouds with Puritan collars.
Wounds from the Indian wars
cut into the soft plank tables
by the picnic lake, and birches
peel like canoes, and the maple's
leaves tumble like Hessians;
hills froth into dogwood, churches
arrow into the Shawmut sky.

XIX   O lakes of pines and still water,
where the wincing muzzles of deer
make rings that widen the idea
of the state past the calendar!
Does this aging Democracy
remember its log-cabin dream,
the way that a man past fifty
imagines a mountain stream?
The pines huddle in quotas
on the lake's calm water line
that draws across them straight as
the stroke of a fountain pen.
My shadow's scribbled question
on the margin of the street
asks, Will I be a citizen
or an afterthought of the state?

XX   Can I bring a palm to my heart
and sing, with eyes on the pole
whose manuscript banner boasts
of the Union with thirteen stars
crossed out, but is borne by the ghosts
of sheeted hunters who ride
to the fire-white cross of the South?
Can I swear to uphold my art
that I share with them too, or worse,
pretend all is past and curse
from the picket lines of my verse
the concept of Apartheid?
The shadow bends to the will
as our oaths of allegiance bend
to the state. What we know of evil
is that it will never end.

XXI   The original sin is our seed,
and that acorn fans into an oak;
the umbrella of Africa's shade,
despite this democracy's mandates,
still sprouts from a Southern street
that holds grey black men in a stoop,
their flintlock red eyes. We have shared
our passbook's open secret
in the hooded eyes of a cop,
the passerby's unuttered aside,
the gesture involuntary, signs,
the excessively polite remark
that turns an idea to acid
in the gut, and here I felt its

poison infecting the hill pines,
all the way to the top.

XXII   Sir, you urge us to divest
ourselves of all earthly things,
like these camphor cabinets
with their fake-pine coffins;
to empty the drawer of the chest
and look far beyond the hurt
on which a cross looks down,
as light floods this asphalt
car park, like the rush Tower
where Raleigh brushes his shirt
and Villon and his brothers cower
at the shadow of the still knot.
There are things that my craft cannot
wield, and one is power;
and though only old age earns the
right to an abstract noun

XXIII   this, Sir, is my Office,
my Arkansas Testament,
my two cupfuls of Cowardice,
my sure, unshaven Salvation,
my people's predicament.
Bless the increasing bliss
of truck tires over asphalt,
and these stains I cannot remove
from the self-soiled heart. This
noon, some broad-backed maid,
half-Indian perhaps, will smooth

this wheat-coloured double bed,
and afternoon sun will reprint
the bars of a flag whose cloth—
over motel, steeple, and precinct—
must heal the stripes and the scars.

XXIV I turned on the TV set.
A light, without any noise,
in amber successive stills,
stirred the waves off Narragansett
and the wheat-islanded towns.
I watched its gold bars explode
on the wagon axles of Mormons,
their brows and hunched shoulders set
toward Zion, their wide oxen road
raising dust in the gopher's nostrils;
then a gravelly announcer's voice
was embalming the Black Hills—
it bade the Mojave rejoice,
it switched off the neon rose
of Vegas, and its shafts came to
the huge organ pipes of sequoias,
the Pacific, and *Today*'s news.

Stillness

The fury of war passed by and left the silence of the ages. In the Wilderness campaign in northern Virginia in May 1864, the forest caught fire and burned to death wounded men on both sides.

HERMAN MELVILLE (1819–1891) ❦

An Uninscribed Monument on One of the Battlefields of the Wilderness

Silence and Solitude may hint
   (Whose home is in yon piny wood)
What I, though tableted, could never tell—
The din which here befell,
   And striving of the multitude.
The iron cones and spheres of death
   Set round me in their rust,
      These, too, if just,
Shall speak with more than animated breath.
   Thou who beholdest, if thy thought,
Not narrowed down to personal cheer,
Take in the import of the quiet here—
   The after-quiet—the calm full fraught;
Thou too wilt silent stand—
Silent as I, and lonesome as the land.

View of the Wilderness, Virginia

HERMAN MELVILLE (1819–1891)

Shiloh, a Requiem
(April 1862)

Skimming lightly, wheeling still,
   The swallows fly low
Over the field in clouded days,
   The forest-field of Shiloh—
Over the field where April rain
Solaced the parched ones stretched in pain
Through the pause of night
That followed the Sunday fight
   Around the church of Shiloh—
The church so lone, the log-built one,
That echoed to many a parting groan
      And natural prayer
   Of dying foemen mingled there—
Foemen at morn, but friends at eve—
   Fame or country least their care:
(What like a bullet can undeceive!)
   But now they lie low,
While over them the swallows skim,
   And all is hushed at Shiloh.

The poet meditates on the grave of
the dashing Confederate cavalry
commander "Jeb" Stuart. It echoes
Thomas Gray's "Elegy Written in
a Country Churchyard."

MARGARET JUNKIN PRESTON (1820–1897) ❧

A Grave in Hollywood Cemetery, Richmond (J. R. T.)

I read the marble-lettered name,
    And half in bitterness I said,
"As Dante from Ravenna came,
    Our poet came from exile-dead."
And yet, had it been asked of him
    Where he would rather lay his head,
This spot he would have chosen. Dim
    The city's hum drifts o'er his grave,
    And green above the hollies wave
Their jagged leaves, as when a boy,
    On blissful summer afternoons,
    He came to sing the birds his runes,
And tell the river of his joy.

Who dreams that in his wanderings wide
    By stern misfortunes tossed and driven,
    His soul's electric strands were riven
From home and country? Let betide
What might, what would, his boast, his pride,

Ruins of Richmond, Virginia

Was in his stricken mother-land,
    That could but bless and bid him go,
Because no crust was in her hand
    To stay her children's need. We know
The mystic cable sank too deep
    For surface storm or stress to strain,
Or from his answering heart to keep
    The spark from flashing back again!

Think of the thousand mellow rhymes,
    The pure idyllic passion-flowers,
Wherewith, in far-gone, happier times,
    He garlanded this South of ours.
Provençal-like, he wandered long,
    And sang at many a stranger's board,
The tenderest pathos through his song.
We owe the Poet praise and tears,
    Whose ringing ballad sends the brave,
Bold Stuart riding down the years.
    What have we given him? Just a grave!

A solemn reverie on the tumult
of war, ended in silent death.

UNKNOWN ❧

Confederate Memorial Day

The marching armies of the past,
  Along our Southern plains,
Are sleeping now in quiet rest
  Beneath the Southern rains.

The bugle call is now in vain
  To rouse them from their bed;
To arms they'll never march again—
  They are sleeping with the dead.

No more will Shiloh's plains be stained
  With blood our heroes shed,
Nor Chancellorsville resound again
  To our noble warriors' tread.

For them no more shall reveille
  Sound at the break of dawn,
But may their sleep peaceful be
  Till God's great judgment morn.

We bow our heads in solemn prayer
    For those who wore the gray,
And clasp again their unseen hands
    On our Memorial Day.

A long and somewhat effusive poem by a Confederate veteran honoring Lincoln and begging the reunited nation to stand true to Lincoln's democratic and humane vision. The poem was written in 1894 as the United States was becoming more and more active on the international scene.

MAURICE THOMPSON (1844–1901)

Lincoln's Grave
(1894)
(Read at Sanders Theater to the Phi Beta Kappa Brotherhood
of Harvard College)

I   May one who fought in honor for the South
    Uncovered stand and sing by Lincoln's grave?
    Why, if I shrunk not at the cannon's mouth,
    Nor swerved one inch for any battle-wave,
    Should I now tremble in this quiet close,
    Hearing the prairie wind go lightly by
    From billowy plains of grass and miles of corn,
            While out of deep repose
    The great sweet spirit lifts itself on high
    And broods above our land this summer morn?

II Yon little city bumbles like a hive,
    And yonder fields are rolling like the sea,
    From lake to gulf our peaceful millions strive;
    Old notes of discord sink to harmony;
    And here beside this grave I stand apart
    Clothed in my birthright's plentitude of power
    And feel the thought within me rise and yearn,
            And overflow my heart!

I am the poet of this golden hour;
A whole world's aspirations in me burn.

III   And, erst a rebel, I am not a saint;
For dear as life the memory of those days,
Those comrades, that young banner; not a taint
Of shame my record holds. I speak the praise
Unbounded of my camp-mates who yet live,
Or those, with honor shining bright as gold,
Who went to death, as to a banquet going;
      And proudly do I give
A song to you who kept the banner old,
The dearest flag o'er any country blowing!

IV   Whose children walk with bright uplifted heads
Under that flag by bullets rent and cloven,
By factions torn and ravelled into shreds,
By loving hands untangled and rewoven?
Both mine and thine, no matter where we fought,
Our wedded veins now spill a warmer flood
Than poured at Wilderness and Rocky-face;
      The victory we sought,
Each fighting for what seemed his children's good,
Came when that banner reached its rightful place.

V   Broad is our view and broad our charity,
Deep calls to deep, and height to height appeals,
With the foregathering voice of prophecy,
And boundless is the scope our morn reveals!
Blue as an iris-petal bending over,
And violet-sweet this cloudless sky of ours;

Thrills in our air the vital fire of truth,
  And o'er us swarm and hover,
Like golden bees o'er nectar-burdened flowers,
The rare imperious potencies of youth.

VI Oh, is there now a North so arrogant,
A South so narrow and so bitter still,
It bosoms any thought malevolent
Under that flag on freedom's stately hill?
Not those who charged between the batteries,
Crashing midway like meeting cannon-shot,
Can ruminate old hatreds o'er again,
  Stifling warm sympathies
And friendships true that cowards value not;
Not soldiers good, for they are gentlemen.

VII O Federal soldiers, ours, as well as thine,
The passionate wild love of home and land!
When Georgia called I felt the thrill divine,
And who could quell my heart or stay my hand?
We rushed together on the field of death,
Unmindful of ourselves; behind us lay
Home, mother, country—all that life is worth!
  Even now I feel the breath
Of courage that did hurl me through the fray,
And strand me by the ramparts of the North!

VIII Right seems to dally as it strolls along;
But still it moves and never backward goes;
Each pace is certain, every pose is strong;
Crushed in its vestiges it leaves its foes,

And yet no man escapes its loving care,
Or dies in vain its honest combatant,
Or fails to conquer fighting by its side!
  Like incense on the air
Went up brave souls where bayonets crossed aslant
And every bosom held a patriot's pride!

IX Old soldiers true, ah, them all men can trust,
Who fought, with conscience clear, on either side;
Who bearded Death and thought their cause was just;
Their stainless honor cannot be denied;
All patriots they beyond the farthest doubt;
Ring it and sing it up and down the land,
And let no voice dare answer it with sneers,
  Or shut its meaning out;
Ring it and sing it, we go hand in hand,
Old infantry, old cavalry, old cannoniers.

X And if Virginia's vales shall ring again
To battle-yell of Moseby or Mahone,
If Wilder's wild brigade or Morgan's men
Once more wheel into line; or all alone
A Sheridan shall ride, a Cleburne fall,
There will not be two flags above them flying,
But both in one, welded in that pure flame
  Upflaring in us all,
When kindred unto kindred loudly crying
Rally and cheer in freedom's holy name!

XI   Great heart that bled on every awful field,
Deep eyes that wept for every soldier dead,
What time the Blue or Gray swept on or reeled,
What time, triumphant, Meade or Johnston led;
True heart that felt our country one and whole,
Kind eyes that saw to love beyond the strife,
Inspire me, fill me, hold me close and long,
     My every source control,
So that the richest veins of human life
Thrilled through by thee may consecrate my song!

XII   I, mindful of a dark and bitter past,
And of its clashing hopes and raging hates,
Still, standing here, invoke a love so vast
It cancels all and all obliterates,
Save love itself, which cannot harbor wrong;
Oh for a voice of boundless melody,
A voice to fill heaven's hollow to the brim
     With one brave burst of song
Stronger than tempest, nobler than the sea,
That I might lend it to a song of him!

XIII   Meseems I feel his presence. Is he dead?
Death is a word. He lives and grander grows.
At Gettysburg he bows his bleeding head;
He spreads his arm where Chickamauga flows,
As if to clasp old soldiers to his breast,
Of South or North no matter which they be,
Not thinking of what uniform they wore,
     His heart a palimpsest,

Record on record of humanity,
Where love is first and last forevermore.

XIV His was the tireless strength of native truth,
The might of rugged, untaught earnestness;
Deep-freezing poverty made brave his youth,
And toned his manhood with its winter stress
Up to the temper of heroic worth,
And wrought him to a crystal clear and pure,
To mark how Nature in her highest mood
    Scorns at our pride of birth,
And ever plants the life that must endure
In the strong soil of wintry solitude.

XV Close to the ground what if his life began,
In rude bucolic self-denial keyed,
Fed on realities, yet hearing Pan
Along the brookside blow a charmèd reed!
O flocks of Hardin, you remember well
The awkward child, and had he not a look
Of one forechosen of grand destiny?
    In field or forest dell
Did he not prophesy to bird and brook,
And shape vague runes of what was yet to be?

XVI Born in the midway space where freedom seemed
To sport with slavery, and half way o'er
From where the South in golden luxury dreamed
To that old rock of Plymouth on the shore
Made holy by the touch of pilgrim feet,
He grew to stature of the largest mold,

A stalwart burden-bearer trudging on
    And up to that high seat,
Which never more the like of him shall hold,
Over rough ways, through pain and sorrow drawn.

XVII   Giant of frame, of soul superbly human,
Best measure of true greatness measures him;
Crude might of man, the native sweet of woman,
The immanence of destiny strange and dim,
Brawn-building labor with the axe and maul,
Braced and enriched him to the uttermost,
And filled those founts that wisdom bubbles from,
    Made him so kingly tall,
So notable of mien 'mid any host,
The leader and the master strong and calm.

XVIII   He, the last product and the highest power
Of elemental righteousness and worth,
Gave all his life, that in Time's darkest hour,
Dear Freedom should not perish from the earth,
And steadfast in the centre of the storm,
Grim as a panther for its cubs at bay,
He was the one, the fixed, the president,
    The overtowering form,
That broke the bolts of every thunderous day,
And made itself the nation's battlement.

XIX   Set for the right his vision absolute
Compassed all charity, nor failed to see
That highest sense of right may constitute
Grant's glory and the noble strength of Lee;

His eyes were never narrowed to the line
By which the bigot gauges every look;
In Sherman's will, in Stonewall Jackson's prayer
    He felt the force divine
Wherewith the soul of loftiest manhood shook
When war with its wild glamor filled the air.

XX   While all the world on Freedom gazed askance,
Ere yet more than her shadowy form they saw,
He spoke the foresay and significance,
The finest intimation of her law;
Wisdom so tender, justice so kind and good,
The warm appeal of limitless faith in man,
The goal toward which our widening cycle rolls,
    The perfect brotherhood;
These flushed his spirit; and with him began
The universal league of human souls.

XXI   Speak not of accident or circumstance,
He was the genius of primeval man
Evolved anew, despite the waves of chance;
Along his nerves the human current ran,
Pure as the old far fountain in the shade
Of God's first trees. He knew the score right well,
And note by note, of Nature's simple staff,
    Yodled in grove and glade;
He loved the story and the honest laugh,
The rustic song, the sounds of field and fell.

XXII   His humor, born of virile opulence,
Stung like a pungent sap or wild-fruit zest,

And satisfied a universal sense
Of manliness, the strongest and the best;
A soft Kentucky strain was in his voice,
And the Ohio's deeper boom was there,
With some wild accents of old Wabash days,
    And winds of Illinois;
And when he spake he took us unaware
With his high courage and unselfish ways.

XXIII And fresh from God he had the godlike power
Of universal sympathy with life,
Or high or low; he knew the day and hour,
Felt every motive actuating strife,
Lived on both sides of every aspiration,
And saw how men could differ and be right,
How from all points the waves of truth are driven
    To one last destination;
How prayer that battles prayer with awful might
Eternally tempestuous rolls to heaven.

XXIV He heard the rending of the bonds of love,
And he was rent with every snapping strand;
Toppled the temple's base and dome above,
Yawned a black chasm across our lovely land;
And yet he could not let the fragments go,
Or loose his hold on that firm unity
Welded at Valley Forge and Bunker Hill;
    He heard the bugles blow
On either side, and yet how could it be?
He prayed for peace, forebore and trusted still!

XXV   He was the Southern mother leaning forth,
At dead of night to hear the cannon roar,
Beseeching God to turn the cruel North
And break it that her son might come once more;
He was New England's maiden pale and pure,
Whose gallant lover fell on Shiloh's plain;
He was the mangled body of the dead;
    He writhing did endure
Wounds and disfigurement and racking pain,
Gangrene and amputation, all things dread.

XXVI   He was the North, the South, the East, the West,
The thrall, the master, all of us in one;
There was no section that he held the best;
His love shone as impartial as the sun;
And so revenge appealed to him in vain,
He smiled at it, as at a thing forlorn,
And gently put it from him, rose and stood
    A moment's space in pain,
Remembering the prairies and the corn
And the glad voices of the field and wood.

XXVII   Oh, every bullet-shock went to his heart,
And every orphan's cry that followed it,
In every slave's wild hope he bore a part,
With every master's pang his face was lit;
But yet, unfaltering, he kept the faith,
Trusted the inner light and drove right on
Straight toward his golden purpose shining high
Beyond the field of death,

Beyond the trumpets and the gonfalon,
Beyond the war-clouds and the blackened sky.

XXVIII Annealed in white-hot fire he bore the test
Of every strain temptation could invent,
Hard points of slander, shivered on his breast,
Fell at his feet, and envy's blades were bent
In his bare hand and lightly cast aside;
He would not wear a shield; no selfish aim
Guided one thought of all those trying hours;
      Nor breath of pride,
No pompous striving for the pose of fame
Weakened one stroke of all his noble powers.

XXIX And so, vicariously all suffering,
Over stupendous ills he rose supreme,
Set Freedom free, made that a real thing
Which all the world had thought a splendid dream!
Across the red and booming tide of war
He sped the evangel of eternal right,
The message brave that broke the ancient spell
      And rang and echoed far;
Above the battle at its stormiest height
He heard each chain of slavery as it fell!

XXX And then when Peace set wing upon the wind
And Northward flying fanned the clouds away,
He passed as martyrs pass. Ah, who shall find
The chord to sound the pathos of that day!
Mid-April blowing sweet across the land,
New bloom of freedom opening to the world,

Loud pæans of the homeward-looking host,
    The salutations grand
From grimy guns, the tattered flags unfurled;
But he must sleep to all the glory lost!

XXXI   Sleep! Loss! But there is neither sleep nor loss,
And all the glory mantles him about;
Above his breast the precious banners cross,
Does he not hear his armies tramp and shout?
Oh, every kiss of mother, wife or maid
Dashed on the grizzly lip of veteran,
Comes forthright to that calm and quiet mouth,
    And will not be delayed,
And every slave, no longer slave but man,
Sends up a blessing from the broken South.

XXXII   Shall we forget what other slaves to-day
Delve, freeze and starve and wear the iron chain?
What women feel the lash, what children pray
For mother, father, home, and pray in vain?
Beware of treaties with a tyrant power,
One manly peasant's worth a thousand Tzars,
One woman struck calls for a million sabres!
    Ring, ring, O golden hour,
Foreseen of patriots in a myriad wars!
Great soul, march on and end thy glorious labors!

XXXIII   Hero and hind, thy strong, familiar pace,
Outreaching Time, is that the world must take,
If it shall find at last the lofty place
Where Glory flames and Freedom's banners shake!

Imperial hands, that never touched the helve
Of plough or hoe, may glove themselves in scorn,
At mention of those palms so hard and brown,
  Those knuckles formed to delve;
But what empurpled despot ever born
Could buy one whiff of freedom with a crown?

XXXIV Oh, nevermore the tide of life shall turn
Backward upon the dark and savage past;
The flame he lit shall grow and stronger burn
With incense farther blowing to the last!
Why build for him a monument or tomb,
Or carve his name on any temple's stone,
Or speak of him as one whose soul has fled?
  No mausoleum's gloom,
No minster space, no pyramid grand and lone,
Can shut on him or prove that he is dead.

XXXV He is not dead. France knows he is not dead;
He stirs strong hearts in Spain and Germany,
In far Siberian mines his words are said,
He tells the English Ireland shall be free,
He calls poor serfs about him in the night,
And whispers of a power that laughs at kings,
And of a force that breaks the strongest chain;
  Old tyranny feels his might
  Tearing away its deepest fastenings,
And jewelled sceptres threaten him in vain.

XXXVI Years pass away, but freedom does not pass,
Thrones crumble, but man's birthright crumbles not,

And, like the wind across the prairie grass,

A whole world's aspirations fan this spot

With ceaseless panting after liberty,

One breath of which would make dark Russia fair,

And blow sweet summer through the exile's cave,

    And set the exile free;

For which I pray, here in the open air

Of Freedom's morning-tide, by Lincoln's grave.

A meditation on the death of the
great and the well known.

CARL SANDBURG (1878–1967) ❧

Cool Tombs

When Abraham Lincoln was shoveled into the tombs, he forgot the copperheads and the assassin . . . in the dust, in the cool tombs.

And Ulysses Grant lost all thought of con men and Wall Street, cash and collateral turned ashes . . . in the dust, in the cool tombs.

Pocahontas' body, lovely as a poplar, sweet as a red haw in November or a pawpaw in May, did she wonder? does she remember? . . . in the dust, in the cool tombs?

Take any streetful of people buying clothes and groceries, cheering a hero or throwing confetti and blowing tin horns . . . tell me if the lovers are losers . . . tell me if any get more than the lovers . . . in the dust . . . in the cool tombs.

A visit to the battlefield of
Gettysburg in October when the
summer tourists have gone and the
scene of Pickett's charge is empty
except for the silent monuments.

EDGAR LEE MASTERS (1869–1950)

Gettysburg

Amid the hush of the distant hills which house
The sleeping meadows, oak leaves loose and fall
Across the sunlight, and along the rhythmical
Wash of the air upon this shore of boughs.

Leaves drift around the bronzes. But over the grass
Of the field where Pickett's men defied
The grape shot and the cannon, and who died,
The shadows of October's clouds repass.

No shouts arise from the vanished garrisons;
No sound is here of wounded man or steed;
Meade stares at Lee, and Lee at Meade
Across a mile of pasture, eyed in bronze,

Where flies the solitary crow. Beyond
The spires of Gettysburg the skies implore;
And near the cattle graze, and grackles soar
Where the air is tranced as by a wizard's wand.

Part of Gettysburg battlefield, 1863

Till now it is a suspended mood whose gleam
Is like an invisible crystal which enspheres
The souls it veils, who with Elysian ears
List the far voice of undiscovered dream.

This stillness is the indifference of the sky,
The tranquil Muses behind the mountains hid,
Who suffer the Fate's beginning, nor forbid,
Nor ask the battle, nor mourn the tragedy.

Still they are brooding in their fanes afar;
And now they stir the oak leaves with their breath,
Saying there is no life, neither is death,
Nor victors, nor defeated, nor fame, nor war;

But only music at last out of the dreams of these,
As the one reality which overtones the mime,
The landscape, nations, races, even Time,
Quiring eternal Nature whose heart is peace.

*At an unnamed battlefield, the poet
contemplates the dead who once
lay in these fields as though they
were mysterious and foreign to the
tranquil present.*

ROBERT PENN WARREN (1905–1989) ❧

History among the Rocks
From: "Kentucky Mountain Farm"

There are many ways to die
Here among the rocks in any weather:
Wind, down the eastern gap, will lie
Level along the snow, beating the cedar,
And lull the drowsy head that it blows over
To startle a cold and crystalline dream forever.

The hound's black paw will print the grass in May,
And sycamores rise down a dark ravine,
Where a creek in flood, sucking the rock and clay,
Will tumble the laurel, the sycamore away.
Think how a body, naked and lean
And white as the splintered sycamore, would go
Tumbling and turning, hushed in the end,
With hair afloat in waters that gently bend
To ocean where the blind tides flow.

Under the shadow of ripe wheat,
By flat limestone, will coil the copperhead,

Fanged as the sunlight, hearing the reaper's feet.
But there are other ways, the lean men said:
In these autumn orchards once young men lay dead—
Gray coats, blue coats. Young men on the mountainside
Clambered, fought. Heels muddied the rocky spring.
Their reason is hard to guess, remembering
Blood on their black mustaches in moonlight.
Their reason is hard to guess and a long time past:
The apple falls, falling in the quiet night.

Davidson was one of the more romantic and nostalgic of the Vanderbilt Fugitives. They were not sympathetic to black hopes for equality and dignity, and Davidson was perhaps the most passionate among them in upholding the racial attitudes of the Confederacy, as this poem shows.

DONALD DAVIDSON (1922–) ❧

Sequel of Appomattox

A whisper flies to the empty sleeve
Pinned on the braidless coat,
And a rumor flushes the scarred young cheek
Of a man in butternut.

The riders go past fenceless fields.
They meet by the ruined wall.
And the gaunt horses crop and stray
While voices mutter and drawl.

The crow starts from the blackberry bush,
But the windowless house won't tell.
Darkness watches the ravished gate.
No hand swings the fallen bell.

Till roads are white with columns
Of phantom cavalry
That move as by the dead's cool will
Without guns or infantry.

And the hoofbeats of many horsemen
Stop and call from the grave:
Remember, I was your master;
Remember, you were my slave.

At midnight a town's four corners
Wake to the whistles' keening;
The march of the dead is a long march.
Certain its meaning.

Something for grandfathers to tell
Boys who clamor and climb.
And were you there, and did you ride
With the men of that old time?

Dickey is a South Carolinian,
a poet and novelist. Here the
narrator and his brother look for
metal relics of a skirmish, and the
narrator is thrown into a meditation
on the war that blazed briefly over
this calm place.

JAMES DICKEY (1923–) ✍

Hunting Civil War Relics at Nimblewill Creek

As he moves the mine detector
A few inches over the ground,
Making it vitally float
Among the ferns and weeds,
I come into this war
Slowly, with my one brother,
Watching his face grow deep
Between the earphones,
For I can tell
If we enter the buried battle
Of Nimblewill
Only by his expression.

Softly he wanders, parting
The grass with a dreaming hand.
No dead cry yet takes root
In his clapped ears
Or can be seen in his smile.
But underfoot I feel

The dead regroup,
The burst metals all in place,
The battle lines be drawn
Anew to include us
In Nimblewill,
And I carry the shovel and pick
More as if they were
Bright weapons that I bore.
A bird's cry breaks
In two, and into three parts.
We cross the creek; the cry
Shifts into another,
Nearer, bird, and is
Like the shout of a shadow—
Lived-with, appallingly close—
Or the soul, pronouncing
"Nimblewill":
Three tones; your being changes.

We climb the bank;
A faint light glows
On my brother's mouth.
I listen, as two birds fight
For a single voice, but he
Must be hearing the grave,
In pieces, all singing
To his clamped head,
For he smiles as if
He rose from the dead within
Green Nimblewill
And stood in his grandson's shape.

ACKNOWLEDGMENTS ❧

For permission to reprint material in copyright, grateful acknowledgments are made to:

Brandt & Brandt Literary Agents, Inc. "John Brown's Body," from *Selected Works of Stephen Vincent Benét*. Copyright © 1927–28 by Stephen Vincent Benét and renewed © 1955–56 by Rosemary Carr Benét.

Jonathan Cape, Inc. "The Black Cottage," from *The Poetry of Robert Frost*, edited by Edward Connery Lathem. Copyright © 1958 by Robert Frost; copyright © 1967 by Lesley Frost Ballantine; copyright © 1930, 1939, © 1969 by Henry Holt and Co., Inc.

Ecco Press. "Fabrication of Ancestors," by Alan Dugan. Copyright © 1961, 1962, 1968, 1973, 1974, 1983 by Alan Dugan. From *New and Collected Poems 1961–1983*. First printed by The Ecco Press in 1983. Used by permission.

Faber and Faber Ltd. "Boston Common," from *Collected Poems 1937–1971*, by John Berryman. "A Description of Some Confederate Soldiers," from *The Complete Poems of Randall Jarrell*. "For the Union Dead," from *For the Union Dead*, by Robert Lowell. "Ode to the Confederate Dead," from *Collected Poems*, by Allen Tate. "The Arkansas Testament," from *The Arkansas Testament*, by Derek Walcott.

Farrar, Straus & Giroux. "Boston Common," from *Collected Poems 1937–1971*, by John Berryman. Copyright © 1989 by Kate Donahue Berryman. "From Trollope's Journal," from *The Complete Poems 1927–1979*, by Elizabeth Bishop. Copyright © 1979, 1983 by Alice Helen Methfessel. "Tintype of a Private of the Fifteenth Georgia Infantry," from *Songs After Lincoln*, by Paul Horgan. Copyright © 1965 and renewed © 1993 by Paul Horgan. "A Description of Some Confederate Soldiers," from *The Complete Poems*, by Randall Jarrell. Copyright © 1942 by Randall Jarrell and renewed © 1969 by Mrs. Randall Jarrell. "For The Union Dead," from *For the Union Dead*, by Robert Lowell. Copyright © 1964 by Robert Lowell and renewed © 1992 by Harriet Lowell, Sheridan Lowell, and Caroline Lowell. "Ode to the Confederate Dead," from *Collected Poems 1919– 1976*, by Allen Tate. Copyright © 1977 by Allen Tate. "The Arkansas Testament," from *The Arkansas Testament*, by Derek Walcott. Copyright © 1987 by Derek Walcott.

Hamish Mamilton Ltd. "Richmond," from *Facing Nature*, by John Updike (first published by Alfred A. Knopf, Inc.). Copyright © 1985 by John Updike.

Harcourt Brace Jovanovich. "The Long Shadow of Lincoln, a Litany," from *The Complete Poems of Carl Sandburg*, by Carl Sandburg. Copyright © 1950 by Carl Sandburg and renewed © 1978 by Margaret Sandburg, Helga Sandburg Crile, and Janet Sandburg. "Cool Tombs," from *Cornhuskers*, by Carl Sandburg.

Henry Holt and Co., Inc. "The Black Cottage," from *The Poetry of Robert Frost*, edited by Edward Connery Lathem. Copyright © 1958 by Robert Frost; copyright © 1967 by Lesley Frost Ballantine; copyright © 1930, 1939, © 1969 by Henry Holt and Co., Inc.

Houghton Mifflin Company. "A Soldier on the Marsh," "After the Wilderness," "Around the Campfire," "At Chancellorsville," " Burial Detail," and "Serenades in Virginia," from *After the Lost War*, by Andrew Hudgins. Copyright © 1988 by Andrew Hudgins.

Alfred A. Knopf, Inc. "Frederick Douglass: 1817–1895," from *The Panther and the Lash*, by Langston Hughes. Copyright © 1967 by Arna Bontemps and George Houston Bass. "Lincoln Monument: Washington," from *The Dream Keeper and Other Poems*, by Langston Hughes. Copyright © 1932 by Alfred A. Knopf, Inc., and renewed © 1960 by Langston Hughes. "Richmond," from *Facing Nature*, by John Updike. Copyright © 1985 by John Updike.

Liveright Publishing Corporation. "Frederick Douglass," from *The Collected Poems of Robert Hayden*, edited by Frederick Glaysher. Copyright © 1966 by Robert Hayden.

Macmillan Publishing Company. "Abraham Lincoln Walks at Midnight," from *Collected Poems of Vachel Lindsay*, by Vachel Lindsay (originally published by Macmillan, 1925). "The Master," from *Collected Poems of Edwin Arlington Robinson*, by Edwin Arlington Robinson (originally published by Macmillan, 1937).

Ellen C. Masters. "Anne Rutledge," from *Spoon River Anthology*, by Edgar Lee Masters (originally published by Macmillan); "The Battle of Gettysburg," from *Poems of the People*, by Edgar Lee Masters (originally published by D. Appleton–Century); "Gettysburg," from *Invisible Landscapes*, by Edgar Lee Masters (originally published by Macmillan); "Veterans of the Wars," by Edgar Lee Masters.

Milkweed Editions. "General John Cabell Breckinridge; My Recurring Dream: December 2, 1865," from *Civil Blood*, by Jill Breckenridge. Copyright © 1986 by Jill Breckenridge.

The New Yorker. "Gettysburg, July 1, 1863" (originally published in *The New Yorker*). Copyright © 1992 by Jane Kenyon.

Harold Ober Associates. "Lincoln Monument: Washington" and "Frederick Douglass: 1817–1895," by Langston Hughes.

Dudley Randall. "Memorial Wreath," by Dudley Randall. Copyright © by Dudley Randall.

Random House. "A Confederate Veteran Tries to Explain the Event," from *Selected Poems 1923–1975,* by Robert Penn Warren. Copyright © 1966 by Robert Penn Warren. "History among the Rocks" and "Two Studies in Idealism: Short Survey of American and Human History," from *Selected Poems 1923–1975,* by Robert Penn Warren. Copyright © 1936 and renewed © 1964 by Robert Penn Warren.

Suzanne Rhodenbaugh. "The Civil War," by Suzanne Rhodenbaugh. Copyright © by Suzanne Rhodenbaugh.

William Rukeyser. "The Soul and Body of John Brown," from *Collected Poems,* by Muriel Ruykeyser (originally published by McGraw-Hill, 1978).

University of Arkansas Press. "Lincoln," from *The Selected Poems of John Gould Fletcher,* by John Gould Fletcher.

University of California Press. "Anecdotes of the Late War," from *The Collected Poetry of Charles Olson,* edited by George Butterick.

University of Minnesota Press. "Lee in the Mountains" and "Sequel of Appomattox," from *Collected Poems,* by Donald Davidson. Copyright © 1966 by University of Minnesota.

University Press of New England. "Hunting Civil War Relics at Nimblewill Creek," from *Drowning with Others,* by James Dickey. Copyright © 1962 by James Dickey (originally published by Wesleyan University Press).

Stuart Wright, Publisher. "This Year's Drive to Appomattox" and "A Few Days in the South in February," from *New and Selected Poems,* by Eleanor Ross Taylor.

ILLUSTRATIONS ✍

Grateful acknowledgment is made to the Library of Congress for permission to reproduce "107th United States Colored Infantry guard and guardhouse, Fort Corcoran," and also to the National Archives for permission to reproduce all other illustrations.

Interior view of a military hospital (probably Carver Hospital, near Washington, D.C.)   16

Grand Review, Washington, D.C.   24

Battlefield of Bull Run   28

Jefferson Davies, President of the Confederate States   34

Confederate General John C. Breckinridge, of Kentucky   39

"Overseer Artayou Carrier whipped me. I was two months in bed sore from the whipping. My master came after I was whipped; he discharged the overseer." *The very words of poor Peter as he sat for his picture, April 2, 1863*   50

Ruins of Charleston, South Carolina, 1865   68

Harriet Beecher Stowe   80

Union General William Tecumseh Sherman   107

Slave pen of Price, Birch & Co., Alexandria, Virginia   110

John Brown   124

D. W. C. Arnold, private in the Union Army   142

Ruins of Henry House, first battle of Bull Run   145

Battlefield of Atlanta, where General James McPherson was killed   151

Chaplain conducting Mass for the 69th New York Militia   154

Emory Eugene King, private in the 4th Michigan Infantry   163

Winter quarters: Soldiers in front of their wooden hut, "Pine Cottage"   165

The Drummer Boy of Shiloh, John L. Clem, aged 10   169

Pioneers Camp, Lookout Mountain, Tennessee   173

Engineer Camp, 8th New York Militia   177

Surgeons of Harwood Hospital, Washington, D.C.   181

Union General Philip H. Sheridan   188

107th United States "Colored" Infantry guard and guardhouse, Fort Corcoran   207

Inside the Confederate lines, 1865, Petersburg, Virginia   214

John Wilkes Booth   218

Ruins of Galligo Mills, April 1865, Richmond, Virginia   236

Union and Confederate dead, Gettysburg battlefield   239

Union General Ulysses S. Grant at Cold Harbor   259

Confederate General Robert E. Lee   266

Admiral David G. Farragut   270

Confederate General Albert Sidney Johnston   280

Confederate General Robert E. Lee   284

Confederate cavalry commander J. E. B. ("Jeb") Stuart   289

Confederate General Stonewall Jackson   297

John Burns (with wife) and cottage, Gettysburg, Pennsylvania   301

Frederick Douglass   320

Ford's Theatre chair in which President Lincoln was sitting when shot   332

Walt Whitman   336

Abraham Lincoln, President of the United States   346

Mrs. Abraham Lincoln   358

President Lincoln and his generals at Antietam   362

Union General George B. McClellan   388

Part of the Chickamauga battlefield   390

Band, 4th Michigan Infantry   395

Dead Confederate soldier in the trenches, April 3, 1865, Petersburg, Virginia   400

Union infantry private on post   415

Edmund Ruffin, private in the Confederate Army   420

National Cemetery, Andersonville, Georgia   456

Group of black workers   467

Inside the trenches before Petersburg, Virginia   472

View of the Wilderness, Virginia   496

Ruins of Richmond, Virginia   499

Part of the Gettysburg battlefield, 1863   519

INDEX

of Authors, Titles, and First Lines

Titles of poems are set in italic type, first lines are set in roman type and enclosed in quotation marks; if the title and first line of a poem are identical, or virtually so, only the title is given.

Abraham Lincoln Walks at Midnight, 355

Address by an Ex-Confederate Soldier to the Grand Army of the Republic, An, 439

"After the eyes that looked, the lips that spake / Here," 402

After the Wilderness, 43

"Ah, Douglass, we have fall'n on evil days," 315

Albert Sidney Johnston, 279

All Quiet along the Potomac Tonight, 20

"Amid the hush of the distant hills which house / The sleeping meadows," 518

Anecdotes of the Late War, 217

Anne Rutledge, 351

Arkansas Testament, The, 478

"Arms reversed and banners craped," 150

Army Corps on the March, An, 176

Around the Campfire, 45

Artilleryman's Vision, The, 174

"As far as statues go, so far there's not / much choice," 36

"As he moves the mine detector," 525

As I Lay with My Head in Your Lap Camerado, 162

"At anchor in Hampton Roads we lay," 147

At Chancellorsville, 41

At Harper's Ferry Just before the Attack, 116

Ball, Caroline Augusta (b. 1825).
  Jacket of Gray, The, 399

Ball's Bluff, a Reverie, 8

Barbara Frietchie, 306

Battle Autumn of 1862, The, 369

Battle-Cry of Freedom, The, 57

Battle Hymn of the Republic, The, 55

Battle of Gettysburg, The, 198

"Be sad, be cool, be kind," 361

Bear Track Plantation: Shortly after Shiloh, 32

Beat! Beat! Drums!, 168

"Before the solemn bronze Saint Gaudens made," 130

Bell, James Madison (1826–1902).
  Poem Entitled the Day and the War, A, 190

Bell (*continued*)

Though Tennyson, the Poet King,
190

Benét, Stephen Vincent(1898–
1943). *Congressmen Came Out to
See Bull Run, The,* 27

John Brown's Body, 27, 120

John Brown's Prayer, 120

"Beneath the trees," 261

Berryman, John (1914–1972). *Bos-
ton Common,* 460

"Between each layer of tattered,
broken flesh," 246

Bierce, Ambrose (1842–1914?).

Confederate Flags, The, 430

Death of Grant, The, 436

General B. F. Butler, 438

Hesitating Veteran, The, 433

To E. S. Salomon, 426

Bishop, Elizabeth (1911–1979).

From Trollope's Journal, 36

Bishop, Thomas Brigham. *John
Brown's Body,* 53

Bivouac on a Mountain Side, 172

Black Cottage, The, 450

Blue and the Gray, The, 411

Boston Common, 460

Boston Hymn, 75

"Brave Grant, thou hero of the
war," 258

Breckenridge, Jill. *Civil Blood,* 38

*General John Cabell Breckinridge;
My Recurring Dream: December
2, 1862,* 38

"Bring the good old bugle, boys,
we'll sing another song," 106

Bryant, William Cullen (1794–
1878). *Death of Abraham Lincoln,
The,* 331

Death of Slavery, The, 71

"Build me straight, O worthy Mas-
ter!" 85

Building of the Ship, The, 85

Burial Detail, 246

Burial of Latané, The, 293

" 'But why did he do it, Grandpa?'
I said," 213

"By the flow of the inland river,"
411

"Calm as that second summer which
precedes / The first fall of the
snow," 67

Carolina, 63

Cavalry Crossing a Ford, 171

Charleston, 67

Civil Blood, 38

Civil War, The, 237

"Cloud possessed the hollow field,
A," 194

College Colonel, The, 158

Colored Soldiers, The, 206

"Column of lemon sky lit one hill,
A," 237

"Combat raged not long, but ours
the day, The," 293

"Come, stack arms, men. Pile on the
rails," 296

Come Up from the Fields Father,
178

Confederate Flags, The, 430

Confederate Memorial Day, 501

*Confederate Veteran Tries to Explain
the Event, A,* 213

Conflict of Convictions, The, 153

*Congressmen Came Out to See Bull
Run, The,* 27

Cool Tombs, 517

Cumberland, The, 147

Davidson, Donald (1922–). *Lee in
the Mountains,* 323

Sequel of Appomattox, 523

"Dawn of a pleasant morning in
May," 283

Death of Abraham Lincoln, The,
331

Death of Grant, The, 436

Death of Slavery, The, 71

*Description of Some Confederate Sol-
diers, A,* 225

"Despot treads thy sacred sands,
The," 63

"Despot's heel is on thy shore, The,"
59

"Dey was talkin' in de cabin, dey
was talkin' in de hall," 211

Dickey, James (1923–). *Hunting
Civil War Relics at Nimblewill
Creek,* 525

"Did all the lets and bars appear,"
144

"Did you ask dulcet rhymes from me?," 392

Dirge for McPherson, A, 150

Dirge for Two Veterans, 12

Dixie, 114

Douglass, 315

"Douglass was someone who, / Had he walked with wary foot," 319

Driving Home the Cows, 423

Dugan, Alan (1923–). *Fabrication of Ancestors,* 469

Dunbar, Paul Laurence (1872–1906). *Colored Soldiers, The,* 206
Douglass, 315
Frederick Douglass, 313
Robert Gould Shaw, 312
Unsung Heroes, The, 317
When Dey 'Listed Colored Soldiers, 211

Dying Words of Stonewall Jackson, The, 310

"Edwin, your father has never ceased to be / My admiration," 446

Emerson, Ralph Waldo (1803–1882). *Boston Hymn,* 75
Voluntaries, 79

Emmett, Daniel Decatur (1815–1904). *Dixie,* 114

Enlisted Today, 141

"Every night I dream we're fighting, armies raised / high to celestial fields," 38

Fabrication of Ancestors, 469

Farragut, Farragut, 269

"Father! whose hard and cruel law / Is part of thy compassion's plan," 436

Few Days in the South in February, A, 227

Finch, Francis Miles (1827–1907). *Blue and the Gray, The,* 411

"Flags of war like storm-birds fly, The," 369

"Flesh to earth, The, thy soul to God," 438

Fletcher, John Gould (1886–1907). *Lincoln,* 357

"Flying word from here and there, A," 352

"Fold away all your bright-tinted dresses," 180

"Fold it up carefully, lay it aside," 399

For the Union Dead, 471

"Forth from its scabbard, pure and bright," 267

Frederick Douglass (Paul Laurence Dunbar), 313

Frederick Douglass (Robert Hayden), 316

Frederick Douglass: 1817–1895, 319

From Trollope's Journal, 36

From Year to Year the Contest Grew, 109

Frost, Robert (1874–1963). *Black Cottage, The,* 450

Furnace Blast, The, 99

"Gallant foeman in the fight, A," 265

General B. F. Butler, 438

General Grant—the Hero of the War, 258

General John Cabell Breckinridge; My Recurring Dream: December 2, 1862, 38

Gettysburg 518

Gettysburg, July 1, 1863, 238

Gettysburg Ode, 402

Gilmore, Patrick Sarsfield (1829–1892). *When Johnny Comes Marching Home,* 414

Give Me the Splendid Silent Sun, 166

"Good Friday was the day / of the prodigy and crime," 333

Grave in Hollywood Cemetery, Richmond (J. R. T.), A, 498

Hall, Charles Sprague. *John Brown's Body,* 53

"Hanging from the beam, / Slowly swaying," 255

"Happy are they and charmed in life," 391

Harte, Bret (1836–1902). *John Burns of Gettysburg,* 300

Second Review of the Grand Army, A, 23

Harvard '61: Battle Fatigue, 33

"Have you heard the story that gossips tell," 300

Hayden, Robert (1913–). *Frederick Douglass*, 316

"He is dead, the beautiful youth," 6

"He rides at their head," 158

"He was an Indiana corporal," 41

Hesitating Veteran, The, 433

High Tide at Gettysburg, The, 194

"His life is in the body of the living," 123

History among the Rocks, 521

Horgan, Paul (1905–). *Tintype of a Private of the Fifteenth Georgia Infantry*, 322

Horton, George Moses (1797?–1883?). *General Grant—the Hero of the War*, 258

Hospital Duties, 180

"Hour, the spot, are here at last, The," 116

House-Top, The, 160

Howe, Julia Ward (1819–1910). *Battle Hymn of the Republic, The*, 55

Robert E. Lee, 265

Hudgins, Andrew (1951–). *After the Wilderness*, 43

Around the Campfire, 45

At Chancellorsville, 41

Burial Detail, 246

Serenades in Virginia, 242

Soldier on the Marsh, A, 250

Hughes, Langston (1902–1967). *Frederick Douglass: 1817–1895*, 319

Lincoln Monument: Washington, 366

Hunting Civil War Relics at Nimblewill Creek, 525

"Hush is over all the teeming lists, A," 313

"I didn't mind dying—it wasn't that at all," 33

"I hear again the tread of war go thundering through the land," 279

"I know the sun shines, and the lilacs are blowing," 141

"I read last night of the Grand Review," 23

"I read the marble-lettered name," 498

"I see before me now a traveling army halting," 172

"I was a rebel, if you please," 439

"I wish I was in de land ob cotton," 114

"If the muse were mine to tempt it," 206

In 'Fifty Congress Passed a Bill, 49

"In this green month when resurrected flowers," 466

Irving, Minna (b. 1872). *Marching still*, 448

"It is done!," 103

"It is portentous, and a thing of state," 355

Jacket of Gray, The, 399

Jarrell, Randall (1914–1965). *Description of Some Confederate Soldiers, A*, 225

John Brown's Body (S. V. Benét), 27, 120

John Brown's Body (Unknown), 53

John Brown's Prayer, 120

John Burns of Gettysburg, 300

Kentucky Belle, 273

Kentucky Mountain Farm, 521

Kenyon, Jane (1947–). *Gettysburg, July 1, 1863*, 238

Killed at the Ford, 6

Lanier, Sidney (1842–1881). *Dying Words of Stonewall Jackson, The*, 310

"Last sunbeam, The, / Lightly falls from the finish'd Sabbath," 12

Laus Deo!, 103

Lee in the Mountains, 323

Lee to the Rear, 283

"lethargic vs violence as alternatives of each other for los americanos, the," 217

"Let's go see Old Abe," 366

"Like a gaunt, scraggly pine," 357

Lincoln, 357

Lincoln Monument: Washington, 366

Lincoln, the Man of the People, 348

Lincoln's Grave, 503

Lindsay, Vachel (1879–1913). *Abraham Lincoln Walks at Midnight*, 355

"Line in long array, where they wind betwixt green islands, A," 171

Little Giffen, 256

Long Shadow of Lincoln, The, 361

Longfellow, Henry Wadsworth (1807–1882). *Building of the Ship, The*, 85

Cumberland, The, 147

Killed at the Ford, 6

"Low and mournful be the strain," 79

Lowell, James Russell (1819–1891). *Memoriae Positum R. G. Shaw*, 261

Ode Recited at the Harvard Commemoration, July 21, 1865, 372

Lowell, Robert (1917–1977). *For the Union Dead*, 471

"Lynx-eyed, cat-quiet, sleepy mild," 322

Malvern Hill, 387

"March comes, / and Eastern bluebird shows himself," 476

March in the Ranks Hard-prest and the Road Unknown, A, 14

March into Virginia, The, 144

"Marching armies of the past, The," 501

Marching Still, 448

Marching through Georgia, 106

Markham, Edwin (1852–1940). *Lincoln, the Man of the People*, 348

Martyr, The, 333

Master, The, 352

Masters, Edgar Lee (1869–1950). *Anne Rutledge*, 351

Battle of Gettysburg, The, 198

Gettysburg, 518

Spoon River Anthology, 351

Veterans of the Wars, 446

"May one who fought in honor for the South," 503

Melville, Herman (1819–1891). *Ball's Bluff, a Reverie*, 8

College Colonel, The, 158

Conflict of Convictions, The, 153

Dirge for McPherson, A, 150

House-Top, The, 160

Malvern Hill, 387

March into Virginia, The, 144

Martyr, The, 333

Memorial on the Slain at Chickamauga, 391

Portent, The, 255

Sheridan at Cedar Creek, 187

Shiloh, a Requiem, 497

Uninscribed Monument on One of the Battle-fields of the Wilderness, An, 495

Memoriae Positum R. G. Shaw, 261

Memorial on the Slain at Chickamauga, 391

Memorial Wreath, 466

Memories of President Lincoln, 335, 345

Meredith, William Tuckey (b. 1839). *Farragut, Farragut*, 269

"Mine eyes have seen the glory of the coming of the Lord," 55

Moody, William Vaughn (1869–1910). *Ode in Time of Hesitation, An*, 130

Music in Camp, 394

My Maryland, 59

"No sleep. The sultriness pervades the air," 160

O Captain! My Captain!, 345

"O subtle, musky, slumbrous clime!," 443

"O thou great Wrong, that, through the slow-paced years," 71

Obsequies of Stuart, 288

Ode ("Sleep sweetly in your humble graves"), 417

Ode in Time of Hesitation, An, 130

Ode Recited at the Harvard Commemoration, July 21, 1865, 372

Ode to the Confederate Dead, 455

"Oh, I'm a good old Rebel," 419

"Oh, slow to smite and swift to spare," 331

"Old man bending I come among new faces, An," 17

"Old South Boston Aquarium stands, The, / in a Sahara of snow now," 471

"Old wound in my ass, The, / has opened up again," 469

Oliver, Thaddeus (1826–1864). *All Quiet along the Potomac Tonight,* 20

Olson, Charles (1910–1970). *Anecdotes of the Late War,* 217

"Omnipotent and steadfast God," 120

"On leave, I sat on marsh grass, watched / bees tremble into new red blooms," 250

"On starry heights / A bugle wails the long recall," 153

"One noonday, at my window in the town," 8

"One ship, one only," 227

Osgood, Kate Putnam (1841–1910). *Driving Home the Cows,* 423

"Out of me unworthy and unknown," 351

"Out of the clover and blue-eyed grass," 423

"Out of the focal and foremost fire," 256

"Over Fayetteville, Arkansas," 478

Palmer, John Williamson (1825–1906). *Stonewall Jackson's Way,* 296

"Peace! Peace! God of our fathers grant us Peace!," 3

Poem Entitled the Day and the War, A, 190

Poem on the Fugitive Slave Law, A, 49

Poem Written for the Celebration of the Fourth Anniversary of President Lincoln's Emancipation Proclamation, 109

Portent, The, 255

Prayer for Peace, A, 3

Preston, Margaret Junkin (1820–1897). *Grave in Hollywood Cemetery, Richmond (J. R. T.), A,* 498

Randall, Dudley (1914–). *Memorial Wreath,* 466

Randall, James Ryder (1839–1908). *My Maryland,* 59

Randolph, Innes (1837–1887). *Rebel, The,* 419

Read, Thomas Buchanan (1822–1872). *Sheridan's Ride,* 184

Rebel, The, 419

Rhodenbaugh, Suzanne (1944–). *Civil War, The,* 237

Richmond, 235

Robert E. Lee, 265

Robert Gould Shaw, 312

Robinson, Edwin Arlington (1869–1935). *Master, The,* 352

Rogers, Elymas Payson (1815–1861). *In 'Fifty Congress Passed a Bill,* 49

Poem on the Fugitive Slave Law, A, 49

Root, George Frederick (1820–1895). *Battle-Cry of Freedom, The,* 57

"Row after row with strict impunity," 455

Ruykeyser, Muriel (1913–1980). *Soul and Body of John Brown, The,* 123

Ryan, Abram Joseph (1839–1894). *Sword of Robert Lee, The,* 267

Sandburg, Carl (1878–1967). *Cool Tombs,* 517

Long Shadow of Lincoln, The, 361

Second Review of the Grand Army, A, 23

Sequel of Appomattox, 523

Serenades in Virginia, 242

"Shadows in his eye sockets like shades, The, / upon a bearded hippie," 235

"She is old, and bent, and wrinkled," 448

Sheridan at Cedar Creek, 187

Sheridan's Ride, 184

Sherwood, Kate Brownlee (1841–1914). *Albert Sidney Johnston*, 279

Shiloh, a Requiem, 497

"Shoe the steed with silver," 187

Sight in Camp in the Daybreak Gray and Dim, A, 164

Silence and Solitude may hint, 495

"Skimming lightly, wheeling still, / The swallows fly low," 497

"Sleep sweetly in your humble graves," 417

"Slumped under the impressive genitals / Of the bronze charger," 460

Snowden, Thomas *and* Ellen. *Dixie*, 114

Soldier on the Marsh, A, 250

"Song for the unsung heroes who rose in the country's need, A," 317

Soul and Body of John Brown, The, 123

Spirit Whose Work Is Done, 393

Spoon River Anthology, 351

"Stars of Night contain the glittering Day, The," 310

Stonewall Jackson's Way, 296

"Summer of 'sixty-three, sir, and Conrad was gone away," 273

Sword of Robert Lee, The, 267

Tate, Allen (1899–1979). *Ode to the Confederate Dead*, 455

Taylor, Bayard (1825–1878). *Gettysburg Ode*, 402

Taylor, Eleanor Ross (1920–). *Few Days in the South in February, A*, 227

This Year's Drive to Appomattox, 476

"There are many ways to die," 521

This Year's Drive to Appomattox, 476

Thompson, John Reuben (1823–1873). *Burial of Latané, The*, 293

Lee to the Rear, 283

Music in Camp, 394

Obsequies of Stuart, 288

Thompson, Maurice (1844–1901). *Address by an Ex-Confederate Soldier to the Grand Army of the Republic, An*, 439

Lincoln's Grave, 503

To the South, 443

Thompson, Will Henry (1848–1914). *High Tide at Gettysburg, The*, 194

Though Tennyson the Poet King, 190

"Thy flesh to earth, thy soul to God," 438

Ticknor, Francis Orrery (1822–1874). *Little Giffen*, 256

Timrod, Henry (1829–1867). *Carolina*, 63

Charleston, 67

Ode ("Sleep sweetly in your humble graves," 417

Tintype of a Private of the Fifteenth Georgia Infantry, 322

To a Certain Civilian, 392

To E. S. Salomon, 426

To the South, 443

"Torn hillside with its crooked hands, The," 225

"Tut-tut! give back the flags—how can you care," 430

" 'Twas a battle of States," 198

"Two armies covered hill and plain," 394

Two Studies in Idealism: Short Survey of American and Human History, 32

"Two things a man's built for, killing and you-know-what," 32

Uninscribed Monument on One of the Battle-fields of the Wilderness, An, 495

Unknown. *Confederate Memorial Day*, 501

Dixie, 114

Enlisted Today, 141

John Brown's Body, 53

Unsung Heroes, The, 317

"Up from the meadows rich with corn," 306

"Up from the South, at break of day," 184

Updike, John (1932–). *Richmond*, 235

Veterans of the Wars, 446

*Vigil Strange I Kept on the Field
One Night,* 10

Voluntaries, 79

Walcott, Derek (1930–). *Arkansas
Testament, The,* 478

"Walking into the shadows, walking
alone," 323

Wallis, Severn Teackle (1816–
1894). *Prayer for Peace, A,*
3

Warren, Robert Penn (1905–
1989). *Confederate Veteran Tries to
Explain the Event, A,* 213

   History among the Rocks, 521

   Kentucky Mountain Farm, 521

   *Two Studies in Idealism: Short
Survey of American and Human
History,* 32

"We chanced in passing by that af-
ternoon," 450

"We could not pause, while yet the
noontide air," 288

"We wait beneath the furnace-blast,"
99

"Weak-winged is song," 372

"What! Salomon! such words from
you," 426

"When Abraham Lincoln was shov-
eled into the tombs," 517

"When Clifford wasn't back to camp
by nine," 43

When Dey 'Listed Colored Soldiers,
211

"When I was young and full of
faith," 433

"When it is finally ours, this free-
dom, this liberty, this beautiful /
And terrible thing," 316

*When Johnny Comes Marching
Home,* 414

*When Lilacs Last in the Dooryard
Bloom'd,* 335

"When the Norn Mother saw the
Whirlwind Hour," 348

"When we heard of a lady who /
was said to be a stunning beauty,"
242

"While my wife at my side lies slum-
bering, and the wars are over
long," 174

"Whisper flies to the empty sleeve,
A," 523

Whitfield, James Monroe (1822–
1871). *From Year to Year the
Contest Grew,* 109

   *Poem Written for the Celebration
of the Fourth Anniversary of
President Lincoln's Emancipation
Proclamation,* 109

Whitman, Walt (1819–1892).

   Army Corps on the March, An,
176

   Artilleryman's Vision, The, 174

   *As I Lay with My Head in Your
Lap Camerado,* 162

   Beat! Beat! Drums!, 168

   Bivouac on a Mountain Side,
172

   Cavalry Crossing a Ford, 171

   Come Up from the Fields Father,
178

   Dirge for Two Veterans, 12

   Give Me the Splendid Silent Sun,
166

   *March in the Ranks Hard-prest
and the Road Unknown, A,* 14

   Memories of President Lincoln,
335, 345

   O Captain! My Captain!, 345

   *Sight in Camp in the Daybreak
Gray and Dim, A,* 164

   Spirit Whose Work Is Done, 393

   To a Certain Civilian, 392

   *Vigil Strange I Kept on the Field
One Night,* 10

   *When Lilacs Last in the Dooryard
Bloom'd,* 335

   Wound-Dresser, The, 17

Whittier, John Greenleaf (1807–
1892). *Barbara Frietchie,* 306

   Battle Autumn of 1862, The,
369

   Furnace Blast, The, 99

   Laus Deo!, 103

"Why was it that the thunder voice
of Fate," 312

Williams, Edward W. (1863–1891).
*At Harper's Ferry Just before the
Attack,* 116

"With its cloud of skirmishers in advance," 176

Woolson, Constance Fenimore (1840–1894). *Kentucky Belle*, 273

"Word of the Lord by night, The," 75

Work, Henry Clay (1832–1884). *Marching through Georgia*, 106

Wound-Dresser, The, 17

"Ye elms that wave on Malvern Hill," 387

"Yes, we'll rally round the flag, boys, we'll rally once again," 57

"Young man, hardly more, The, / than a boy," 238